The Amateur Historian's Guide to
Medieval and Tudor England
Day Trips South of London

✝

+ The Amateur Historian's Guide to +

Medieval and Tudor England

DAY TRIPS SOUTH of LONDON

Sarah Valente Kettler
&
Carole Trimble

Capital Books, Inc.
Sterling, Virginia

Capital Books, Inc.
P.O. Box 605
Herndon, Virginia 20172-0605

Printed in the United States of America on acid-free paper that meets the American National Standards Institute Z39-48 Standard.

First Edition

10 9 8 7 6 5 4 3 2 1

Design and composition by Melissa Ehn at Wilsted & Taylor Publishing Services
Illustrations and maps by Chadwick Design, Inc.

LIBRARY OF CONGRESS CATALOGING-IN-PUBLICATION DATA

Kettler, Sarah.
    The amateur historian's guide to medieval and Tudor England: day trips south of London / Sarah Valente Kettler, Carole Trimble.
       p.   cm.
    Includes index.
    ISBN 1-892123-73-8 (alk. paper)
    1. Historic buildings—England—London Region—Guidebooks.
2. Great Britain—History—Medieval period, 1066–1485—Anecdotes.
3. Great Britain—History—Tudors, 1485–1603—Anecdotes.   4. Historic sites—England—London Region—Guidebooks.   5. Historic buildings—England, Southern—Guidebooks.   6. Historic sites—England, Southern—Guidebooks.   7. London Region (England)—Guidebooks.   8. England, Southern—Guidebooks. I. Title: Amateur historian's guide to medieval and Tudor England: day trips south of London.   II. Trimble, Carole.   III. Title.
DA650.K43 2002
942.205—dc21   2001047206

CONTENTS

ACKNOWLEDGMENTS

Where to begin? As ever, we thank our families for their infinite patience and support: we couldn't do this without you. Warm thanks to our publisher and friend, Kathleen Hughes of Capital Books, for continuing to believe in us and continually encouraging us . . . to our wise agent, Gail Ross, for her sage advice . . . to all of our many friends who have listened to our travelogues and "did you knows" with (apparently) unfailing enthusiasm . . . to the countless docents, tour guides, information centre personnel, librarians, merchants and "locals" in England who generously and graciously assisted in our quest for information . . . to the outstanding management and staff of the Franklin Hotel in London for providing us with a home away from home . . . to our excellent driver, Roy Adair, for paving the way with humor . . . to the ever-reliable and oh-so-generous Hector Benedi, our computer guru and website master . . . to the mighty Michael Kahn and the Shakespeare Theatre family for introducing us and cheering us on . . . and to one another: best friends, co-authors, business partners and enthusiastic travel companions after two books and eight trips to England. Amazing!

INTRODUCTION

When we finished our first book, *The Amateur Historian's Guide to Medieval and Tudor London*, it was with a degree of sadness. We felt we were leaving London behind. We love that city, particularly its rich and vivid history that served as the inspiration for this series. It was with some trepidation that we set forth to explore the rest of England.

We quickly found that we were equally intrigued by the wealth of medieval and Tudor sites and history to be found very close to London. Our challenge was to find a way to share our discoveries with you in an entertaining, useful and attractive format. We settled on "day trips," grouping sites that would make for easy, enjoyable and compelling one-day excursions. Using London as a base, you can depart in the morning and return in time for dinner or the theater. *(Another motive was entirely selfish. This way we could have our cake and eat it, too. We could stay in London while researching this book, still enjoying the pleasures of the city in the evening while immersing ourselves in medieval and Tudor history during the day. Works for us!)*

We started our explorations with day trips to the south of London, picking up the trail of England's medieval history at our starting point, William the Conqueror's invasion and subsequent victory at the Battle of Hastings in the fall of 1066, and encompassing the myriad castles, manor houses, cathedrals, abbeys, churches and other structures that played prominent roles in England's history through the reign of Elizabeth I. In our next book, we will be tackling trips to the English Midlands, most of which also are within a day's trip from London.

We wanted to share with you a couple of points about our approach to this book and thereby hopefully answer your questions before you ask them.

WILLIAM WHO?

Much of the history you will encounter in this book is steeped in the Norman Conquest—you know, "1066 and all that." Throughout the book, we make reference to the instigator (perpetrator, mastermind, aggressor, etc.) of the Conquest as "William the Conqueror" . . . or "William of Normandy" . . . or "William, *Duke* of Normandy" . . . or "William the Bastard" . . . or "William I." A king by any other name . . .

In most other instances when a person is known to history by more than one name—such as Empress Matilda (a.k.a. Maude) or King Stephen's wife Maud (a.k.a. Matilda)—we have chosen the name we like best and stuck with it.

In the case of Henry VIII's many wives, we *do* realize that the "Catherines" were each also known as "Katherine," and occasionally also as "Kathryn." For the sake of clarity, we refer to Katherine of Aragon, Catherine Howard and Katherine Parr. Apologies to those of you who might strongly prefer another spelling.

BUT WHAT ABOUT . . . ?

As much as we tend to joke about "leaving no ancient stone unturned," we have a confession to make: there are a small handful of sites *(mere pebbles in the historical landscape)* that we have not investigated and several that we have "turned," but have decided, for various reasons, to cast aside for purposes of this book. Southeast England offers a wealth of medieval and Tudor buildings—more than could be conveniently covered in the time and space allocated to this project. Since our interest and expertise is in the realm of history, rather than architecture, we have tended to place primary focus on those sites of historical importance—places connected to the people and events that shaped England from 1066 to 1600. Secondary focus has been given to the "lesser" sites that can be conveniently visited in tandem with the major sites. Finally, we have included a smattering of attractions that we found just too unique (*or too peculiar*) to overlook. In your travels, you will probably come upon a guildhall or two, several manor homes, many churches and perhaps even a village that you feel was a "glaring omission" on our part. Rest assured: we probably know *of* it but felt there wasn't enough to say *about* it to make it worth our while—or yours.

We had a great time working on this project. Once again, the medieval and Tudor sites of this part of England are exhilarating to explore, the history is lively and fascinating, the people are vivid and real to us. We hope we have managed to bring all of this just as alive for you and that you have every bit as much fun with your own tour of *Medieval and Tudor England: Day Trips South of London.*

TIME LINE

1066   *September 28*
William, Duke of Normandy, lands at Pevensey
with an invasion force of an estimated 7,000 men
and builds a "temporary" castle within the
remains of a Roman and Saxon fortress.

September 29
William moves on to Hastings, constructing
a "prefab" motte and bailey castle to serve as
his base.

October 11
King Harold leads an army out of London, moving south to confront William of Normandy.

October 14
The Norman and Saxon armies meet in an open
field called Senlac. King Harold is killed, and the
Saxon forces are decimated by William's better
trained and equipped men.

Christmas Day
William the Conqueror is crowned King of
England.

1070   William the Conqueror orders a church to
be constructed commemorating the Battle of
Hastings with the altar to be placed on the spot
where King Harold was killed; he also founds an
abbey on the site.

1087   William II succeeds to the throne of England.

1100   Henry I succeeds to the throne of England.

1135   Stephen of Blois usurps the crown of Henry I's designated heir, his daughter the Empress Matilda, and ascends the throne of England.

1139   Empress Matilda arrives in England to begin pressing her claim to the English crown. She is received at Arundel Castle. Fourteen years of civil war commence.

1154   Henry II, son of Empress Matilda, succeeds to the throne of England.

1155   Henry II issues a Royal Charter establishing the Cinque Ports.

1170   Thomas à Becket, Archbishop of Canterbury, is murdered in Canterbury Cathedral by knights who believe they are acting on the wishes of King Henry II.

1173   Thomas à Becket, Archbishop of Canterbury, is canonized by Pope Alexander III.

1189   Richard the Lionheart succeeds to the throne of England.

1199   King John succeeds to the throne of England.

1215   Magna Carta is signed by King John, who immediately reneges on the agreement. Barons begin a rebellion and seize Rochester Castle. John conducts a successful siege of the castle, collapsing one tower through undermining.

1216   France's Prince Louis invades England at the invitation of barons rebelling against King John. The prince unsuccessfully besieges Dover Castle although he captures both Farnham and

Guildford Castles. John dies and nine-year-old
Prince Henry succeeds to the throne of England
as Henry III. The barons' rebellion ceases.

1262   Richard of Wych, Bishop of Chichester, is
        canonized; his shrine in Chichester Cathedral
        becomes an important pilgrimage site.

1264   A baronial army led by Simon de Montfort,
        Earl of Leicester, and Gilbert de Clare, Earl of
        Gloucester, wins a resounding victory over the
        royal forces at the Battle of Lewes, capturing
        King Henry III, his son Prince Edward and his
        brother Richard, Earl of Cornwall.

1272   Edward I succeeds to the throne of England.

1307   Edward II succeeds to the throne of England.

1327   Edward III succeeds to the throne of England.

1377   Ten-year-old Richard II succeeds to the throne
        of England. French forces invade southeast
        England, razing the ports of Rye and Hastings
        before being driven back.

1381   Peasants' Revolt occurs.

1399   Henry Bolingbroke usurps the crown of Richard
        II and ascends the throne of England as Henry IV.

1413   Henry V succeeds to the throne of England.

1422   Henry VI succeeds to the throne of England.

1461   Edward IV deposes Henry VI and ascends the
        throne of England.

1470   The House of Lancaster wins back the crown for
        Henry VI; Edward IV flees in exile.

1471   Edward IV returns from exile and deposes Henry
       VI a second time. Henry is subsequently
       murdered in the Tower of London.

1483   Edward V inherits the throne of England but is
       never crowned because his uncle Richard, Duke
       of Gloucester, claims the crown as Richard III.

1485   Henry Tudor deposes Richard III and ascends
       the throne of England as Henry VII; his marriage
       to Elizabeth of York, daughter of Edward IV,
       ends the Wars of the Roses.

1509   Henry VIII ascends the throne of England.

1525   Cardinal Wolsey "gives" the grand palace of
       Hampton Court to Henry VIII.

1533   Henry VIII divorces Katherine of Aragon and
       marries Anne Boleyn.

1535   John Fisher, Bishop of Rochester, is executed as a
       traitor for his refusal to acknowledge Henry VIII
       as the Supreme Head of the Church of England.
       He was the first English bishop ever to be
       executed by a monarch.

c. 1535–1539   The Dissolution of the Monasteries occurs.

1536   Anne Boleyn is executed on charges of treason;
       Henry VIII weds wife number three, Jane
       Seymour.

1537   Jane Seymour dies of "childbed fever" after
       giving birth to the future Edward VI.

1539   The fourth wife-to-be of Henry VIII, Anne of
       Cleves, arrives at Deal Castle in England.

1540   Henry VIII marries (in January) and divorces (in
       July) Anne of Cleves and then marries (also in

July) his fifth wife, Catherine Howard. (Henry
and Catherine were first married in June —
before his marriage to Anne officially was
declared "null and void" — in a secret ceremony at Hampton Court. *It was a busy year
for Henry.*)

1542   Catherine Howard is arrested at Hampton Court
and charged with committing adultery. She is
taken to the Tower of London, where she is
executed after her trial and conviction.

1543   Henry VIII marries his sixth — and last — wife,
Katherine Parr.

1547   Edward VI succeeds to the throne of England.

1551   Thomas Arden is murdered by his wife and her
lover, a servant, in Faversham; the event serves as
the plot of the first English play to be based on a
contemporary event.

1553   Lady Jane Grey is declared Queen of England
and reigns for nine days before the crown is
claimed by her cousin Princess Mary Tudor.

1554   Nicholas Ridley, Bishop of Rochester, is burned
at the stake by Mary I for his refusal to renounce
Protestantism.

1558   Elizabeth I succeeds to the throne of England.

1564   The Elizabethan playwright Christopher
Marlowe is baptized in St. George's Church,
Canterbury.

1603   Elizabeth I dies at Richmond Palace.

The Amateur Historian's Guide to
Medieval and Tudor England
Day Trips South of London

✝

CONTENTS

Getting There & Getting Organized

f you are a London diehard, the prospect of going to England and NOT staying in London is just too shocking for words, no matter how much you might be hankering for a fresh glimpse of ancient English history. Despair not! There are countless medieval and Tudor sites that you can visit within an easy drive or train ride from London. This book focuses on the myriad attractions to the southeast of London. Numerous castles, abbeys, cathedrals, guildhalls and manors—great and small—are scattered throughout Kent, Sussex and Surrey. We have grouped these into "day trips," the premise being that you can wake up in London, venture into the countryside for your daily dose of history, and be back in time for dinner in the capital city. Travel time to most sites is under two hours, and many (though by no means *all*) of the attractions can be reached by train.

Tip!

The trips in this book have been organized geographically, starting with the sites closest to London and sweeping in a clockwise arc through southeast England.

∿

Let us begin with a few caveats. The first involves mode of travel. Yes, we have taken every trip in this book and we have visited almost every attraction—in some cases, several times. For some visits, we relied on train travel; although this was certainly convenient and affordable, it did leave us rather weary at the end of the day. Most recently, we engaged the services of a car and driver. While we recognize that this can be quite expensive, it may be a luxury worth considering if you are traveling with several companions who can help share the cost, or if you have a specific evening deadline for returning to London—such as a 7:30 p.m. curtain for a "not-to-be-missed" play. Of course, if you're handy with a map and are confident driving in a foreign country, renting your own car and heading off on your own is always an option—albeit one that we've never tried.

Our second caution involves "quality" vs "quantity"; while we have never *(well, hardly ever)* seen a medieval or Tudor site we didn't at least *appreciate*, we have found that there inevitably comes a point when even we suffer from historical overload. There is only so much you can take in, absorb and enjoy in a day. Although some of these day trips offer you a cornucopia of options, you may find it more pleasurable to pick and choose among the available sites—particularly if you face a busy evening back in London.

Whether you opt to "see it all," leaving no ancient stone unturned, or choose to enrich your London vacation with just a glimpse of southeast England, we are confident that you'll enjoy the varied pleasures that await you in Kent, Sussex and Surrey.

BEFORE YOU LEAVE HOME
(assuming home is not England)

This book assumes that you will be traveling *to* London and using that city as the base from which you explore southeast England. Because you will want to have the maximum amount of time to enjoy medieval and Tudor sites—and the minimum amount of time consumed with in-London hassles—we offer you some tried-and-true advice to help your trip run smoothly. Years of London travel, both for business and pleasure, have proven that this system works for us. *(Friends and readers who have taken our words of wisdom to heart swear that it works for them, too!)*

~ Make your hotel reservations in advance

Trial and error have led us to the London hotel that works best for our needs, whether it be business or relaxation *(we take both very seriously)*. If you are a regular visitor to London, you have most likely found a hotel that suits your fancy. If not, there are plenty of travel books and websites that can help you find London accommodations to match your budget and your preferences. The important thing is to do this well in advance. London is a tremendously popular destination, and it is not uncommon to find "your" hotel fully booked months ahead of time. Making your room reservations as early as possible not only gives you the widest choice of hotels, it also gives you immediate access to your hotel's concierge service, which will help you with our next two suggestions.

~ If you have a "must" on your restaurant list, book it now

If you do not hail from a big city, you may find this hard to believe, but believe it you must: many of London's most popular restaurants fill their premium dining hours (7:30–10:00 p.m.) weeks or even months in advance. Keep some flexibility in your evening plans—you don't want to have to race back from every day trip you make. However, if there is a restaurant on your list that has come highly recommended—one you'll be bitterly disappointed not to experience—book it when you plan your trip. Chances are your hotel will be glad to make these reservations for you.

~ Purchase tickets for at least one performance ahead of time

Again, you do not want to fill every evening with written-in-stone plans . . . flexibility and spontaneity can be fun *(or so we've heard . . .)*. Still, if you feel your trip will be less than perfect without a performance by the Royal Shakespeare Company or an evening at the "hottest" West End show, then by all means buy in advance! Several great Internet services offer on-line theater tickets; we use *www.whatsonstage.com*. You can also call the box office directly or prey upon your congenial hotel concierge when you make room reservations.

~ Local currency

While it is not necessary to convert all of your cash into British currency, you will want to have at least a day's worth of spending money in your wallet when you arrive in London. That can be as much as £100, depending on your "day one" plans. Be sure to factor in transportation from the airport and tips for drivers and hotel staff.

Day trips out of London require more cash than a day in London. Whether you bring your pounds from home or acquire them in the UK is a matter of preference. If you are planning to bring traveler's checks, we highly recommend that you bring them in pounds sterling, rather than in the currency of your homeland. Although *bureaus de change* and most banks will cash traveler's checks in foreign currency, many shops and restaurants do not. Be advised that most tellers will require you to present your passport when cashing traveler's checks. If the idea of jaunting around southeast England, passport in hand (as opposed to securing it in your hotel safe), makes you nervous, you will need to cash your traveler's checks before departing London for the day, or upon returning in the evening.

Nearly every London establishment takes credit cards, and the exchange rate usually works in your favor if you pay with plastic. However, as you venture out of London, your need for ready cash increases. Many sites do not accept credit cards or large-denomination traveler's checks for entry fees. Likewise, many pubs and some ancient inns and eateries function on a "cash-only" basis. Automatic teller machines abound in London and are not hard to find in most towns in southeast England. If you do not have a PIN for cash advances on your credit card, acquire one before you leave home.

~ Pack wisely

First and foremost, don't forget to bring this book. If you're planning on spending some of your days in London, you'll also want to be sure to pack the *first* book in our series, *The Amateur Historian's Guide to Medieval and Tudor London*. You'll thank us for that self-serving bit of promotion, believe us! Properly armed with insights into ancient sites, you'll also find that these following items from home make touring all the more enjoyable.

* *Slightly upscale leisure clothes.* As you venture out of London by day, you'll want to dress for comfort, particularly if castles and abbey ruins are on the agenda. Still, jeans that are *too* comfy and shorts that are *too* short are probably not the wisest choice if you're planning on visiting a cathedral or privately owned manor home. There is not a dress code per se, but you will feel more at ease and be treated with more respect if you dress with respect.

* *At least one "smart" outfit for evening.* A cultural and political hub, London is a cosmopolitan city, and attire—at least in the evening—tends to be "smart" rather than super-casual. Even if you are planning to spend the evening out-

side of London—perhaps in one of our suggested ancient inns and eateries—you'll want to bring along a nice outfit and change out of your "touring clothes" before dinner.

- *Walking shoes: a pair and a spare.* Many of the sites in this book involve negotiating stone stairways that are exposed to the elements. Surfaces can be slick and footing less than secure. Your shoes should be comfortable for both standing and walking. Take the time to find comfortable shoes that don't look like they've run too many laps on the treadmill and *break them in ahead of time.* Also, since you are very likely to encounter wet weather, we recommend a spare pair of walking shoes, unless yours are particularly waterproof.

- *Mad dogs and Englishmen.* Both may be able to ignore the elements! You, on the other hand, will find it easier to scoff at the inevitable rain if you've packed a waterproof wind-breaker (preferably with a hood) and a small, well-made (i.e., wind-resistant) umbrella. Should you forget *(or choose to ignore us),* the gift shops at most sites sell these, along with the ubiquitous can't-have-too-many-of-'em souvenir sweatshirts.

- *A lightweight pair of binoculars.* We forgot ours on our most recent trip and regretted every gargoyle, statue, carved boss and painted ceiling that went under-appreciated!

- *A roomy, collapsible tote.* We never leave home without this extra piece of luggage because we always leave England with *way* more than we carried upon arrival. If you have a weakness for guidebooks, postcards, history tomes, biographies and free fliers, then trust us—you'll need a way to get those goodies home! *(Much as we'd like to believe that this book replaces the need for all that extraneous literature, we know too well the temptations of on-site bookshops.)*

NOW THAT YOU'RE THERE,
HOW TO GET *THERE*

Somehow, we suspect that getting in and out of London was really easier when there were just three or four roads and all you had to do was hop on your trusty steed . . . oh well! Gone are those days, and so are the highwaymen, wild beasts and washed-out bridges that were the downside of such convenience. Truly, travel from London to southeast England is really pretty easy. After all, we've made it out and back several times—and are here to tell you about it. *(A true indication that it would have to be at least relatively simple!)*

• *Trains.* Each section of this book is divided into specific day trips. In each instance, we have assumed that London is the point of departure. Most—but not all—of the day trips have at least one major site that is accessible by train. For these sites, we have provided the station from which you'll depart London (i.e., Victoria Station, Charing Cross, etc.) and the station for which you're bound. We have not, however, provided you with train schedules or fares. These you can easily research on your own, once you have plotted out your basic itinerary. The fastest and most efficient way to do this is on the Internet. Go to *www.raileurope.com* and click on Brit Rail (now offering a new Southeast England Rail Pass) or visit *www.railtrack.co.uk.* Enter your departing city (London) and your destination (i.e., Rochester), you will be given all of the train schedules for the day you intend to travel. Alternatively, you can call Brit Rail from home (in the USA, call 1-877-456-RAIL) or Rail Track at 020-7557-8000 upon arrival in London. Most hotel concierges also keep a current rail directory on hand, although we have yet to become adept at reading it.

   Note: In some cases, the town you are visiting is accessible by train, but the site you want to see is farther than walking distance from the station. In these instances, you will need to use a taxi service. Most train stations have cab service on hand; all have phones from which you can call the local service if no cabs are waiting. Also note that in some of the day trips, the primary site may be accessible by train, but the outlying sites are not. Again, taxis are your best option here.

• *Motorcoach/bus.* Many sites are also accessible by motorcoach (upscale buses that run specialty tours to specific destinations) or by bus (by which we mean your basic public transportation). Since we have not tried this method of traveling through southeast England, we have not published bus or motorcoach details in this book. However, there are two relatively easy ways to check this out, if you're interested. The first is to call the site—which we *always* urge you to do before you drop by, for reasons which we'll explain further on. The second is to log on to *www.south eastengland.uk.com*, an indispensable website, about which we'll wax eloquent in a moment.

• *Car rental vs. car hire.* Some people don't think twice about arriving at a foreign airport, hopping into a rental car and heading out on the highway, armed with great maps, an unerring sense of direction and a healthy dose of derring-do. We are not some of those people. We find that European drivers travel at breakneck speeds, which makes it rather dangerous to make that spur-of-the-moment stop when an ancient ruin catches your eye (or you've missed your turn . . .). Nor have we ever quite mastered that "opposite" thing England has going—not only do the cars travel in the left-hand lane, but the steering column is on the right-hand side of the car. We prefer to sit back, check our manuscript and leave the driving to someone else. However, if you are one of those people who appreciates both the autonomy and the economy of driving yourself—and you're comfortable doing so—go to it! We have provided you with the most direct routes from London to each of the listed sites, using main arteries and the best-marked roadways. Ours are not always the *fastest* routes, but they are, in our minds, the clearest. Still, you will want to invest in at least one, and possibly two, great maps. We recommend both the A–Z series (they produce one on southeast England, as well as individual maps for Kent, Sussex and Surrey) and the Great Britain Ordinance Surveys, which do a grand job of giving you landmarks and obscure markers that will help you get your bearings.

♦ Another option is to hire a car and driver. Convenience is the advantage here—you will be picked up at your hotel, driven directly to all of the sites of your choice, and returned to your hotel as close as possible to the time you specify. Cost is the disadvantage. You can expect fees to run in the range of £30–£35 per hour, or a flat rate of about £200 for a full day of touring. Should you choose this method of travel, ask your hotel for recommendations. Most hotels have a service that they use on a regular basis (although they may add a mark-up to the driver's fees, so ask). Do not hesitate to request several recommendations, so that you can comparison-shop. You can also use the Internet to search for firms. We used Google to search for "Cars & Drivers, London," checked references, bartered bids and discovered a driver who was top-notch in every way. You can, too.

LEARN TO LOVE BRITISH TELECOM

You will note that every site in this book has a phone number. USE IT! We cannot stress how important it is to get into the habit of calling sites ahead of time. The numbers we give in the book are preceded by a zero (0); this is the number you will use when calling a site from London or from anywhere else in England. If you wish to call from another country, you will drop the zero, and add the international code and the country code. When calling from the USA, for instance, you would dial 011-44-(drop zero)-number.

Why is it important to call ahead? There are several reasons. One is to verify opening hours. Although we have made every effort to give you accurate, up-to-the-minute opening times, these can (and do!) change. Many a time, we have stood before a locked gate or closed door and wished we'd made that simple call before leaving London. Another reason to call is to see if any special events are occurring during your stay, which may dictate a change in your plans. Festivals, workshops, concerts, lectures and school tours are but a few of the "surprises" you might encounter at any given site—knowing about them ahead of time will allow you to join in (or avoid them). Perhaps you'll want to call and get details for bus or motorcoach service from London—most sites have this printed out and will fax it to you at your hotel if you ask; all will be glad to give you advice by phone. Most staff can also give you directions on how best to travel from one site on your agenda to the next, provided those sites are fairly close to one another (and the sites in each day trip are). Finally, we have found the staff at the sites throughout southeast England knowledgeable, helpful and genuinely enthused by amateur historians. If you call your primary site ahead of time, you may be able to arrange a special tour or gain access to a part of the property that's officially closed. With advance notice, most sites will try to accommodate your needs and interests.

SOUTHEAST ENGLAND WEBSITE

We cannot say enough great things about this website. In addition to finding brief summaries about the sites in this book, you'll obtain transportation information, locator maps, updates on special events, dining and accommodations, shopping and suggestions of "non-historical" ways to spend your time in this beautiful part of England. Spend enough time browsing this website and you may rethink your plans to use London as your home base. Go to *www.southeastengland.uk.com*. Have fun!

INSIGHTS, ASIDES
AND OTHER HANDY TIPS

~ Admission fees

For the sake of brevity, we have listed the basic adult and basic child admissions for all attractions that charge an entry fee. We have also let you know if there is a "family ticket" or discounted admission for families. Please note, however, that every attraction seems to have a different policy on discounts ("concessions") for senior citizens, students, groups and visitors with special physical needs. Don't hesitate to ask; you may well find a few pence savings over the price we've quoted.

In addition, there are widely divergent policies on the age of a "child" (anything from over 3 to under 15) and what constitutes a family (two adults and two children, two adults and three children, etc.). You can assume the price we quote is the highest price an adult or child would have to pay (as of the time of publication). In many cases, you'll be in for a pleasant surprise, in the form of a lower-priced ticket!

You will also want to note that although most churches do not officially charge an admission fee, a donation is both encouraged and appreciated. Let's face it—the cost of maintaining these ancient buildings is staggering. In most instances, we have found a donation of £2.00 per person is about right; the prices for church literature range from 20p to £1.00 per handout.

Finally, both **English Heritage** and the **National Trust** have overseas membership opportunities. Essentially, you make a donation to the organization and, depending on the level of your contribution, you obtain reduced admission to several (or all) of the sites run by that group. We have not taken advantage of this plan—they tend to include too many "après-Elizabeth" sites for our purposes—but if you plan to include attractions beyond the medieval and Tudor eras, check it out. From the USA, call 011-44-870-333-1182 for English Heritage's member services department. The National Trust's Royal Oak Foundation for American members can be contacted at 1-800-913-6565 or at *www.royal-oak.org.*

~ Open hours

Let us be *very* clear: the farther you go from London, the more "flexible" the open hours . . . that's our euphemism for wildly inconsistent. We've had more than a small number of disappointments after showing up at a site with clearly posted open hours, only to find the site locked up tight. On the other hand, we've also happened by sites that were supposedly closed and, to our delight, found them . . . open! We've visited castles where the portcullis started to groan threateningly because it was a) raining b) dusky c) within an hour of the posted closing time for the day. Some sites close if a large group has booked the facility for a special function. And, due to the age of all of these sites, closures for maintenance are not uncommon. We don't mean to sound negative, but if there's a site you simply *must* see, we recommend calling in advance, *both* when planning your itinerary and again before you leave London.

With regard to holidays, it is safe to assume that all sites are closed on December 24 and 25; most sites are closed on Good Friday, Easter and New Year's Day as well. Then there's the maddening issue of Bank Holiday Mondays; some sites that are typically closed on Mondays are open on Bank Holiday Mondays, while others that are usually open on Mondays may opt to *close* due to the holiday. Again, call in advance!

There are, however, some general rules of thumb that will help you as you start to plan your trip. Generally, most attractions in England have "summer" hours and "winter" hours. The summer season tends to stretch from Easter Monday through mid-to-late October. Winter hours are generally in effect from November 1 through March. In almost every instance, historic attractions are open more days of the week, for longer hours each day, during the summer.

You will note that we have not included the open hours for

tourist information centers. They are widely divergent. However, you can assume that most are open Monday through Friday during that particular town's retail business hours. Weekend hours may be more limited. All information centers post their hours; if you arrive too early, check back later in the day.

Note: It is also important to note that, despite the stated "closing" hour, the last admission to many sites is actually one hour before closing (i.e., if a site "closes" at 5 p.m., the latest you will be admitted may well be 4 p.m.).

~ Churches

The good news is that southeast England abounds with ancient churches. The bad news is that so many of them are open on an extremely limited basis. Nor is showing up on Sunday necessarily the answer. In towns with more than one church of a particular denomination, the churches tend to split the worship schedules, with one offering weekday (or evening) services and the other Sunday services. In your travels, you will probably happen upon several churches with *portions* of their architecture dating from the Middle Ages. Consider them a bonus—particularly if you can gain access. For the reasons cited above, we have not attempted to include all the ancient churches of southeast England in this book. We *have* included several churches, close to primary sites, where the history, the architecture or the ability to get in is out of the ordinary.

ANCIENT INNS AND EATERIES

Frankly, we love our history, but we also love our cushy Knightsbridge hotel and the culinary (and liquid!) delights of London at the end of a long day of sightseeing. We realize, however, that many of you can't get enough of all things medieval and Tudor. For you, we have nosed around and come up with a list of B&Bs, country hotels, inns, pubs and restaurants where you can indulge in a total immersion experience. We are confident you'll enjoy every minute. At the end of most trips, you'll find a listing of **Ancient Inns and Eateries**. These are establishments where at least a portion of the "public" areas date from the Middle or Tudor Ages. In cases where we have actually experienced the hospitality on offer, we indicate as much, waxing eloquent as we are prone to do. In most cases, however, we have *not* visited the listed establishments. Therefore, please do not assume that the listing of a particular spot in our book is an endorsement; it is not. *(We are amateur historians, not hotel/restaurant critics, although some would beg to differ!)* In any (and every!) case, call ahead for directions, open hours and prices. Where we were able to find phone numbers, we have included them.

If you are keen on an even more in-depth "slice of life" experience and your vacation schedule allows, be sure to check out the many intriguing overnight accommodations operated by the **Landmark Trust**. The Trust maintains a host of ancient buildings where you can spend an evening or a week, depending on the property. None of these facilities offer meals — "self-catering" (you shop, you cook, you clean up . . . or you find a restaurant in town) is the name of the game. Still, the chance to stay in very-close-to-original-period surroundings is one you may not want to miss. We were particularly tempted by the lure of a night or two at **Hampton Court Palace**. In order to obtain listings, prices and terms, you must purchase the Trust's guidebook, which costs about $25.00. In the USA, phone 1-802-254-6868 or go to *www.landmarktrust.co.uk*.

Tip!

We have encountered some B&Bs that do not have in-room or public phones for their houseguests. If it is important for you to be available by telephone, check the policy before checking in. A cell phone with an international calling plan could solve this problem.

CAROLE AND SARAH'S GREATEST HITS

Suppose you're not quite ready for total immersion in the history of southeast England, amateur or otherwise. Maybe you only have a day or two to spare, or perhaps you'd rather just sample some of the delights outside of London before committing to the full menu. Or maybe you'd rather just cut to the chase and have us prioritize your travels for you. That's what we're here for . . . glad to be of help!

The following is our very subjective list of *not-to-be-missed* sites in southeast England, with some extra-added help in planning "theme" trips for all you specialists. When you've seen 'em all, we'd love to know *your* top picks!

~ When time is of the essence . . .

See **Eltham Palace**. It's less than a half hour from London, the history is compelling and the interior design is unlike any "medieval" site you've ever seen.

~ Best close-in day trip . . .

This is a toss-up between **Faversham** and **Rochester**. For some, a trip isn't worth its salt if there's not a castle or a cathedral involved; Rochester has both, and a very nice side trip to the charming village of Cobham as well. However, for our money, Faversham has the slight edge. No castle, no cathedral, but an incredibly well-preserved medieval town, with houses, churches, inns and a guildhall that date from the Middle Ages.

~ Want to go farther afield?

It has to be **Dover**. Although almost too far to qualify for a day trip (two hours, each way), Dover is easily accessible by direct train, bus and motorcoach. The castle is one of the very best we've ever visited, with fascinating history and engaging displays. If you have the time, you must visit!

~ Sleeping away from London, forsooth!

We suggest you set your sights on **Rye**. Rye is a convenient stopover between day trips to **Maidstone** or **Sevenoaks** and Dover. There are a whole host of ancient inns and eateries in a wide range of prices, and the medieval sites in Rye can be enjoyed in a few very easy hours.

~ Totally Tudor . . .

See **Sevenoaks**. The entire day trip is devoted almost exclusively to Tudor manor homes, including Anne Boleyn's childhood home, **Hever**. There are so many sites you'd be hard-pressed to see them in a day.

~ Castle crazed . . .

The **Arundel** day trip is all about castles—although you'll have to spend the night in one in order to see it firsthand. If you choose to spend the night and want to stick to the castle theme, combine this trip with a visit to **Lewes**.

~ Best cathedral . . .

We are taking a *big* risk here, but we both agree: **Chichester Cathedral** edges out most others we've visited, with fewer tourists and a very evocative sense of the spiritual. Of course, you can't beat the history of **Canterbury Cathedral**, and the town of Canterbury offers more than enough to keep you busy for the day. Your choice; we've given you *our* opinion!

~ Shopping spree!

All right, all right, we admit it. Sometimes we've just had *enough* history and need some attitude adjustment to set us back on track. When it's too early for happy hour, shopping does the trick, and we have found the best shopping outside of London in the town of **Guildford**. By the way, the historic sites here are top-notch, too.

LOOKING BACK ON LONDON

Much as we enjoyed every hour we spent in southeast England researching this book, there were times when our action-packed itinerary simply demanded that we "stay put" for the day. Staying put, for us, meant a day spent in London, revisiting some of our favorite ancient sites *(and shops, and restaurants, and museums, too!)*. If you find yourself inclined to spend a day or two in London — and you haven't had the opportunity to purchase and enjoy the first book in our series — here are a few "not-to-be-missed" suggestions. You'll find details on these and many more attractions in *The Amateur Historian's Guide to Medieval and Tudor London.*

~ One day in London? Off the beaten path!

We really don't think you can do justice to the Tower and Westminster Abbey in under a half day each, so avoid the crowds and take home pictures your friends and neighbors are less likely to have in their scrapbooks! We suggest you see:

* *The 11th-century church of St. Bartholomew the Great, Smithfield*
* *The knights' effigies at Temple Church, Holborn*
* *The Guildhall*

or

* *Shakespeare's Southwark:* cathedral, palace, prison and theater, all within walking distance

~ Ready for exercise?

Walk the Wall! The ancient medieval wall, which enclosed the one-square-mile City of London, can be traced on foot . . . provided you have comfortable walking shoes, the right mix of curiosity and patience, and a helpful guide *(you'll find the 21 Wall remnants detailed in our first book)*. It gets your legs moving, your blood pumping, and your mind stretching.

~ It's raining, it's pouring?

It's London. Ignore it. *(Although this may not be the best time to catch an open-air performance at Shakespeare's Globe.)*

CONTENTS

Laying the Foundation

SOUTHEAST ENGLAND

 eginning as long ago as prehistoric times, the story of the people who populated England is one of migration and invasion. The southeast coast, lying so close to the Continent, played a prominent role in the settlement and conquest of the country. Offering good, natural harbors and a short crossing of the English Channel, the southeast coast was the most logical landing point. From here, both peaceful settlers and invading armies spread inland. This pattern was followed by the first nomadic tribes to move from the Continent to England and by all subsequent invaders—from the Celts to the Romans to the Saxons to the Normans.

The lessons learned and the tactics employed by those who preceded the Normans outlined a strategy that William the Conqueror and his followers were careful to follow as they moved to gain the English crown for William and solidify his hold on the throne. Understanding at least the basics of England's earliest history helps us better comprehend the plan William implemented after the Battle of Hastings in 1066. The attention he and his followers lavished on the defense of this most vulnerable part of the country continued to pay dividends through the 20th century.

THE ROMANS (55 BCE–450 CE*)

It was from the Romans that England first got its name "Britannia." Curious as to how this little-known land could enhance his empire, Julius Caesar invaded England in 55 BCE. Dover had already been well fortified by the Celts, so Caesar bypassed it, landing north of Dover and marching inland, conquering Celtic tribes as he moved. Caesar was content just to demand payment of annual tribute from the local chieftains . . . "render unto Caesar" suited his purposes just fine. This remained the state of affairs between Rome and Britannia until 43 CE when the Emperor Claudius decided it was beneficial to make this frontier land a full part of the Roman Empire (so much more to render!).

To enforce the emperor's plan, Roman legions landed in Kent and constructed a supply base at **Richborough** (near Sandwich). The remains of the fortress they constructed can still be seen today. The legions met fierce resistance along the River Medway, but tribal forces were no match for the redoubtable Roman troops. There was hardly a pause in the forward march of the legions.

As they spread throughout southeast England, the Romans built other forts and settlements at strategic sites. It was a classic case of "location, location, location." The wisdom they showed

---

*For years, the accepted method of historical dating has been to use "BC" ("before Christ," for those years prior to the birth of Jesus, arbitrarily designated as year 1) and "AD" (Anno Domini: the years following Jesus' birth). Many religions, however, do not recognize the birth of Christ, and some cultures use other methods of historical dating. In recent years, an increasing number of authors and historians have adopted the more inclusive "Common Era" dating system. We have chosen to follow course. When you see "BCE" (Before Common Era), know that we are referring to the years familiarly known as "BC." Similarly, "CE" refers to the period of time traditionally known as "AD."

in selecting these points of control, particularly along the coast, is underscored by the fact that the invaders who came later often employed the same strongholds, building their own style of fortifications on top of the Roman ruins. This is true of **Pevensey**, Dover, Herne Bay, Rochester and almost every other strategic point of southeast England. Roman, Saxon, Norman, later medieval and Tudor ruins are all mixed together—which presents no small challenge to amateur historians poking among the ancient rocks and rubble, trying to separate one period from another! (*Don't worry; we'll help you.*) In particular, traces of the Roman occupation can be found in a lighthouse converted to a church bell tower at Dover Castle; well-preserved wall paintings in what was once a hotel for Roman soldiers at the **Roman Painted House**, also in Dover; the fascinating remains of elaborate Roman villas at **Lullingstone**, **Fishbourne** (near Chichester), **Bignor** and the **Roman Museum in Canterbury**; another fort at **Reculver** in Herne Bay; and the ruins of the only known Roman temple that became a Christian church, **Faversham Stone Chapel**.

THE SAXONS (450–1066)

It didn't take long after the collapse of Roman control of England early in the 5th century for the Saxons, those fierce warriors who came across the North Sea from Denmark and Saxony, to take advantage of the now defenseless Britons. By the end of the 5th century, they had firmly established themselves in southeast England, carving out turf and creating the kingdoms of the South Saxons (Sussex) as well as the East (Essex) and the West (Wessex). From these strongholds, the Saxons, joining forces with the Angle invaders from Germany, spread slowly, but inexorably, throughout the rest of England.

• •
☞ Did you know?
The Saxon kings of Kent in the 8th century were the first to mint the "pennies" that became the bedrock of English currency.
• •

Christianity traveled with them. The Saxon King Ethelbert of Kent was among the first to embrace the new religion at the end of the 6th century. It was he who greeted St. Augustine when the monk came to England in 597 on a mission sanctioned by Pope Gregory.

Because of the Saxon endorsement, Christianity spread rapidly throughout southeast England, with Canterbury serving as the central spoke from which the Church's tentacles branched. Traces of the old Saxon churches can be found at **St. Martin's** in Canterbury, at **St. Mary-in-Castro** on the grounds of Dover Castle, in **Rochester Cathedral** (site of the second oldest bishopric in England), at **Reculver** and in many of the medieval parish churches scattered throughout southeast England. You also will find the tombs of several Saxon saints and kings among the ruins of **St. Augustine's Abbey** in Canterbury.

◆ ◆

☞ **Did you know?**

Legend has it that it was at Herne Bay, site of the old Roman stronghold, that St. Augustine first set foot on English soil.

◆ ◆

Southeast England remained a Saxon stronghold as Danish invaders took over much of the rest of England in the 11th century. Therefore, this wave of invaders left little mark on this part of the country. It wasn't until the Norman invasion and conquest of 1066 that the Saxons lost their hegemony in southeast England.

THE NORMAN INVASION

Borrowing a page from Julius Caesar's book, William the Conqueror began his invasion of England by bypassing Dover. It would be the last successful invasion of England. He landed at Pevensey on September 28, 1066, building upon the fortifications left by his Roman and Saxon predecessors to create a beachhead. From there, he began moving up the English coastline, raiding as he went to goad the last Saxon king, Harold Godwinson, into joining battle in the south. Following his victory at the **Battle of Hastings**, William continued moving up the coast and then inland, building fortifications and putting brutal, reliable men in charge as he went to secure his line of retreat and forcibly subdue the land and people *(perhaps the real reason behind his nickname William the Bastard!)*. He never varied from this early method of success—dividing England into fiefdoms, rewarding his followers

> ☛ **Did you know?**
>
> It wasn't just Julius Caesar who gave Duke William clues as to how to stage a successful invasion of England. The Conqueror may have learned from the Saxons as well. Pevensey was also the 491 CE landing site of Aelle, the first king of Sussex.

with control of vast tracts of land and ordering them to construct strong castles from which a few men-at-arms could venture forth to defend large territories. Thus was England conquered and a new way of life introduced to the island nation.

THE LAST SAXON KING: HAROLD II (C. 1020–1066)

Big, bold, brash, brave; vainglorious, rash, intemperate and lusty—all are adjectives that could be applied to Harold Godwinson, the last Saxon king who, ironically, had not one drop of royal blood in his veins. His death at the Battle of Hastings ended 600 years of English rule by Saxon kings.

Harold was the second of six sons of Godwin, Earl of Wessex. An able, ambitious man, Godwin was the leader of an aggressive family which had gathered much wealth and power. His daughter Edith was married to King Edward the Confessor (reigned 1042–66) and the family, at the height of its power, controlled four of the six great earldoms in England. Needless to say, this abundance of riches caused much jealousy among the other lords and left the king in a resentful and fearful frame of mind.

Edward took action to break the family's power in 1051 and managed to drive Earl Godwin and his sons into exile. Their lands were confiscated and divided among royal favorites. Edith was sent to a nunnery. But in 1052, the family regrouped, and Godwin and Harold led a two-pronged invasion into England, overwhelming Edward's forces and pressuring the king into negotiations that fully restored the family to its former glory.

Harold inherited his father's title and power in 1053 (his elder brother, Sweyn, died in September 1052 on the return leg of a pilgrimage to the Holy Land). As the most powerful lord in England, Harold dominated Edward and was effectively the de facto king of England for the last 13 years of Edward's reign.

On the day Edward the Confessor died, January 5, 1066, Harold boldly stepped forward to claim the Crown of England for himself, announcing to the world that the saintly king, with his dying breath, had bequeathed the throne to him. Thus, Harold usurped the throne from Edward's blood heir, his young nephew Edgar the Ætheling, and ignored competing claims from William, Duke of Norway, and Harold Hardraada, King of Norway. Harold was coronated the next day in Westminster Abbey—the day of Edward the Confessor's funeral.

This was the beginning of Harold's real troubles. According to the *Anglo-Saxon Chronicle*, "Eorl Harold was also hallowed king—and he had little peace during the time he ruled the kingdom." Needless to say, neither William of Normandy or Harold Hardraada was going to peacefully accept Harold's assumption of the throne. Both began immediate preparations for pressing their claims with military might. Between guarding against invasion threats from rival claimants and subduing recalcitrant nobles, Harold had little time to enjoy his brief kingship. The last Saxon king spent almost all of the 10 months of his reign in battle of one form or another.

• •

☞ Did you know?

The whole issue of the succession to the English monarchy was further complicated by Harold's 1064 sojourn at the court of William, Duke of Normandy. Historians differ on the reasons why Harold paid a visit to William. Some believe it was because Harold had been sent on a diplomatic mission by Edward the Confessor. Others maintain that Harold was shipwrecked, captured and turned over as a prisoner. Regardless of the reason why he was there, Norman chroniclers, in particular that magnificent piece of political propaganda known as the Bayeux Tapestry, reported that during his stay, Harold swore to be William's liege man and to uphold the duke's claim to the throne of England. Thus, the Normans viewed (*or at least spun*) Harold's usurpation of the crown as a treasonous betrayal and a repudiation of an oath swore on holy relics—a major sin in those days.

• •

DIVVYING UP THE SPOILS

From a pre-Conquest perspective, William the Bastard's proposed invasion of England to gain a crown was no sure thing. In fact, it was a very risky venture, pitting a small invasion force against the might of all of Anglo-Saxon England, with no sure means of supply and/or escape should the need arise.

Recruitment, therefore, was a tricky business. William was forced to lure support with the promise of rich booty and lavish rewards. Needless to say, it was the most greedy, adventurous and unscrupulous of men who thus flocked to William's banner. Their only reward would come through victory and so they fought hard at the Battle of Hastings to win it.

They achieved their objective and expected their rewards. But one narrow victory did not win a country. William still had to subdue the rest of England and force the nobles who had not died at the Battle of Hastings, the English church and the people to succumb to his rule. His strategy for meeting both needs — rewarding his supporters and subduing the English people — was to give custody of huge tracts of land to key supporters who would then construct fortified castles from which they could control their new territories.

William was too wise to concentrate too much power in the hands of one man — especially men like the ones who had followed him to England. He knew he would be absent from England for long periods of time when he traveled to the Continent to oversee his lands there. (He was still Duke of Normandy and held numerous neighboring lands that he had conquered over the years.) And the instability of a newly conquered domain could pose a great temptation when the king's back was turned. So William divided authority, particularly in southeast England. He awarded control of Kent to his half brother Odo, Bishop of Bayeux. The Isle of Wight went to William Fitz Osbern. Sussex was divided into five "rapes": Hastings, which went first to Humphrey de Tilleul but soon passed to Robert, Count of Eu; Pevensey, granted to William's other half brother, Robert, Count of Mortain; Lewes, awarded to William de Warenne; Bramber, given to William de Braose; and Arundel, bestowed upon Roger de Montgomery. This division of spoils set the pattern for the way all of England would be governed by the Normans as solidification of control moved across the land.

These men and their descendants became some of the most powerful magnates of the post-Conquest era. They all acquired estates in other parts of England as the Conquest spread inland and established power bases throughout the country. Their names echo down through medieval and Tudor history, associated with most of the famous — and infamous — events of the times.

◇◇

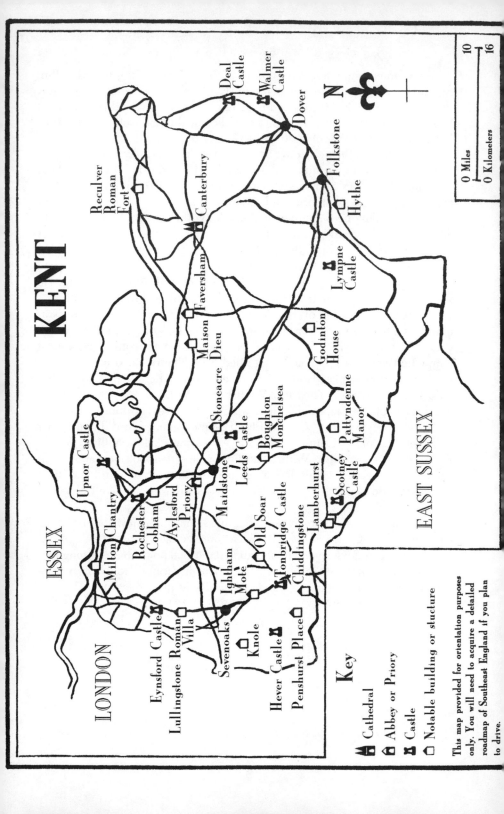

·····3·····

Kent

◇

◇   ◇   ◇

CONTENTS

Greater London

Testing the Waters

hen we first started writing this chapter, we thought the heading "Greater London" was a misnomer. What could be "greater" than London, our favorite city in the world, chock-full of medieval and Tudor treasures, all of which are enhanced by the glamour and pizzazz of a very cosmopolitan cultural experience. But as we began to venture further afield, we found—to our surprise and delight—a wonderful assortment of ancient castles, palaces, abbeys, priories, cathedrals and common buildings, enhanced in their own way by beautiful scenery and a far more leisurely pace.

If you find yourself with only a half day—or even just a couple of hours—to indulge in the history outside of London, you'll be happy to realize that there are some wonderful attractions just minutes beyond the capital. All are easily accessible by public transportation and each is bound to whet your appetite for sampling the many grand attractions just slightly further afield.

By the way, don't be surprised if you run into us at Eltham Palace . . . we are sure no one would mind much if we simply made ourselves at home!

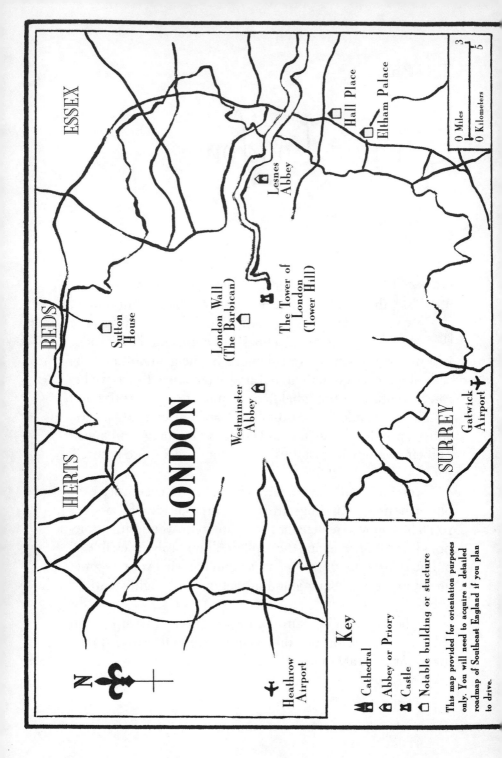

✝ Eltham Palace
Eltham Palace Courtyard
Eltham

>>

PHONE
020-8294-2548

LOCATED
M25 to junction 3, then A20 and follow signs to Eltham; from central
London, take the A2 to Eltham.

TRAVEL
Trains depart Charing Cross and Victoria Stations for Eltham Station. From there, turn left onto Well Hall Road, continue over
Eltham High Street, then walk along Court Yard to the palace
gates. Travel time is approximately 30 minutes.

OPEN
10:00 a.m.–6:00 p.m. Wednesday–Friday and Sunday, April–
September
10:00 a.m.–5:00 p.m. Wednesday–Friday and Sunday, October
10:00 a.m.–4:00 p.m. Wednesday–Friday and Sunday, November–
March
Also open Bank Holiday Mondays, year-round; phone for hours.

ADMISSION
£6.00 Adults
£3.00 Children
£4.40 Seniors

CONVENIENCES
Tearoom and gift shop

>>

Although we had read about Eltham for years, during our earliest visits to London the palace was closed for renovation. During later visits it was open, but on a very limited schedule. Still, our hunch that a visit to Eltham would be well worth the effort was so strong that we rearranged an entire trip to England around our ability to gain access to the palace. We were not disappointed. Surprised, yes . . . but not disappointed.

The "Eltham surprise" is that there are two separate, very different buildings on the palace grounds: the medieval Great

Hall, which dates from the reign of Edward IV, and a 20th-century Art Deco showpiece that left us itching to redecorate our homes. *(We'll let you in on a little secret: our hearts may belong to the Middle Ages, but our tastes are firmly rooted in 1930s Hollywood!)*

Christmas retreat of the Plantagenets, nursery palace for the Tudors—Eltham was, perhaps, the "coziest" residence of the English monarchs from the 13th century through the reign of Henry VIII. Its convenient location, on a hillside just 5 miles southeast of London, afforded easy access to Westminster, with commanding views of the capital and air considerably sweeter than that of the malodorous City. The name is believed to stem from the Saxon word *ealdham,* meaning "old [*eald*] settlement [*ham*]"—an indication that Eltham may be one of London's oldest suburbs. The village dates at least as far back as the Norman Conquest, when a local manor was granted by William the Conqueror to his brother Odo, Bishop of Bayeux and Earl of Kent.

Despite these ancient roots, little of historic importance seems to have occurred in Eltham's early years. At some point in the late 11th century, the estate reverted to the Crown; it was eventually divided between the monarchy and the powerful de Mandeville family . . . perhaps to sweeten the pot in an attempt to purchase the loyalty of the fair-weather Geoffrey de Mandeville during the civil war between King Stephen and his cousin the Empress Matilda. There are 12th-century references to "Eltham de Mandeville"; the nature of that property, however, is lost to history.

We do know that by 1297, a manor of considerable proportion existed at Eltham. It was owned by Anthony Bek, Bishop of Durham. Although Bek was a contemporary of Edward I, his sympathies and support lay with the king's controversial son, the first Prince of Wales. Bek was quick to show his fondness for the prince when Edward II succeeded his father to the throne in 1307.

Although Eltham was surely not as sumptuous as the second

Edward's other royal digs, it was apparently adequate for the needs of his haughty consort, Isabella, "She-Wolf of France." Isabella retreated to Eltham in 1312, following the birth of her first son (the future Edward III), believing it to be "healthier" than either Windsor or Westminster. She returned four years later for the birth of her second son, John of Eltham. It's a darn good thing Isabella was partial to the place; as dowager queen, she spent a good amount of time at Eltham under "house arrest" . . . a relatively benevolent punishment for the role she played in Edward II's brutal murder.

◆◆◆◆◆◆◆◆◆◆◆◆◆◆◆◆◆◆◆◆◆◆

☞ Did you know?

Although he was the oldest surviving son of Edward I, Edward II was, in fact, his parents' 14th child. His three elder brothers, John, Henry and Alphonso, all preceded the Prince of Wales to the grave, while the laws of primogeniture (and several premature deaths) prevented any of his 11 older sisters from inheriting Edward I's crown.

◆◆◆◆◆◆◆◆◆◆◆◆◆◆◆◆◆◆◆◆◆◆

During the reign of Edward III, Eltham finally began to evolve from a cozy country getaway to a manor befitting a monarch. Royal residences were beginning to rely less upon fortification and more upon beautification as a means for overawing the public. This trend is evident in the attention Edward gave Eltham—he lavished a then-staggering £2,237 on the palace in the 1350s. He constructed a massive wooden bridge across the moat and built separate great chambers for himself and Queen Philippa, which were connected by a covered walkway. Special attention was given to the gardens and a vineyard was added (*presumably for ambience and not for wine*). The Eltham deer park was expanded and bountifully stocked with a variety of game; for the next 300 years, Eltham would be one of the monarchy's most-frequented hunting grounds.

This emphasis on Eltham's "great outdoors" was reflected in life at the palace. During the 1340s, Eltham was a favorite proving ground for Edward III's son the Black Prince and his fellow knights-in-arms. When not waging war on France, the young warriors spent many hours parading their prowess on Eltham's tournament grounds. So rigorous was the "sport" at these competitions that during a 1341 joust celebrating the visit of the Black Prince's uncle the Count of Hainault, the guest of honor himself was wounded.

Eltham also provided Edward's family with a safe haven from the devastation of the Black Death. It is recorded that the king and his loved ones, along with the royal physician, Master Gaddesen, retreated to the healthier confines of the palace to weather the 1348 outbreak of the plague.

Enthusiastic as the Black Prince was about Eltham's grassy fields, it was his son Richard II who cultivated a particular fondness for the palace proper. As a young king, Richard masterminded extensive improvements to the royal residence, sparing little expense in making Eltham one of the most luxurious palaces of the era. Nearly fanatical when it came to personal hygiene, Richard (the king who introduced the linen handkerchief to nobles accustomed to blowing their nose into their bare palms) constructed a state-of-the-art bathhouse at Eltham where the royal family could soak, primp and preen in relative comfort and privacy. A spectacular painted chamber and a separate dancing chamber reflected Richard's love of art and music. Many palace windows were replaced with brilliant stained glass and the surrounding gardens were laid with turf.

Richard enjoyed entertaining on a lavish scale. He added both a spicery and a saucery to aid in the preparation of elaborate feasts and constructed luxurious accommodations for his overnight guests. His powerful uncle John of Gaunt maintained private apartments at Eltham, as did Lady Lutell ("housemother" for the queen's handmaids) and royal favorites Robert de Vere and Thomas Mowbray.

All of this effort was not for naught. Richard spent consider-

• • • • • • • • • • • • • • • • • • • •

☞ Did you know?

The great English poet Geoffrey Chaucer could not earn his keep by pen alone *(we can sympathize)*. During the reign of Richard II, Chaucer was the king's Clerk of the Works for the Greenwich area and Eltham Palace came under his direct supervision. Allusions to Eltham, as well as to the palaces of Sheen and Greenwich, can be found in some of Chaucer's earlier works.

• • • • • • • • • • • • • • • • • • • •

able time at Eltham, particularly whenever relations with parliament went sour. He would abandon Westminster in times of duress and seek the solace of his country palace. Together with Queen Anne of Bohemia, Richard could be found strolling the vine-covered walkways and fragrant gardens of Eltham. The king and queen kept Christmas at Eltham in 1392–93, enjoying entertainment by mummers from London and receiving remarkable gifts, such as a one-hump camel and a rather ungainly pelican.

Yet, despite its comparative tranquility, Eltham was no stranger to strife. During the tempestuous autumn of 1386, young King Richard essentially boycotted the "Wonderful Parliament," infuriated by its intent to interfere in his choice of close advisors and counselors. He was pursued to Eltham by his uncle the Duke of Gloucester and Thomas Arundel, Bishop of Ely, who badgered Richard with complaints and pleaded with him to acquiesce on at least *some* of parliament's demands. It was also at Eltham that John of Gaunt, clad in chain mail and escorted by an armed retinue, nearly came to blows with Richard over rumors of the king's plot to kill him. Clearly, wherever Richard went, trouble was bound to follow.

Richard's successor, the usurper Henry Bolingbroke, also cultivated an affection for Eltham. As Henry IV, he oversaw the addition of a handsome library to house his impressive literary collection. Henry also selected the palace as the site of his second marriage. A widower for eight years, the 36-year old monarch chose as his new wife Joan of Navarre, widow of Duke John IV of Brittany. The wedding was held in the Eltham chapel on April 3, 1402; unfortunately, the bride was unable to attend. Her envoy, Anthony Riez, had the honor of standing in for Joan *(one can't help but wonder if he was the pleased recipient of the king's traditional wedding kiss)*. On a more solemn note, Henry IV spent his last Christmas at Eltham, just a few short months

• • • • • • • • • • • • • • • • • • •
☞ Did you know?
Henry IV is the only monarch to have died at Westminster Abbey and one of the few not to be buried there. He was laid to rest in Canterbury Cathedral.
• • • • • • • • • • • • • • • • • • •

before his 1413 death in the Jerusalem Chamber at Westminster Abbey.

Little is known about Henry V's relation with Eltham Palace, with one interesting exception involving the Lollard uprising. In January 1414, a band of would-be kidnappers, led by Henry's onetime friend Sir John Oldcastle, disguised themselves as mummers and set out to capture the king at Eltham, where he was celebrating Twelfth Night. Their plot was foiled. Oldcastle managed to escape and flee the country; his co-conspirators were arrested and hanged. Oldcastle would live on in infamy: he is believed to be the prototype for Shakespeare's character Sir John Falstaff, the pub-crawling partner of Prince Hal in *Henry IV: Parts I and II.*

History does note, however, that the next monarch, Henry VI, shared both his grandfather's love of Eltham and his penchant for books. This Henry expanded the Eltham study, adding seven massive windows fitted with 42 square feet of stained glass. In 1445, he honored his bride, Margaret of Anjou, with lavishly renovated apartments for her use prior to her coronation. On May 28 of that year, the new queen rode from Eltham to Blackheath, where she was officially welcomed by the Lord Mayor of London, before proceeding to Westminster Abbey for the coronation ceremonies. A new hall, scullery and additional lodgings were also added to Eltham during this time. Unfortunately, the palace was hit by lightning during a freak thunderstorm in February 1450; a substantial portion of Eltham was destroyed, including the new hall, a storeroom, a kitchen and many of the private apartments. Henry's library seems to have been left unscathed.

Although each of the Plantagenet monarchs from Edward I on lent a hand in the shaping of Eltham, it is Edward IV who is most closely connected with the palace today. Edward had always shown a special affinity for the Thames Valley—he spent as much time as possible at Greenwich, Sheen, Westminster and Windsor, and he spared no expense in making each of these palaces as striking as possible; indeed, no king since Edward III devoted as much of his treasury to building and renovation. But in the 1470s, a particular pet project captured Edward IV's imagination: the building of a "family palace" at Eltham—and from this point on, a considerable amount of Edward's money and attention went toward making his vision come to life.

In 1475, under the direction of Roger Appelton, the newly appointed Master and Surveyor of the King's Works, work began on a spectacular new hall—the only substantial part of the medieval palace still standing. The striking similarities between the Eltham Great Hall and London's Crosby Hall (an earlier home of Edward IV) have led some architectural historians to conclude that both structures were the masterpieces of the King's Mason Thomas Jurdan. The spectacular hammerbeam roof was designed by the leading carpenter of the day, James Needham—it is the third largest roof of its kind in England, trailing only Westminster Hall and Christ Church, Oxford.

◆◆◆◆◆◆◆◆◆◆◆◆◆◆◆◆◆◆◆◆◆◆

☞ Did you know?

James Needham was one busy carpenter indeed! In addition to building the hammerbeam roof at Eltham, Needham was responsible for work at the Tower of London, Rochester, Greenwich, Petworth and **Knole**. He also designed the roof for the great hall at **Hampton Court**. *(And you thought it was hard trying to get on your handyman's schedule . . .)*

◆◆◆◆◆◆◆◆◆◆◆◆◆◆◆◆◆◆◆◆◆◆

Apparently, Edward was frequently on hand to supervise construction—Eltham was his preferred love nest for visits with his mistress Jane Shore *(so much for all that talk about a "family" palace).*

During the advent of the Tudors, Eltham's primary focus began to change. The close-in rural setting made the palace a natural nursery for the children of Henry VII and his queen, Elizabeth of York. Although only one of their eight children was actually born at Eltham (Elizabeth Tudor, 1492–1495), all of them spent considerable time at the palace, where great emphasis was placed on their education and "royal" upbringing. *(A dyed-in-the-wool skinflint, Henry VII was careful not to scrimp on any efforts that would shore up the legitimate claim of his heirs to the throne he usurped from their great-uncle Richard III!)*

Henry also made significant improvements to the chapel at Eltham, providing the funds for Mass to be celebrated daily, whether the king was in residence or not (*did we say anything about a guilty conscience?*).

In 1499, Desiderius Erasmus of Rotterdam was escorted by his friend Sir Thomas More on a visit to Eltham. Erasmus was impressed with the intellectual aptitude of the young Tudors, although he was more than a tad chagrined when eight-year-old Prince Henry demanded that the scholar "challenge something from his pen." Clearly, Erasmus (*unlike some of us*) was not prepared to write on demand!

Despite its associations with his childhood, Henry VIII spent relatively little time at Eltham, preferring to use it for brief visits. During the early years of his reign, the palace functioned as a Tudor "conference center"—a convenient site for important meetings with the king's top advisors. The nature of those "meetings" and "brief visits" changed once Anne Boleyn entered his life. During their courtship, Henry and Mistress Anne were frequent visitors to the palace. Indeed, Eltham eventually became a favorite playground for the king's randy humors; one William Webbe had the misfortune of riding past the property with his fiancée when Henry was "in the mood" . . . the maiden was quickly claimed by the king, only to be returned to Webbe several hours later, rather the worse for wear! These risqué pastimes might explain Henry's improvements to Eltham. He built an underground tunnel (which still exists) from the palace to the southern end of the moat and spent great sums on increasing privacy throughout the palace, adding a high brick wall, screening and a secluded garden.

Like his parents before him, Henry eventually came to use Eltham as a royal nursery. Princess Elizabeth spent her first Lent at Eltham and was visited by her parents when Easter rolled around. Her mother, Anne, apparently planned to give birth to her second child at Eltham. The queen's chambers were renovated in anticipation of her lying-in, the walls painted in yellow ochre, which was Anne's favorite color. Unfortunately, that pregnancy ended in a miscarriage, the final straw in what was, by then, a disintegrating marriage. During Anne's trial on trumped-up charges of adultery, it was alleged that one of her many supposed dalliances was to have occurred at Eltham just weeks before that 1535 stillbirth.

No wonder that as queen, Elizabeth harbored little fondness for Eltham! Although she would occasionally host hunting parties in the fabled deer park, she rarely sought the pleasures of the palace for any other purpose. Eltham's heyday as a preferred royal retreat had passed. Gradually, the palace fell into a sorry state of disrepair; many of its buildings were destroyed during the Cromwellian war and others succumbed to the ravages of time.

In the 1930s, the property was purchased by Stephen and Virginia Courtland, whose vision was to link the medieval ruins to a chic, sleek, modern-day "palace." Preserving—albeit in a heavily "medievalized" manner—Edward's Great Hall, the Courtlands proceeded to fashion a cutting-edge Art Deco mansion that showcased the very best in contemporary 20th-century design. Recently restored by English Heritage,

> ☞ Did you know?
>
> By the 1930s, the Eltham Great Hall was in such disrepair that the Courtlands had to "re-create" the medieval atmosphere, drawing heavily from Hollywood's interpretation of England in the days of yore. In the process of replicating the stained glass and carved bosses of ancient buildings, some interesting liberties were taken. For instance, there are glass panels depicting most of Eltham's owners from Bishop Odo to Henry VIII, but Edward II is notably "missing." And, in case you're wondering, the carved initials on the tracery of the rood screen are those of 20th-century persons integral to the restoration of the Great Hall—not medieval personages, as one might assume.

the two "palaces" coexist in a manner that is both thoughtful and thought-provoking (our thoughts running to "how can we finagle a way to take up residence here?"). Not to be missed are the expansive Eltham grounds, where a sunken rose garden, lawn theater and "white wood" meld with the ancient ruins. If the weather is cooperative, you could easily while away an afternoon strolling the palace grounds. Simply stunning!

☩ Sutton House

2 and 4 Homerton High Street
Hackney, London

>>>

PHONE
020-8986-2264

E-MAIL
suttonhouse@smtp.ntrust.org.uk

LOCATED
At the corner of Homerton High Street and Isabella Road

TRAVEL
Take the Highbury and Islington Tube, connect to the Silverlink
Line or Bethnal Green, then take the 106, 253 or D6 bus *(don't
despair—this is easier than it sounds. Hackney is a mere 3 miles
from the City of London).*

OPEN
House:
11:30 a.m.–5:30 p.m. Wednesday, Sunday and Bank Holiday Mondays, February–November
Café/bar:
11:30 a.m.–5:00 p.m. Wednesday and Sunday, year-round

ADMISSION
£2.10 Adults
50p Children
Family ticket available

CONVENIENCES
Book and gift shop; art gallery

TIP!
Throughout the year, Sutton House hosts special Discovery Days,
with themes such as "Tudor Times" and "Ghost Stories from Sutton
House." Arts and crafts, historic cooking classes, storytelling and the
chance to dress in period costumes make these events a great diver-
sion, especially if you're traveling with children. Admission is free of
charge. Call Sutton House for details and schedule.

>>>

Too often overlooked, even on the itineraries of amateur historians, Sutton House is well worth a visit. This rare red-brick Tudor home was built by Henry VIII's Secretary of State Sir Ralph

(Rafe) Sadleir in 1535. Oddly, it takes its name from Sir Thomas Sutton, founder of Charterhouse in London, who was once erroneously believed to have owned the house (he actually lived next door). As for Sadleir, he merely referred to his home as "Bryk Place."

Although the home was expanded in the 18th century, many of the original details can still be appreciated. Next to Hampton Court Palace, Sutton House features the finest Tudor kitchen we've encountered. Although the lovely painted staircase postdates "our" era, the Linenfold Parlour, Little Chamber and Great Chamber bear significant 16th-century vestiges. In the lobby, be certain to note the "Armada" window, allegedly crafted from the timber of a Spanish galleon.

◆◆◆◆◆◆◆◆◆◆◆◆◆◆◆◆◆◆◆◆◆◆

🐭 Did you know?

Ralph is not the only Sadleir whose name is linked to the Elizabethan era. His cousin Hamnet Sadleir was godfather to Shakespeare's twins, Hamnet and Judith.

◆◆◆◆◆◆◆◆◆◆◆◆◆◆◆◆◆◆◆◆◆◆

SIR RALPH SADLEIR

His name might not be readily recognizable to most amateur historians (*including, we admit, us*), but Ralph Sadleir played a significant role in the reigns of both Henry VIII and Elizabeth I. Ralph was born in 1507, the son of Henry Sadleir. The senior Sadleir hit pay dirt when he was appointed purveyor of all the canvas and buckram needed to stage Henry VIII's extravagant 1520 tournament, Field of the Cloth of Gold (*that was one heck of a lot of canvas*). Papa Sadleir used the proceeds to purchase and renovate an alehouse in Hackney on the site of the present Sutton House. The family moved from their home in Warwickshire, and young Ralph was placed in the London household of the Sadleirs' family friend Thomas Cromwell.

A better position could hardly be found to apprentice in statecraft. Ralph was a quick study and he followed Cromwell's impressive ascent up the ranks of the Tudor power structure. By 1535, Sadleir was tapped for service to the king, first as an "overseer" for specific Dissolution missions and later as a diplomat to France and Scotland. By this time, Ralph had married a cousin of Thomas Cromwell, Helen Barre, and begun work on the new Sadleir family home, replacing the former Hackney alehouse with his new "Bryk Place." This residence was just a small part of his extensive property in the Hackney area—clearly, Henry VIII was pleased with Ralph's service and was paying him accordingly. Sadleir was knighted in 1540 and elevated to the position of Principal Secretary of State.

Such honors did not, however, keep him from a trip to the Tower when his mentor, Thomas Cromwell, was arrested for treason that same year. Sadleir's incarceration was mercifully brief and he was quick to distance himself from Cromwell as he resumed his position at court. The king, however, had other challenges in mind for Sadleir; in 1544, Henry named him ambassador to Scotland, a position he held through the reigns of Edward VI and Elizabeth. (An avowed Protestant, Sadleir lived in retirement at his estate in Hertfordshire during the reign of the Catholic queen, Mary Tudor.) His vast knowledge of the people and politics of Scotland earned him the dubious honor of serving as a judge during the 1586 trial of Mary, Queen of Scots.

The ordeal of sentencing Mary Stuart to death—and bearing Elizabeth's subsequent displeasure—proved to be incredibly taxing on Sir Ralph Sadleir. He died the following year at the age of 80. His magnificent marble effigy can be seen today in the parish church of Standon near Ware in Hertfordshire.

◇◇◇◇◇◇◇◇◇◇◇◇◇◇◇◇◇◇◇◇◇◇◇

☞ Did you know?

Ralph Sadleir's exquisite tomb depicts the Tudor courtier and all seven of his children . . . but his wife, Helen, is conspicuously absent from the family scene. Why? The answer lies in a scandal worthy of politicos from our own era. When Ralph met Helen Barre, she and her two children were suffering the humiliation of having been abandoned by her first husband, a ne'er-do-well whom Helen claimed had subsequently "died in Ireland" *(a euphemism if we ever heard one)*. If numbers of offspring are any indication, things were going swimmingly between Helen and Ralph; they had seven children of their own, in addition to her two. But while Ralph was on embassy to Scotland in 1544, who should arrive on the scene? You got it: husband number one. Sadleir hurried home from Scotland and pulled every string in the book, eventually obtaining an Act of Parliament that annulled Helen's first marriage and saved their children from the stigma of illegitimacy. One can assume, however, that it put a strain on the Sadleirs' happy home, which is why Helen is not depicted on Ralph's tomb *(we have to wonder whose tomb she does adorn)*.

Also close to London . . .

☩ Lesnes Abbey
Abbey Road
Abbey Wood, London

>>

PHONE
020-8303-9052

LOCATED
Approximately 5 miles outside of London, ¾ mile beyond the village of Woolrich, just past the Abbey Wood Station

OPEN
Daylight hours daily, year-round

ADMISSION
Free of charge

>>

We know all you baby boomers are going to ask, so we feel compelled to tell you now: yes, it's *that* "Abbey Road." What set us off in this direction was not, however, hopes of replicating the famous Beatles' album cover, but rather the search for yet another medieval ruin. Lesnes may not be the most spectacular abbey ruin you'll come across in your adventures, but it is exceedingly handy to central London if you find yourself pressed for time. It also has a rather interesting history. The abbey was built in 1178 by Henry II's Chief Justiciar, Robert de Lucy, as an act of contrition for his role in Thomas à Becket's fatal dispute with the king. De Lucy, one of the most influential royal advisors of the era, retired to the abbey a year before his death, having traded his robes of state for the humble habit of an Augustinian canon. The abbey thrived until 1524, when it fell beneath Cardinal Wolsey's harsh hand. The ancient buildings were demolished at that time; their foundations were rediscovered in the 20th century.

✝ Hall Place
Bourne Road
Bexley

>>

PHONE

01322-526574

LOCATED

Just off the A2, junction 2 or the A20, junction 3, approximately 15 miles outside of London

TRAVEL

Trains depart for Bexley on a regular basis from Charing Cross, Cannon Street, London Bridge and Waterloo East Stations.

OPEN

10:00 a.m.–5:00 p.m. Monday–Saturday, year-round
2:00–6:00 p.m. Sunday, April–October

ADMISSION

Free of charge

>>

• •
☞ Did you know?

The origins of Bexley are believed to stem from the Stone Age; artifacts from this era, as well as from the Bronze, Iron and Roman Ages, have been found in the vicinity. The name Bexley—which translates as "clearing in the box wood"—was first recorded in 814 when the Saxon King Kenulph of Mercia granted the lands to Wulfred, Archbishop of Canterbury.
• •

The close proximity of Hall Place to the City of London gives a clue to the stately home's ancestry. Hall Place was constructed in 1540 by then–Lord Mayor of London Sir John Champneys. It is a fine example of a Tudor "country" home, serenely sited on the banks of the River Cray, with the requisite formal gardens and handsome Great Hall. Perfect for a quick excursion, if your time "out of London" is limited.

While you're in the area . . .

ANCIENT CHURCHES

The borough of Bexley offers a treasure trove of ancient churches, most of which can be easily reached from Hall Place.

We recommend that you ask specific directions from the very friendly and knowledgeable docents at Hall Place. They will gladly point you in the right direction. It is also wise to phone ahead, as access to the interior of some of these churches can be erratic.

~ All Saints
Foots Cray
020-8303-7096

Although this ancient church was heavily restored in the 19th century, it still houses its original 12th-century baptismal font.

~ Greek Orthodox Church
Welling
020-8301-3858

Originally known as the parish church of St. Michael, this 13th-century house of worship bears traces of medieval wall murals.

~ St. John the Baptist
Erith
01322-332555

This Norman church dates from the 12th century. There are several ancient brasses and memorials, including a lovely homage to Elizabeth, Countess of Shrewsbury (d. 1567).

~ St. Mary the Virgin
Bexley
01322-528622

Parts of the building date from the 12th and 13th centuries. Royal-watchers will want to know that the "other" Queen Elizabeth's grandparents were married here in 1853.

~ St. Paulinus
Crayford
01322-522077

Another ancient church with traces of 12th-century and late medieval architecture.

CONTENTS

Eynsford

Mostly Roman

ust on the outskirts of London (*or should we say "Londinium"?*) lies the Roman settlement now known as Eynsford. One of the most important Roman-British discoveries was unearthed at Eynsford: Lullingstone Roman Villa. With architecture spanning three centuries and its stunning mosaic floor tiles, this villa is, indeed, the cornerstone of this trip. Add to this the bits and pieces of two castles, a manor home and a priory and you'll agree: a visit to Eynsford is an easy "something-for-everyone" jaunt out of London.

~

✝ Lullingstone Roman Villa
Eynsford

>>

PHONE
01322-863467

LOCATED
½ mile southwest of the village of Eynsford, 600 yards north of Lullingstone Castle; take the A225 or the M25, junction 3.

TRAVEL
Trains leave Victoria Station for Eynsford at hourly intervals. There is taxi service for the ¾ mile ride to the villa and castle from Eynsford Station. Travel time is approximately 30 minutes.

OPEN
10:00 a.m.–6:00 p.m. daily, April–September
10:00 a.m.–5:00 p.m. daily, October
10:00 a.m.–4:00 p.m. daily, November–March

ADMISSION
£2.50 Adults
£1.30 Children

>>>

For many years, *the* reason for visiting the village of Eynsford was **Lullingstone Castle**. And while we would never typically rate a medieval attraction as "second best," we must say that Lullingstone Roman Villa does give the castle a run for its money.

It was during grounds work on the castle in the mid-1700s that workers first discovered the beautiful Roman floor mosaic that lay just below the earth's surface. Over 200 years later, painstaking archeological excavations finally revealed one of the most dramatic Roman villas in England. Artifacts discovered on the site indicate that this was probably the farmhouse of an important agricultural facility, erected around 80 CE and occupied for nearly three centuries. During that time, its owners converted to Christianity and a chapel was added to the original structure; this and St. Augustine's Abbey number among the earliest Christian sites in Britain.

A large part of Lullingstone Villa is now under roof. You can admire the spectacular floor mosaics depicting the four seasons and the abduction of Europa and enjoy an imaginative audio tour, which brings to life the everyday events of a middle-class Roman family. The Lullingstone Villa museum displays statues, wall paintings and some of the villa's roof tiles, whimsically etched with the prints of various farm animals.

✝ Lullingstone Castle
Eynsford

>>>

PHONE
  01322-862114

LOCATED
  West of the A225, 1 mile south of the village of Eynsford; the Lullingstone Roman Villa is 600 yards beyond.

TRAVEL
  See Lullingstone Roman Villa entry.

OPEN
  2:00–6:00 p.m. Saturday, Sunday and Bank Holiday Mondays,
  May–August

ADMISSION
  £4.00 Adults
  £1.50 Children

>>>

Interestingly, there are three separate components to Lullingstone Castle. The parish church that graces the property dates
from the Norman era—although it is full to the brim with 18th-
century furnishings. The gatehouse, built in 1497, has the distinction of being the first brick gatehouse in England, and is arguably the property's most compelling feature. The main house
bears an 18th-century facade, although the interior walls are
considerably older.

Lullingstone Castle is still a family home; hence the very
limited viewing hours. Inside, the elaborate staterooms and
handsome family portraits are impressive, but alas, little remains from the medieval or Tudor eras. Still, if you need to have
a "castle" to justify your visit to the nearby Roman villa, Lullingstone will give you a perfectly pleasant alibi.

While you're in Eynsford . . .

✝ Eynsford Castle
Eynsford, Dartford

>>

PHONE
  None

LOCATED
  On the A225 in the village of Eynsford

TRAVEL
  Trains depart Victoria Station for Eynsford hourly. Taxi service is available from the station. Travel time is about ½ hour.

OPEN
  Daylight hours daily, year-round

ADMISSION
  Free of charge

>>

Well, if you're looking for the medieval castle *closest* to London, this is it. *(Yes, we promise you, closer than Windsor or Berkhampstead!)* Built by William de Eynsford in 1110, this Norman castle once consisted of a free-standing wooden hall protected by a separate curtain wall. By 1130, the hall had been reconstructed out of local flint. The Eynsford family died out in 1312 and the castle's hall was abandoned in the 14th century. The walls, however, served a variety of purposes over the centuries, including as kennels for hunting hounds. The walls—which, at 30 feet, are unusually high for a castle of this era—are the only part of Eynsford Castle that remain.

Ghost Alert!

Eynsford townfolk claim that the castle grounds are haunted by a mysterious "white lady"—to date, the phantom has done nothing more dastardly than startle unsuspecting tourists.

✝ Milton Chantry
New Tavern Fort Gardens
Gravesend

≫≫≫

PHONE

01474-321520

LOCATED

M25 to junction 2, then follow the A227 and head toward Gravesend; the Chantry is ¼ mile east of Gravesend, in New Tavern Fort Gardens.

TRAVEL

Frequent train service runs from Charing Cross Station to Gravesend; taxi service is available from the station to the Chantry. Travel time is approximately 1 hour.

OPEN

Noon–5:00 p.m. Wednesday–Saturday, May–September
10:00 a.m.–5:00 p.m. Sunday, May–September
Noon–4:00 p.m. Saturday, March, April and October–December
10:00 a.m.–4:00 p.m. Sunday, March, April and October–December
Closed January and February

ADMISSION

£1.50 Adults
75p Children

≫≫≫

For such a minute building, Milton Chantry has certainly had a varied past! The oldest surviving house in the vicinity, it was built in the 14th century by Edward II's cousin Aymer de Valence, Earl of Pembroke. Here prayers were offered for the repose of the de Valence and Montechais family-member souls. Subsequently, it became a house of worship for local lepers, a role it served until the Reformation. A tavern and a fortress's outpost were but two of its "modern" uses, before becoming a mini-museum of local history and crafts. As you tour today, you will be treated to the "voice of Aymer de Valence," who acts as your audio docent, pointing out details of interest in the 700-year-old building.

CONTENTS

Rochester

A Castle, Cathedral and More

nother ancient city of narrow streets and byways, Rochester is one more of those strategic southeast England sites that loomed so large in medieval history. Located at the lowest fordable point of the River Medway, Rochester is believed to have first been settled in prehistoric times. Certainly, the Romans recognized the critical nature of the site. They built a fort here in 43 CE, dubbing the settlement "Dorobrivae" after the early Briton name of "Doubris." The name "Rochester" is derived from the Anglo-Saxon name "Hrofeceaster." Christianity also took root early in Rochester. The second-oldest bishopric in England was established here in 604 by St. Augustine.

There is much to see and do in and around Rochester. In Rochester proper, there is, of course, the impressive keep of Rochester Castle, the ancient cathedral and a host of other intriguing spots. All are located within walking distance up and down the main drag of High Street, which is part of Watling Street, the old Roman road that ran from the coast to London. Just outside of Rochester are

> **☞ Did you know?**
>
> If your interests span more than just medieval and Tudor times, you may want to know that Rochester was Charles Dickens's favorite city. Many landmarks in the city are associated with Dickens and his novels; every June, Rochester plays host to a Dickens Festival. Eastgate House, a 16th-century timber and brick building, has been named the Dickens Centre in his honor.

some intriguing manor homes. The village of Cobham, with the lovely Elizabethan Cobham Hall and the church of St. Mary Magdalene, which has the largest collection of effigy brasses in England, is definitely worth a visit.

∾

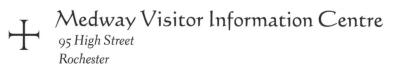

Medway Visitor Information Centre
95 High Street
Rochester

>>

PHONE
01634-843666

E-MAIL
visitor.centre@medway.gov.uk

LOCATED
Rochester is about 30 miles southeast of London via the A2.

TRAVEL
Frequent train service operates from Waterloo, Victoria and Charing Cross Stations. Travel time is approximately 45 minutes.

CONVENIENCES
Book and gift shop

>>

We recommend that you start your visit in Rochester with a stop at the Visitor Information Centre. The one in Rochester is particularly helpful. It is well stocked with travel guides and brochures, and the staff is very knowledgeable. The Centre also serves as a mini-museum, with displays and a video about the history of Rochester.

If you are interested in a thorough introduction to the history of Rochester, schedule your visit for a Wednesday, Saturday or Sunday afternoon from April through September. A guided tour of the city departs from the Dickens Centre at 2:15 p.m. on those days. We warn you, though, that the tour is bound to be packed with information about post-Tudor monarchs and historical figures. Charles II, Victoria and Charles Dickens are favorites of the locals. *(We got so much information on these topics that we thought about creating a button that said, "We stop at 1600!")*

If, like us, you prefer to wander on your own, poking only into those sites related to our favorite period of history, the Visitor Information Centre does provide an excellent walking tour brochure that will help you uncover all the medieval gems that can be found in Rochester.

Tip!

Whatever way you choose to explore Rochester, keep an eye out as you wander around the city for chunks of the medieval city wall. One large section can be found next to a convenient car park just off High Street, a couple of blocks down from the Visitor Information Centre.

〰

✝ Rochester Castle
Castle Hill
Rochester

>>

PHONE
01634-402276

E-MAIL
visitorattractions@medway.gov.uk

LOCATED
By Rochester Bridge on the A2

OPEN
10:00 a.m.–6:00 p.m. daily, April–September
10:00 a.m.–4:00 p.m. daily, October–March

ADMISSION
£3.70 Adults
£2.60 Children
£2.70 Concessions
Family ticket available

CONVENIENCES

Refreshment kiosk on the grounds and gift shop in the forebuilding of the keep.

TIP!

If you plan your visit for August, try to schedule your trip to Rochester for a Saturday. Every Saturday in August features a "Norman experience" at the castle, with actors in period costume and displays of daily life at the time.

>>>

Looming darkly and ominously over the city's skyline, Rochester Castle probably is the best-preserved Norman keep in all of England. Dating from the 12th century, it is also one of the tallest in the country, soaring 113 feet. It covers 70 square feet, with walls that are 11 to 13 feet thick. Sadly, the building is just a shell; the roofs and floors of the three floors that once divided the keep are gone, although a central wall that split the building in half remains. Still, visitors are permitted to enter the keep and, if you have stamina and courage enough to tackle the steep, narrow, spiraling staircase that goes up to the battlements, you will see a breathtaking view of the city and surrounding countryside.

From the wall of the keep, an excellent overview of the cathedral allows you to easily identify the oldest parts of that building. Also visible from this vantage point is the Prior's Gate, the best preserved of the gates that once surrounded the grounds of the monastery attached to the cathedral.

Inside the keep, note the tall, carved archways in the central wall that denote the location of the main hall. A model of the castle as it was in the 13th century can be found in one of the tower rooms.

As is typical of many of the castle strongholds in southeast England, the Normans were not the first to recognize the strategic value of Rochester. The Romans built a fort here to guard a bridge spanning the River Medway. Part of the wall that once surrounded that fort was incorporated into the later curtain wall built by the Normans.

Rochester figured early and importantly in William the Conqueror's scheme for subduing all of England. He put the fief into the hands of one his most trusted advisors, his half brother Odo, Bishop of Bayeux, whom William also named Earl of Kent. Odo immediately set about constructing a strong motte and bailey castle on the site of the present-day keep.

Odo proved not to be such a loyal supporter of the Conqueror's son and successor, William Rufus. The powerful bishop backed his other nephew, the Conqueror's elder son, Robert, Duke of Normandy, when the brothers battled for the crown of England in 1088. As Earl of Kent, Odo controlled the critical strongholds of **Tonbridge**, Pevensey and Dover, as well as Rochester. Rufus moved quickly to suppress his uncle's power, rapidly overrunning the garrison at Tonbridge and achieving the surrender of Pevensey after only six weeks of siege.

In a stroke of luck for William Rufus, Odo was inside Pevensey when it fell and thus became a captive of his nephew. Rufus immediately escorted Odo to Rochester, where the king hoped that his uncle would be able to convince the garrison inside to surrender without further bloodshed. But the keep was being held by hardened veterans from Normandy led by Robert de Belleme. Rather than surrender, they helped engineer Odo's escape from the royal forces. Odo fled inside the castle and Rufus settled down for siege warfare. Eventually, the garrison succumbed to the starvation that generally resulted from prolonged sieges. In an effort to build support, William Rufus was generous with the castle defenders, pardoning most of them and letting the rest off with fines and forfeitures of castles. Only Odo was banished from England.

◇◇

ODO, BISHOP OF BAYEUX (c. 1030–1097)

Odo, Bishop of Bayeux and Earl of Kent, was one of the central figures of the Norman Conquest of England. A half brother of William the Conqueror, Odo was a clever and dangerous man whose greed and ambition ultimately brought about his downfall. He also may have been one of the first great practitioners of the art of political spin. He is widely credited with commissioning the Bayeux Tapestry to justify the Norman invasion of England.

William the Conqueror was the bastard son of Robert, the first Duke of Normandy, and his mistress Herleve. After her affair with the duke ended, Herleve was married to Herluin de Conteville. Odo was most likely born sometime in the early 1030s as a result of this union.

Historical evidence indicates that Odo must have been liked and trusted by his ruling half brother because William appointed Odo the Bishop of Bayeux sometime in 1049 or early 1050, when Odo would still have been a teenager. Odo also was a pivotal player in the planning and preparation of the invasion of England. He was at William's side during the Battle of Hastings, wielding weapons himself and helping to rally the troops at key moments of the battle *(no pacifist priest was our Odo!)*.

Although a man of the cloth, Odo—like many clergy of the time—was more politician than churchman. Ambitious and worldly, Odo was not one to deny himself the sins of the flesh. He compensated for his sins by organizing the construction of a new cathedral at Bayeux and founding an abbey dedicated to St. Vigor on the edge of town. He also patronized poets and scholars in Normandy.

In England, his reputation was quite different. As a key ally of his brother William, Odo ruthlessly helped spread Norman control. William named his brother Earl of Kent and granted him power over great swathes of land. Odo also often acted as William's regent when the king traveled to his domains on the Continent. The bishop was so effective at expanding Norman authority in England that the medieval chronicle at the abbey of Evesham described him as "a ravening wolf."

Odo's ambition ran away with him late in 1082. Not one to easily tolerate rivals, William had Odo imprisoned then for recruiting knights as part of a scheme to make himself pope. A deathbed wish of the Conqueror resulted in Odo's release in September 1087. This was a mistake. Odo quickly became a leader of the opposition to William Rufus, supporting the claims of the Conqueror's eldest son Robert, Duke of Normandy, to the crown of England.

As Earl of Kent, Odo had the critical castles of Dover, Pevensey and Rochester in his control. Pevensey, along with Tonbridge, succumbed relatively quickly to assault and siege by William Rufus. Rochester, garrisoned by a troop of seasoned Norman knights, managed to hold out. After Odo was captured at the end of the six-week siege of Pevensey, he was taken to Rochester to persuade the troops there to surrender. The defenders turned the tables on the besiegers, managing to free Odo, who escaped behind Rochester's strong walls. Eventually, Rochester, too, fell to siege and Odo was banished from England. His lands reverted to the Crown.

After his banishment from England, Odo returned to Normandy. He joined his nephew Robert, Duke of Normandy, on Crusade, but got no farther toward the Holy Land than Sicily, where he died in January 1097. His epitaph, written a generation later, described him as a man "more given to worldly affairs than spiritual contemplation."

❖❖❖

Construction of a stone keep at Rochester was started in 1087 by Bishop Gundulf, William the Conqueror's master architect, who also supervised construction of the White Tower in the Tower of London. Part of the curtain wall built by Gundulf, which incorporated remains of the ancient Roman wall, still surrounds the castle.

The present-day castle dates from 1127. It was built by William de Corbeil, Archbishop of Canterbury, who was appointed by Henry I in 1127 to hold the castle. Henry's instructions to the archbishop were "to make in the same castle a fort or tower, as they pleased, and have guard of it." The result of this order was the formidable stone structure you see today. The castle remained in the hands of the Archbishop of Canterbury until 1215, when Rochester once again became a pivotal point in an English civil war.

Barons rebelling against the infamous King John seized control of Rochester Castle in 1215 in an attempt to stop John from marching from Dover to London. An angry King John soon set siege to the castle, determined to batter it into submission. In describing the siege, an anonymous medieval chronicler known as the Barnwell annalist wrote, "In our age there had never been another siege so determinedly pursued or so vigorously resisted."

Despite pleas to negotiate a surrender, John ceaselessly battered down the outer defenses and then turned his attention to breaking into the keep into which the defenders had retreated. His strategy was to undermine one of the towers, using wooden scaffolding to support the stone structure until the mining operation was completed. In an inspired move, John sent a message demanding delivery "with all speed by day and night forty of the fattest pigs of the sort least good for eating." He used the pigs — and their fat — as fuel for the fire that burned the scaffolding, resulting in the collapse of the southeast tower. (*Talk about your pig roasts!*) Still, the defenders did not surrender. They retreated behind the central wall that divided the keep in half and continued to hold out against John. Altogether, the castle stood firm for two months (October and November), although the 95 knights and 45 men-at-arms inside suffered horribly from hunger and other privations.

According to the Barnwell chronicler, the end of the siege was ugly. John ordered the amputation of the hands and feet of several of the defenders and had the survivors imprisoned in chains. After this savagery, the chronicler reported, "Hearing of the outcome of the siege, the rest of the barons were dismayed and with rising panic gathered in London or stayed in religious houses. There were few indeed who felt secure behind fortifications."

The southeast tower that John collapsed was rebuilt as a round turret during the reign of his son Henry III. That is why Rochester Castle has a distinctive profile of one round and three square towers. (For once, Henry placed military concerns above aesthetics—round towers were considered superior to square for defensive purposes.)

This was not the last time that Rochester Castle was besieged, suffered heavy damage and was restored. It happened again during the barons' revolt led by Simon de Montfort, Earl of Leicester, against Henry III. This time, the castle was not restored until the reign of Edward III. The castle also suffered heavy damage during the Peasants' Revolt of 1381, after which it was repaired by Richard II. Part of Richard's renovation of the castle included construction of the northwest bastion, which still stands today. The bastion was erected to guard the bridge over the River Medway.

◆◆◆◆◆◆◆◆◆◆◆◆◆◆◆◆◆◆◆◆◆◆◆◆
☞ Did you know?
The bridge over the River Medway is maintained through endowments from the Bridge Trust, founded in 1391 and still functioning today.
◆◆◆◆◆◆◆◆◆◆◆◆◆◆◆◆◆◆◆◆◆◆◆◆

◆◆◆◆◆◆◆◆◆◆◆◆◆◆◆◆◆◆◆◆◆◆◆◆
☞ Did you know?
Just outside Rochester Castle is the Esplanade, a lovely walkway that winds along the River Medway. Here you will find the **Bridge Chapel**, erected in 1397. The sole purpose of this chapel was to provide medieval pedestrians with the chance to pause and "give thanks" for the bridge that spanned the river. The chapel is not open to the public, but it's worth a stroll by to admire it and to spot the stone carvings of the heads of Richard II and his first queen, Anne, on either side of the front door.
◆◆◆◆◆◆◆◆◆◆◆◆◆◆◆◆◆◆◆◆◆◆◆◆

Richard's successors were not so enamored with the ancient keep, and gradually the castle fell into disuse and disrepair. Plans were laid in the 18th century to tear down the castle remains, but, thankfully, wiser heads prevailed and at least the shell of the keep has been preserved.

❖❖❖

ROBERT, EARL OF GLOUCESTER (c. 1090–1147)

While Rochester Castle escaped siege during the long civil war between Stephen of Blois and Empress Matilda for control of the English crown, it earned a historical footnote as the prison of Robert, Earl of Gloucester. The oldest illegitimate son of Henry I, Gloucester was a brilliant soldier and respected leader who was the mainstay of his half sister Matilda's struggle to claim the throne. He had managed in 1141 to gain for his sister the upper hand in the war that had already been raging for two years by defeating and capturing King Stephen at the Battle of Lincoln in February.

However, the advantage was lost when a strong army led by Stephen's queen, Maud, and the infamous Flemish mercenary William of Ypres laid siege to Winchester in September, trapping Gloucester, the empress and most of their forces. After weeks of privation, Gloucester staged a dramatic escape that enabled the empress to elude her captors. Unfortunately, her freedom was achieved at the cost of Gloucester's, who was imprisoned in the strongest fortress then under the control of the royal forces—the Norman keep at Rochester. The empress was left with little choice but to bargain for Gloucester's freedom. Without him at her side, she had little chance of wresting the crown from Stephen.

The price Queen Maud demanded was, of course, an exchange of prisoners. Thus, Stephen was restored to the throne, Empress Matilda was in worse straits than she had been before and the struggle for control continued for another 12 years.

❖❖❖

KING JOHN (1167–1216) REIGNED 1199–1216)

"Foul as it is . . . Hell itself is defiled by the fouler presence of King John."
—13th-century chronicler Matthew Paris

The most notorious of all England's monarchs is King John, the evil prince of the Robin Hood tales. John has one nasty reputation; believe us, he earned every bit of it. Some modern historians have attempted to rehabilitate John's reputation, defining him as a conscientious king who was a good administrator and a legal reformer. While there is some historical record to support this contention, the greater truth is that John was a cruel and malicious man who was detested by his subjects.

John's reign marked a notable change in the course of England's monarchy. He was the first of the Norman/Plantagenet kings to spend most of his time in England. This was not necessarily by choice. A disastrous military commander, John managed in the first five years of his reign to lose almost all of the vast continental domains he had inherited from his powerful parents, Henry II and Eleanor of Aquitaine, and his legendary brother and predecessor, Richard the Lionheart. For the first time since William the Conqueror claimed the crown of England in 1066, the monarchy was without a land base in Normandy. For the rest of his life, John struggled to find a way of regaining those lost domains.

* *

☞ Did you know?

The Plantagenet dynasty gained its name from its founder, Geoffrey of Anjou (1128–1151), husband of Empress Matilda and father of Henry II. Geoffrey was awarded his sobriquet as a salute to the jaunty sprig of broom (*genet* in French) that he always wore in his hat.

* *

John began acquiring his villainous reputation early in life, starting with a series of betrayals that signaled the pattern he would follow all his life. The last of the seven children of Henry II and Eleanor of Aquitaine, John was his father's favorite. In the dynastic struggles that marked the later years of Henry's long reign, John first sided with his father, then joined his brothers in rebelling against their father, was forgiven and welcomed back by Henry, only to turn on him one final time and side with Richard in the days just before Henry's death.

John served his brother no better. While Richard was gone on Crusade, John filled his days attempting to usurp his brother's throne (hence the plot of many of the Robin Hood tales). When Richard was captured and held prisoner in Germany on his return from the Holy Land, John actively plotted to have his brother killed or, at the very least, imprisoned for life. After Richard regained his freedom (thanks to his mother, Eleanor of Aquitaine, who coerced the king's barons into financing an extremely heavy ransom), Richard forgave John for his betrayals, but kept a very wary eye upon this unscrupulous brother for the rest of his reign.

The record of John's cruelty and viciousness as king is extensive, starting with the legend that in April 1203 he himself, in a drunken rage, killed his nephew Arthur of Brittany, his rival for the English throne and his prisoner at the time. There are other, even more stomach-turning, examples of the ways John dealt with his enemies—or those he perceived to be enemies. Starving them to death was a favorite technique. He used this method to punish captives from a 1202 battle at Mirebeau in France after they tried a mass escape from Corfe Castle. He employed it again as an effective means of stopping the shrewish mouth of Matilda de Braose, wife of the powerful baron William de Braose.

De Braose, a close confidant and favorite of John, probably was one of the few men who knew the truth behind the disappearance of Prince Arthur. When John suddenly turned against de Braose in 1205, seeking to destroy the family's power and demanding hostages as security for loyalty, Matilda—a very foolish woman—refused to hand them over. She said she was afraid to comply because John had killed his nephew and therefore could not be trusted with the lives of people in his custody. Needless to say, this public accusation did nothing to temper John's ire against the family. The de Braoses fled to Ireland in 1209, but even in that wild and hostile land, they were not able to entirely escape from John's pursuing armies. Matilda and her eldest son returned to England in 1210 and were soon captured and imprisoned in Windsor Castle, where they were starved to death, despite offers of ransom.

Of course, the fact that John could not be trusted with prisoners in his custody was amply demonstrated again just two years later. In 1212, in retaliation for Welsh defiance of a forced treaty, John ordered the execution of 30 Welsh hostages, some as young as five years old.

All of John's unsavory acts, his contemptuous and unscrupulous treatment of his barons, and his lascivious behavior with their wives and daughters caused the nobility to unite in the latter years of John's reign and demand restrictions upon royal power and prerogatives. They were able to apply enough pressure to force John at Runnymede on June 15, 1215, to sign Magna Carta, the first document that defined the rights and responsibilities of monarchs and nobles and served as the foundation of English common law.

Not surprisingly, John reverted to type after the event at Runnymede, denouncing Magna Carta and waging war against his nobles. By now, John's constant deceits and treachery had tremendously eroded his support. So disgusted by John were some of the English barony that they invited Prince Louis of France to invade and claim the throne with their backing. This revolt came close to succeeding and may well have changed the course of the English throne if not for the fortuitous death of John. While marching toward the north in October 1216, John and his army were caught in a tidal flood as they attempted to cross the River Wellstream. The baggage train sank into the quick sand, the royal treasury was lost and John almost drowned. Sick with dysentery and shaking with chills, John was transported to Newark Castle in Nottinghamshire, where he died on October 18. He is buried in Worcester Cathedral.

Support for Prince Louis and the rebellion melted away with John's death, which demonstrated the personal nature of the revolt against the king. The barons rapidly coalesced behind John's nine-year-old heir, Henry III, and the English monarchy was once again firmly in the hands of the descendants of William the Conqueror.

❖❖

✝ Rochester Cathedral (a.k.a. Cathedral Church of Christ and the Blessed Virgin)

70a High Street
Rochester

>>

PHONE
01634-401301

E-MAIL
chapterclerk@rochester.anglican.org

LOCATED
Readily accessible from the M2, junction 3; also signposted on the M20, junction 6 and the A2

OPEN
7:30 a.m.–6:00 p.m. daily, year-round
Limited touring during services

WORSHIP
Sung Matins: 9:45 a.m. Sunday
Sung Eucharist: 10:30 a.m. Sunday
Evensong: 3:15 p.m. Saturday and Sunday
     5:30 p.m. Monday–Friday
Matins: 7:30 a.m. daily
Holy Communion: 8:00 a.m. daily
     1:00 p.m. Thursday

ADMISSION
£2.00 donation requested

CONVENIENCES
Tearoom, brass rubbings and gift shops (one located in the cathedral, the other in High Street); guided tours for groups are available for a charge of £2.50 per person.

>>

The smallest of the Norman cathedrals remaining in England, Rochester Cathedral claims fame by being the second-oldest bishopric in the country. It was founded in 604, simultaneously with the bishopric of London, by St. Augustine, who conse-crated his fellow missionary Justus as the first Bishop of Roches-ter. In celebration of the momentous event, King Ethelbert ordered a church, dedicated to St. Andrew, to be built in Rochester.

Early bishops of Rochester were influential in spreading Christianity throughout England. St. Paulinus, who is buried in the cathedral, founded the bishopric of York. His successor, Ithamar, was the first Anglo-Saxon to be made a bishop. Ithamar also had the honor of consecrating the first Archbishop of Canterbury. A chapel in the crypt of Rochester Cathedral is dedicated to him. This is a lovely, serene space, a good place to pause for a moment of reflection or prayer. The stained glass in the chapel windows is "of the period," according to one of the cathedral's priests, although it is not original to Rochester Cathedral.

The early church on this site was destroyed by the Danes in one of their many raids on southern England in the late 9th century. The footprint of the Saxon building that stood here can be found on the floor in the entrance of the cathedral. A plaque on a nearby pillar explains the church's history.

Construction of the present building was started in 1080 by Bishop Gundulf, the architect for Rochester Castle and the White Tower in the Tower of London, who was named Bishop of Rochester in 1077. The best remaining feature of Gundulf's work is the tower named for him, located on the north side of the cathedral. A statue of Gundulf can be seen in the 13th-century quire screen along with statues of King Ethelbert and bishops Justus, Paulinus and John Fisher.

The Norman cathedral started by Gundulf was not consecrated until 1130. The fact that the ceremony was attended by Henry I and 13 bishops underscores the importance of Rochester Cathedral in medieval times. Six bays of the original nave survive, and the transverse arches are most likely the earliest pointed arches in England.

Two fires in the 12th century destroyed the wooden roof of the cathedral. Scorch marks from these fires can still be seen on the pillars in the nave. After the fires, the cathedral was enlarged and rebuilt in Gothic style.

Medieval features of the cathedral that make it well worth a walk-through are the lovely Lady Chapel (completed in 1492), the fragmentary remains of many wall paintings, some interesting ancient graffiti in the crypt (to be found behind plexiglass just outside the entrance to the Ithamar Chapel) and an intricately carved 14th-century doorway (located to the right of the altar). The night entrance for the monks into the cathedral, the doorway is a brilliant example of the stone carver's art. It was built by Bishop Hamo de Hythe (bishop 1319–52), whose tomb is located to the left of the quire. Tombs and effigies of other medieval and Tudor bishops of Rochester are scattered throughout the cathedral. Some of those worth seeking out include the tomb and effigy of Walter de Merton, Chancellor of England and founder of Merton College, Oxford (bishop 1274–77); the much-worn effigy of John de Bradfield (bishop 1277–83); and the tomb of John de Sheppey (bishop 1353–60; Treasurer of England 1356–58), whose effigy retains much of its brilliant medieval paint.

Piety and respect for miracle-making relics did not stop the forces of King John from plundering the cathedral in 1215. (*Frustration at the recalcitrant barons in the castle must have overcome their good sense and holy terror.*) The cathedral was even more thoroughly desecrated by the troops of the very pious Simon de Montfort when

☞ **Did you know?**

The financial future of Rochester Cathedral was secured—at least for medieval times—in 1201. A baker named William from Perth, who was staying at the priory while on pilgrimage to the Holy Land, was murdered in Rochester and laid to rest in the cathedral. Miracles were soon reported at his gravesite, which became an important pilgrim shrine. Proceeds from their visits paid for the remodeling of the east end of the cathedral, which was awkwardly annexed to the Norman nave. The shrine was destroyed in 1538.

☞ **Did you know?**

The graffiti in the crypt of Rochester Cathedral allegedly was carved by Simon de Montfort's forces in 1264. Such defacing of religious property by the men involved in this rebellion was ironic, given that de Montfort himself was extremely devout and some of the greatest supporters of his revolt against Henry III were bishops.

they captured the city during the barons' rebellion against John's son Henry III.

As so often happened in medieval times, conflicts of interests caused tension between the monks of the Benedictine priory founded at Rochester by Bishop Gundulf and the townspeople. The monks highly resented the intrusions of the "common folk" upon their religious devotions. Ultimately, the conflict resulted in the construction of another church, meant to cater to the religious needs of the townspeople. Thus the parish church of St. Nicholas was erected next to the cathedral in 1423. Today, St. Nicholas serves as the offices for the diocese and is not open to the public.

Between the church and cathedral stands the 15th-century Deanery Gate, once the inner gate to the monastery and the path pilgrims followed to reach the shrine of St. William of Perth. Another 15th-century gate, Chertseys Gate, leads from High Street into the cathedral precincts. It was once part of the wall that separated the cathedral from the town.

The Rochester priory was

* *
☞ Did you know?

It was at the Bishop's Palace on the grounds of the former monastery at Rochester that Henry VIII first laid eyes on wife-to-be number four, Anne of Cleves. The sensuous Henry, as you will recall, had agreed to this political match (promoted by his counselors as a means of establishing closer ties to German Protestants) based on a flattering portrait of Anne by Hans Holbein. After receiving rapturous reports of Anne's reception by her new subjects following her arrival in England on December 26, 1539, Henry was even more eager to meet his bride-to-be. Rather than continue to wait in London for Anne to come to him, as had been planned, the impatient bridegroom set out on New Year's Eve for Rochester, where Anne was scheduled to stay for two nights.

The meeting was a disaster. The discriminating monarch was appalled at Anne's plain appearance and felt betrayed and misused by the counselors who had promoted the match. After leaving Anne, he complained bitterly about being misled and cried to anyone who would listen, "I like her not! I like her not!" Surprisingly, Henry went forward with the wedding ceremony, but the marriage was doomed from the moment Henry first laid eyes on Anne. It didn't take long for him to begin searching for a way out of this fourth — and most unfortunate — bond.

* *

the last monastic house to surrender to Henry VIII's commissioners during the Dissolution of the Monasteries, but the monks finally gave up their fight on April 8, 1540. Subsequently, Rochester was refounded as a cathedral with a dean, rather than a prior, and the monks were turned out. Henry VIII appropriated the priory buildings for himself. He intended to use them as another castle *(just what he needed, since he already owned about a dozen palaces in London alone)*. Almost nothing remains of these buildings.

Time and war—both ancient and modern—have left their marks on Rochester Cathedral, parts of which have been heavily restored and not always with pleasant results. Still, the spirits of the early Norman founders are alive and well in this building, and it is well worth a stroll through the nave and crypt.

❖❖❖

ROCHESTER MARTYRS

The bishopric of Rochester produced two martyrs to the religious struggles of the 16th century. The first was John Fisher, who was executed in June 1535 for his refusal to acknowledge Henry VIII as the Supreme Head of the Church of England. A close friend of Thomas More, Fisher was imprisoned in a chamber above More's in the Bell Tower of the Tower of London prior to their deaths. The first English bishop ever to be executed by a monarch, Fisher preceded More in death by just a few weeks. He was canonized, along with More, in 1935.

The second bishop of Rochester who died for his beliefs was a martyr to the Protestant cause. Nicholas Ridley was appointed Bishop of Rochester in 1547 during the flowering of the Protestant cause in the reign of Edward VI. He was a prime force in spreading the new theology and religious practices throughout England. Ridley paid for his religious convictions after Mary ascended the throne and attempted to restore Catholicism in England. As one of the signatories of Edward VI's will that attempted to designate the Protestant Lady Jane Grey, "the Nine Days Queen," as heir to the throne, Ridley was arrested soon after Mary assumed the crown in 1553. After a public hearing in Oxford in 1554, both Ridley and Hugh Latimer, Bishop of Worcester, were declared heretics and burned at the stake.

In Rochester, you will find a plaque commemorating Ridley on the wall of the Baptist Church in Crow Lane. (This is now a store, although it is still called the Baptist Church. Look on the front of the building for a modern plaque that lists other Protestant martyrs as well.) Another, honoring Fisher, is located on the garden wall of College Green, just south of the cathedral. Part of the 15th-century building that was the Old Bishop's Palace, where Fisher lived, has been incorporated into the existing building on the site.

✧✧

✝ Watts' Charity, The Poor Travellers' House

97 High Street
Rochester

>>

PHONE
  01634-845609

OPEN
  2:00–5:00 p.m. Tuesday–Saturday, March–October

ADMISSION
  Free of charge

>>

This 16th-century hostel for impoverished vagabonds was the result of a bequest in the will of Sir Richard Watts, the Member of Parliament for Rochester. The philanthropist stipulated that a building be constructed that would provide lodging for six poor travelers who, "not being rogues or proctors," could stay free for one night and receive four pence each.

The house in which Watts lived in Rochester and once sumptuously entertained Queen Elizabeth still exists, although it has been greatly modified. You can find it across the street from the far side of the castle, but, we warn you, it is not open to the public. Called Satis House, the home earned its name supposedly from a comment Elizabeth made during her 1573 visit about the quality and quantity of the entertainment provided by her host. "Enough," she reportedly said, using the Latin word "Satis."

✝ Guildhall Museum
High Street
Rochester

>>>

PHONE
  01634-848717

OPEN
  10:00 a.m.–5:15 p.m. daily, year-round

ADMISSION
  Free of charge

>>>

Rochester's Guildhall Museum, built in 1687, offers a historical tour of the city's past. Exhibits are arranged chronologically beginning with prehistoric times, progressing through the Roman occupation and moving on through the medieval and Tudor ages to modern times. It's worth a quick dip into the museum if only to see a very cool scale model of King John's 1215 siege of Rochester Castle.

Tip!

As you wander along High Street, keep an eye out for **Baggins Book Bazaar,** the largest secondhand bookstore in England and one of our favorites. Located at 19 High Street, the store is open daily from 10:00 a.m. to 6:00 p.m. Be careful, though. It is easy to lose track of time wandering through the miles of shelves that hold about a half million books. The knowledgeable staff of Baggins also will tempt you to lighten your wallet by offering to conduct a worldwide book search for anything you can't find in the store. Believe us—they are good at it and very reliable.

Restoration House
Crow Lane
Rochester

>>>

PHONE
   01634-843666

OPEN
   10:00 a.m.–5:00 p.m. Thursday and Friday, July–September

ADMISSION
   £4.50 Adults
   Family ticket available

>>>

A red-brick Elizabethan mansion, Restoration House was named in the 17th century to commemorate Charles II's restoration to the throne. Other than the building itself, there is little here of interest to medieval enthusiasts, but the house does have close associations with Charles Dickens for those who are interested.

~

While you're in Rochester . . .
St. Mary Magdalene Church
Cobham, Rochester

>>>

PHONE
   01474-814262 or 01474-814524

LOCATED
   Off the M2 at Watling Street (A2)

TRAVEL
   Trains depart Victoria Station for Sole Street Station, Cobham.

OPEN
   Call ahead for an appointment *(the church staff will make every effort to accommodate your schedule)*.

ADMISSION
Donation requested

CONVENIENCES
Brass rubbing by prior arrangement, £10.00 per hour.

>>

Just outside of Rochester is the lovely little village of **Cobham**. Of particular note to medievalists *(and even more particularly to Sarah!)* is the 13th-century church of St. Mary Magdalene, which by reputation has the finest collection of medieval memorial brasses in the world, spanning from 1320 to 1529. What makes this so intriguing to Sarah is that the majority of the brasses are in memory of the de Cobham family and their descendants, the Brookes —Sarah's English ancestors, whose genealogy started Sarah on this wild passion for all things medieval! However, whether you are a Brooke or not, you are welcome to try your hand at brass rubbing while visiting St. Mary's, provided you make a prior appointment.

• •
☞ Did you know?

The focal point of St. Mary Magdalene is the grand tomb of Sir George, ninth Baron de Cobham, and Lady Anne (née Bray) Brooke. Sir George and his family were close personal friends of Thomas Cranmer. George's brother, Thomas Brooke, was an official on Cranmer's staff and eventually married Cranmer's niece; they named their first child Cranmer Brooke. Sir George was a leading proponent of the Reformation and played an active role in the Dissolution of the Monasteries at both Rochester and Canterbury. His association with this parish indicates that St. Mary Magdalene would have been one of the earliest parish churches to celebrate the new liturgy, which evolved into the Book of Common Prayer. Inscribed on his tomb is the acclamation that George maintained his Protestant beliefs through the persecutions of Mary Tudor "to his final breath."
• •

Also of note are the medieval sedilia, dating from 1370, and the church's original piscina for the washing of sacred vessels.

The unusual tilting helmets that adorn the chapel, although rare, are copies; the originals may be viewed in the Tower of London.

Immediately behind St. Mary Magdalene is **New College of**

Cobham, a cluster of ancient almshouses, founded by Sir John de Cobham in 1362 as a chantry for the church. The college can be accessed by a footpath at the rear of the church. It is well worth a peek — Henry Yevele is believed to have been the architect. You may make arrangements to tour when you schedule your visit at St. Mary Magdalene.

❖❖❖

HENRY YEVELE (C. 1320–1400)

Henry Yevele was the "architect to the stars" of the 14th century. Considered one of the greatest architects in English history, Yevele had a hand in building or renovating several of the most prestigious castles of medieval times, including Westminster Palace, the Tower of London, Baynard's Castle and the Savoy in London and Eltham, Cooling and Sheen castles in Kent. His ecclesiastical projects included work on Westminster Cathedral, the parish church of St. Dunstan in the East in London and the chapter of St. Paul's Cathedral. The nave of Canterbury Cathedral is considered one of his masterpieces. Yevele also was responsible for the maintenance of London Bridge for more than 30 years.

Yevele did not restrict himself to building projects. He also created some of the most impressive of the medieval tombs with effigies. He is credited with designing those of Edward III, Richard II and his queen Anne and Cardinal Langham in Westminster Abbey. Some historians attribute the tomb and effigy of the Black Prince in Canterbury Cathedral to Yevele.

Born in Derbyshire, probably as a serf, Yevele became a freeman in 1353 after he moved to London. He spent the rest of his life there, marrying the daughter of a London tradesman and becoming a man of property and some wealth due to his construction commissions. He continued to design and build right up to the time of his death.

❖❖❖

✝ Also of note in Cobham . . .
Cobham Hall

>>>

Now a girls' school, Cobham Hall once served as the ancestral home of various de Cobhams, Brookes and Darnleys. The north and south wings date from 1584 to 1603, although they

have been heavily remodeled over the centuries. Queen Elizabeth visited the estate twice during her reign; she would barely
recognize the place now. Cobham Hall is open for (required)
90-minute guided tours on a very limited basis—basically when
the students are not in residence. A sign posted at the property
entrance on the A2 trunk road is your best indication of whether
or not you'll be able to tour, or phone 01474-823371. Admission
is £3.50 adults, £2.75 seniors.

✚ Also while you're in Rochester . . .
Cooling Castle

Located in Cooling, north of Rochester, **Cooling Castle** is a
14th-century ruin that is privately owned and not open to the
public. The castle was built by John de Cobham in the early
1380s to help counter the French invasion threat. To make sure
that no one would misunderstand his purpose in constructing
the castle, de Cobham had a copper plaque affixed to the wall of
the gatehouse:

> *Knouwyth that beth and schul be*
> *That I am made in the help of the cuntre*
> *In knowing of whyche thyng*
> *Thys is chartre and wytnessyng.*

In 1408, the castle and the title of Lord Cobham that went
with it passed into the hands of Sir John Oldcastle, through his
marriage as the fourth husband to the great heiress Joan de la
Pole. Oldcastle was a close friend and ally of Prince Henry of
Monmouth. He also was a secret follower of John Wycliff, the
founder of the heretical "Lollard" sect. Soon after Henry ascended the throne in 1413 as Henry V, Oldcastle's religious beliefs were exposed and Henry was forced to grant permission to
the Church for his friend to be tried for heresy. Oldcastle defied

the order to appear for trial and locked himself in Cooling Castle in August 1413. He held out until the end of September, when he was finally taken into custody and escorted to the Tower of London. Oldcastle used his trial as a platform from which to proclaim his views, thus condemning himself to excommunication. For friendship's sake, Henry held off from signing Oldcastle's death warrant, giving Oldcastle a chance to recant. Oldcastle refused to do so and managed the near impossible feat of escaping from the Tower on the night of October 28. He then became a leader of a short-lived revolt in 1415 that was aimed at overthrowing Henry V.

Oldcastle remained at large, most likely hiding in Wales, until November 1417, when he was captured near Welshpool. He was taken back to London, brought before parliament on December 14 and declared guilty of treason. Sentenced to immediate execution *(no one was taking any chances this time)*, Oldcastle was dragged on a hurdle to St. Giles Field, where he was hanged from a gallows while a fire was lit beneath him.

Today, the gatehouse of Cooling Castle is easily visible from the road, but if you want to check it out, please remember that the property is in private hands.

~~

Also while you're in Rochester . . .

✝ Temple Manor
Knight Road
Strood

>>

PHONE
01634-827980

LOCATED
Just off the A28 in Strood (Rochester)

TRAVEL
Buses travel through Strood, stopping about 1 mile from the site; taxis are available at the train stations in Rochester, Strood and Chatham.

OPEN
10:00 a.m.–6:00 p.m. Saturday and Sunday, April–September
10:00 a.m.–4:00 p.m. Saturday and Sunday, October
Closed November–March
Appointments also can be made

ADMISSION
Free of charge

>>

Although the viewing hours are quite limited, Temple Manor makes an interesting side trip to your tour of Rochester. This 13th-century manor house served as a hostel for Knights Templars traveling between London and the Continent. An impressive stone chamber sits atop the original undercroft. The Knights Templars were banned from England, under dubious circumstances, during the reign of Edward II. From that point on, Temple Manor was privately owned. The brick wing was added on to the west end of the building during the 17th century.

∿

✝ Upnor Castle
Upnor

>>
PHONE
01634-718742

LOCATED
2½ miles from the center of the city of Rochester; 2 miles northeast of Strood at Upnor, located on an unclassified road off the A228

TRAVEL
There is a regular bus route from Rochester; in midsummer, open-topped buses provide transportation; taxis are available at the train stations in Rochester, Strood and Chatham.

OPEN
10:00 a.m.–6:00 p.m. daily, April–September
10:00 a.m.–4:00 p.m. daily, October
Special admission can be arranged for groups November–March

ADMISSION
£3.60 Adults
£2.50 Children
£2.60 Concessions
Family ticket available
>>>

Upnor Castle is a well-preserved 16th-century fort built to accommodate Queen Elizabeth's gunships. Constructed to protect the Chatham Dockyard across the River Medway, the castle failed its mission in 1667 when it was unable to stand fast against a Dutch invasion.

☞ Did you know?
Stone from the decrepit Rochester Castle was used in the construction of Upnor Castle.

ANCIENT INNS AND EATERIES

~ King's Head Hotel and Hogshead Bar
58 High Street
Rochester
01634-831103
Dating from the late 1500s, this restaurant specializes in traditional English meals.

~ Royal Victoria and Bull
16–18 High Street
Rochester
01634-846266
This 400-year-old inn was once a favorite haunt of Dickens (who we believe was a closet medieval enthusiast!)

CONTENTS

TRIP 4

Sevenoaks

To the Manor Born

ings and queens ruled medieval and Tudor England with a pomp and majesty virtually unequaled in history. But when it came to ruling the proverbial roost, it was the nobility whose behind-the-scenes power held sway. That's what we love best about a trip to Sevenoaks: the chance to see how the swells—the knights and nobles, lords and ladies—lived in ages past. Don't get us wrong—nothing thrills us more than poking around a castle! Yet the wealth of stately homes and all-but-royal palaces that dot this pocket of Kent are a welcome change of pace. From the nearly regal palatial estates of Knole, Hever (Anne Boleyn's childhood home) and Penshurst Place to the humbler (but exquisite!) moated manor home of Ightham Mote, a trip to Sevenoaks is a peek at how the privileged used the perks of their peerage. We think you'll be mightily impressed.

✝ Knole
Sevenoaks

>>

PHONE
01732-450608

E-MAIL
kknkmw@smtp.ntrust.org.uk

LOCATED
25 miles southeast of London; off A225 or the M25, at the south end of High Street, Sevenoaks

TRAVEL
The train ride from Charing Cross Station takes about 30 minutes; there is connecting bus service to Knole.

OPEN
Noon–4:00 p.m. Wednesday–Saturday, April–October
11:00 a.m.–5:00 p.m. Sunday and Bank Holiday Mondays, April–October

ADMISSION
£5.00 Adults
£2.50 Children
Family ticket available

CONVENIENCES
Brewhouse Restaurant, serving light meals

>>

Knole was built in 1457 for Cardinal Thomas Bourchier, Archbishop of Canterbury, replacing a much smaller home that had briefly stood on the site. Nearly 100 years later, Thomas Cranmer was blithely enjoying the estate's splendor when it was suddenly snatched away from him by King Henry VIII, in much the same manner that the king wrested Hampton Court from Cardinal Wolsey. A typical Henrican expansion plan followed, and the architecture of Knole largely reflects

••••••••••••••••••••
☞ Did you know?
Knole is known as a "calendar" house; its 365 rooms, 52 staircases and 7 courtyards correspond to the days of the year, weeks of the year and days of the week, respectively.
••••••••••••••••••••

the renovations undertaken by that master of conspicuous consumption.

Henry may have been famed for demanding the properties of those closest to him as a show of homage. His daughter Elizabeth preferred the opposite tack, bestowing homes on those closest to *her,* as a means of securing steadfast loyalty. Elizabeth granted Knole to Sir Thomas Sackville, and the estate has remained the seat of the Sackville-West family ever since.

☞ Did you know?

The andirons in the Great Hall fireplace at Knole belonged to Henry VIII and Anne Boleyn. They are emblazoned with the royal couple's initials. They are believed to have been moved here from Hever Castle.

Today, Knole is the largest private home in Britain. The late medieval architecture is largely overshadowed by the Jacobean influence and the extensive collection of Royal Stuart furnishings.

✜ **Ightham Mote**
   Ivy Hatch
   Sevenoaks

>>

PHONE
   01732-810378

E-MAIL
   kimxxx@smtp.ntrust.org.uk

LOCATED
   Off the A25, 6 miles east of Sevenoaks, or off the A227, 2½ miles south of Ightham

OPEN
   11:00 a.m.–5:30 p.m. daily except Tuesday and Saturday, April–October

ADMISSION
   £5.00 Adults
   £2.50 Children
   Family ticket available

CONVENIENCES
Tea pavilion and gift shop

TIP!
If you are as enthralled by Ightham Mote as we are, you might want to consider booking one of the charming cottages, c. 1475, for an overnight stay. Contact the main number for details and prices.

>>

No visit to Sevenoaks would be complete without a visit to this incredible medieval moated manor home. Dating from about 1340, Ightham Mote thoughtfully blends later periods of architecture into a scheme that is in no way jarring or invasive. The oldest portion of the manor is the handsome 650-year-old Great Hall; it is similar to, though smaller than, the hall at Penshurst Place. The drawing room, chapel and billiard room date from the Tudor era.

• •
☞ Did you know?
The ceiling paintings in the chapel at Ightham Mote are thought to have been created in preparation for a visit from Henry VIII and Katherine of Aragon.
• •

Throughout its early years, Ightham Mote was owned by several different families, all of them knights of local regard. By the late 1500s, the home had been inherited by the Selbys, a family with a high profile in the court of Elizabeth I. Dame Dorothy Selby was one of the queen's ladies-in-waiting, and is best known for the legend that she exposed the Gunpowder Plot (a theory later disproved by scholars).

You will find lots to enjoy during your tour of Ightham Mote, along with helpful exhibitions that highlight both the history and the architectural details of the property.

✝ Old Soar Manor
Plaxtol
Borough Green

>>

PHONE

01732-811145

LOCATED

2 miles south of the A25 at Borough Green, 1 mile east of Plaxtol; you will have to navigate an extremely narrow lane to access the property. **Note:** Although not far from Sevenoaks, Old Soar Manor can be a challenge to find on your own; we recommend that you obtain specific directions while at Ightham Mote. One option is to take the footpath that will lead you along the scenic 3-mile walk connecting the two properties.

OPEN

10:00 a.m.–6:00 p.m. daily except Friday, April–September

ADMISSION

Free of charge

>>

Old Soar was built in 1290 as a manor home for a local knight by the name of Culpeper. It comprises just a couple of rooms, but the ancient solar, chapel and undercroft are beautifully preserved and well worth seeing if you're in the area.

Even though they were not blue bloods, the Culpepers, who lived at Old Soar for 300 years, were most assuredly affluent by the standard of the times. The very fact that the manor boasts a solar is an indication that the family lived well beyond the means of most local knights. Note the marble window seat at the southern end of the room; this luxury is seldom found outside the grandest manors. The family's life, however, must have been extremely quiet: as remote as Old Soar Manor seems today, it was infinitely more so 800 years ago. The Culpepers owed rent and allegiance to the Archbishop of Canterbury—one can easily imagine the knights yearning for a sudden call to arms, just to break the monotony of this "bucolic" setting!

Also in Sevenoaks . . .

✝ **Black Charles**
Underriver
Sevenoaks

>>

This minute 14th-century home was once the residence of John de Blakecherl and his family. Although there are many interesting details, the property is open only by appointment—and then only to groups of 10 or more. Admission is £3.00 per person. Phone: 01732-833036.

〜

✝ **Hever Castle**
Edenbridge

>>
PHONE
  01732-865224

E-MAIL
  mail@HeverCastle.co.uk

LOCATED
  3 miles southeast of Edenbridge, 1½ miles south of B2027 at Bough Bridge

TRAVEL
  Hever is about 1 hour outside of London; from Victoria Station, take the train bound for East Grinstead and disembark at Oxted; transfer to the Uckfield-bound train and exit at Hever Station. It is a 1-mile walk from the train station to the castle; unfortunately, there is no taxi service.

OPEN
  Noon–6:00 p.m. daily, April–October
  Noon–4:00 p.m. daily, March and November
  Closed December–February

ADMISSION
   £8.00 Adults
   £4.40 Children
   £6.80 Seniors
   Family ticket available

CONVENIENCES
   Two restaurants and a gift shop
»»

If you're a Tudor enthusiast, Hever (pronounced *Heever*) is a must-stop, if only for its historical ties to Anne Boleyn and Henry VIII, its romantic visage and its largely unaltered exterior facade. Alas, the "Tudor" village, the formal "period" gardens and the luxurious interior detailing were imaginatively created by American William Waldorf Astor in the early 20th century. Impressive as they are, they are not authentic.

It is more accurate to think of Hever as a fortified manor home than a castle. Semantics aside, the property's history stretches back at least 700 years. It is known that in 1200 the Norman de Hever family secured themselves against small-scale local hostilities by adding a moat and drawbridge to their farmhouse. The history of the present residence is somewhat more veiled. In 1340, a license to crenelate was granted to the manor of Hever; by the time Sir John de Cobham took ownership in the late 1300s, the property boasted a gatehouse, curtain wall and battlement. Although the threat of French invasion justified a second license to crenelate in 1384, Hever was never intended to serve as a defense in serious medieval warfare. Rather, marauding bands of vagabonds and malcontents, such as the local men from Kent who fostered the 1381 Peasants' Revolt, proved more threatening to prosperous manors like Hever.

• •
☞ Did you know?
Hever Castle has been the scene of numerous films and television productions. One of our favorite period pieces, *Anne of a Thousand Days*, was filmed on location at Hever. It may be overly flattering of Anne, but we love it all the same!
• •

Indeed, Hever did not play a significant role in the politics of the time for many generations. However, in 1462 the castle was purchased by the Lord Mayor of London, a prosperous milliner named Sir Geoffrey Bullen, forbear of the infamous Boleyn family and great-great-grandfather of Elizabeth I. Sir Geoffrey left his mark on the grand estate by constructing the massive three-story gatehouse that stands on the property to this day.

More than merely well heeled, the Bullen clan would prove to be sufficiently well shod to climb the political and social ladders of the era. Sir Geoffrey's grandson, Thomas, married into high nobility when he chose as his wife the daughter of the Duke of Norfolk, Lady Elizabeth Howard. Through savvy use of his connections, he was made ambassador to the Emperor Maximilian, as well as envoy to the pope and eventually, ambassador to France under the reign of his future son-in-law, Henry VIII.

Boleyn (as he now called himself) might have ascended no further had he not been blessed with two exceptionally fetching daughters. The eldest, Mary, was the first Boleyn daughter to catch King Henry's eye. A lady-in-waiting to Queen Katherine of Aragon, Mary was conveniently placed to become Henry's mistress. She was frequently courted at Hever by the randy monarch. If Mary's papa had any qualms *(and, somehow, we doubt that he did)*, they were quelled by Henry's heaping even more honors upon him: Treasurer of the Household and Knight of the Garter.

However, the real catalyst in Thomas Boleyn's rapid rise to glory rested upon the wiles of his second daughter, Anne. So taken was Henry upon Anne's return from France that he would settle for nothing short of possessing her . . . so prudent was Anne that she would settle for nothing short of marriage. In the cat-and-mouse game that followed, further family accolades were brought to the bargaining table, and the owner of Hever Castle found himself honored as the new Viscount Rochford; by 1529, he added Earl of Wiltshire and Ormond to his dubiously acquired résumé. Throughout Henry's courtship of Anne, the monarch was a regular guest at Hever, assuring that the castle would be one of the best-known—and most-gossiped-about—addresses in Tudor England!

If the Boleyns rose to fame and fortune through the benevolence of a besotted suitor, they fell with breathtaking speed through the vengeance of a jaded husband. A mere three years after their marriage, Henry had tired of Anne and, in a drastic measure to rid himself of her, had his second queen, her brother and three other hapless men arrested and killed on trumped-up charges of adultery and treason. Sir Thomas was spared the physical effects of Henry's violence, but his final days must have been filled with shame and misery. When Boleyn died two years later, the heartless Henry promptly claimed ownership of his ex-wife's childhood home—after all, Hever would come in ever so handy as a bargaining chit for buying off his *fourth* queen, Anne of Cleves.

Divorced, but well rid of her fickle husband (*and darn lucky to keep her head, we might add!*), the dowager queen Anne retained ownership of Hever until her death in 1557. Her stepdaughter Mary Tudor proceeded to grant the home to one of her closest friends and courtiers, Sir Edward Walgrave. By the turn of the century, Hever Castle had quietly faded from the limelight.

Unfortunately, Hever is rather short on exhibits and displays from its medieval and Tudor past. Scattered throughout the interior are incidental mementos from Henry and Anne's romance, such as Good Time Harry's portable door lock (*wouldn't want any unwelcome interruptions during a midnight rendezvous!*). There are a handful of portraits—each, interestingly, depicts a very "different" look for Anne—and two of the unfortunate young woman's prayer books, inscribed in her own hand.

Ghost Alert!

It has long been a Hever legend that on May 19, the anniversary of her death, Anne Boleyn haunts the castle grounds: a mournful, translucent specter.

◆◆

ANNE BOLEYN (1501?–1536)

Next to Richard III, few luminaries from "our" period of history are as controversial as Anne Boleyn. More than 450 years after her demise, her character, her love life and her influence on the politics of the time continue to be hotly debated. Love her or hate her, Anne is a perennial favorite of biographers and historical novelists—and no wonder! It's all here: family feuds, forbidden love, religious turmoil, court intrigues, falls from power, scandal, untimely death . . . and the posthumous payback of having an "illegitimate" daughter rise to be one of the greatest rulers of all time.

There is some debate over Anne's year of birth—clearly, she's not the only woman in history who may have "fudged" where her age was concerned. She was possibly born in 1507; the more likely date is 1501. In either case, hers was a noble lineage: through both parents, she was descended from Edward I—an ancestry she shared with each of Henry VIII's wives. Her father, Thomas Boleyn, married well in choosing Lady Elizabeth Howard as his wife, a move that certainly helped him secure the ambassadorship to France. Anne's formative years were spent at the French court, where she acquired the language, the social graces, the cultured refinement—and the skill for manipulation—that would accompany her through adulthood.

By the time young Anne returned to England, in 1522, her reputation had preceded her. Although her sister, Mary, was already involved in an adulterous liaison with King Henry, Anne managed to capture the monarch's passionate attention—an "honor" she almost certainly would have preferred to forgo. At the time, Anne was deeply in love with Lord Henry Percy of Northumberland and considered herself betrothed. At the king's command, Cardinal Wolsey forbade the impending marriage. Apparently, Anne was devastated, and her lifelong hatred of Wolsey no doubt had its roots in this sorry incident.

Like her sister before her, Anne became a lady-in-waiting at the court of Queen Katherine of Aragon. If Henry assumed that such a position would guarantee him easy access to (and free rein with) Anne, he was mistaken. Anne was not about to allow herself to be so easily and cheaply used. She rebuffed Henry's amorous overtures for a considerable time, first out of fury over his intervention in the Percy affair . . . and later with an eye to becoming the royal consort, rather than another royal strumpet.

By 1527, Henry was seriously contemplating an end to his marriage with Queen Katherine. Clearly troubled by Katherine's inability to produce a son, he saw Anne not only as fuel for his grand passion, but also as the potential mother of his future male heir. The issues involving Henry's divorce were complex, and the implications for England so far-reaching that they warrant separate discourse. Suffice it to say that this was not your typical "Las Vegas—style, no-fault, three-day-turnaround" end to a marriage; Henry's "Great Matter" would take years to resolve. That did not prevent him, however, from moving Anne into his residence at Greenwich in 1528, nor did it prevent Anne from adopting an increasingly "queenly" profile. By 1531, the couple was openly co-habitating and Anne was queen in all but name. Their marriage was officially announced at Easter 1533, although they had been secretly wed on January 25. Anne, at the time, was already more than "a little pregnant."

How did the English welcome their new queen? They didn't. Anne was despised from the start. Her "Frenchified" ways, her aloof demeanor, her open defiance of sexual mores and religious traditions did nothing to endear her to a population fiercely loyal to Queen Katherine and Katherine's daughter, Princess Mary. The tiny, malformed sixth finger on her left hand led the superstitious to accuse Anne of being a witch; her out-of-wedlock pregnancy allowed the righteous to call her a whore. The populace was open and vocal about their disregard for Mistress Anne. Alas, her husband's disregard was not far behind. No sooner was the marriage declared lawful and binding by Archbishop Cranmer than Henry seemed restless, dissatisfied and disdainful. The king made it increasingly clear that the success of their marriage hinged on Anne's bearing a son. Little did Anne suspect that her very life hung in the balance.

On September 7, 1533, Queen Anne gave birth to a daughter, the future Elizabeth I. Both parents were tremendously disappointed. Had Anne given birth to a son, her fate would certainly have been different. Publicly, Henry went to great lengths to celebrate the birth of his new heir (Princess Mary having been rendered "illegitimate" at the time of her parents' divorce). Behind the scenes, the king was soon wooing a third brood mare, Jane Seymour. Relations between Henry and Anne began to deteriorate rapidly. A brief reprise was enjoyed during Anne's second full-term pregnancy, but their long-awaited son was stillborn on January 29, 1536. The tragedy sealed Anne's fate. She was arrested on May 2, 1536, on charges of adultery that were almost certainly trumped up, and sent to await her fate in the Tower of London—ironically, in the very quarters where she spent the night before her coronation. Anne was found guilty of treason in a trial that was railroaded at astonishing speed by Thomas Cromwell. She was decapitated on May 19 on Tower Green and buried in the Tower's Chapel of St. Peter ad Vincula; her brother and the other three men, with whom she supposedly had her sexual trysts, went to the block at London's Tower Hill.

The name Anne Boleyn will always be linked with the English Reformation. Certainly her relationship with Henry was the catalyst for England's break with Rome, but Anne's religious interests were not merely personal. She seems to have held decidedly modern views on the role of the Church in the life of the individual. While Henry would ever consider himself "Catholic," albeit no longer beholden to the Vatican, Anne's leanings were definitely Protestant. She was well read and well spoken on the European Reformation, and was a generous patron of scholars and clergy whose convictions she supported. Anne was an independent thinker with a sharp tongue, quick wit and more than a small dose of political savvy. She may not have been able to save her own neck, but her strongest attributes blossomed in her daughter, Elizabeth. *(We can't help thinking Anne would have been a proud mama, indeed.)*

◈◈

While you're at Hever ...

Stop by the 14th-century **St. Peter's Church**, located in the village. You'll find the impressive tomb of Sir Thomas Boleyn, Elizabeth I's grandfather.

〜

✝ Penshurst Place
Tonbridge

>>>

PHONE
   01892-870397

E-MAIL
   penshurst@pavillion.co.uk

LOCATED
   M25, junction 5 to the A21 to Tonbridge North, then proceed along the B2027 via Leigh and follow signs to the visitors' entrance at the southeast end of the village, just south of the church

TRAVEL
   Trains run from either Charing Cross or Waterloo to Tonbridge; taxi service is available from the Tonbridge Station.

OPEN
   Noon–5:30 p.m. daily, April–October
   Noon–5:30 p.m. Saturday and Sunday, March
   Closed November–February

ADMISSION
   £6.00 Adults
   £4.00 Children
   Family ticket available

CONVENIENCES

The adventure playground, nature trail and toy museum make Penshurst Place — as stately homes go — a star attraction for children!

>>>

Beautifully situated on the outskirts of a medieval village, Penshurst Place is generally regarded as one of England's finest stately homes. Certainly, it affords the amateur historian an impressive taste of how the gentry lived in the high Middle Ages.

Penshurst Place is over seven centuries old; the first owner is believed to have been Sir Stephen de Penchester (d. 1299), a manservant for Edward I. It is known for certain that the manor was eventually acquired by Sir John de Pulteney, one of the wealthiest and most successful merchants of his time. Of aristocratic birth, Sir John amassed his fortune through wise ventures in the wool trade. Knighted by the Black Prince in 1337, he went on to serve many years as one of London's leading aldermen, and enjoyed a distinguished four-year term as Lord Mayor of that city. Penshurst Place was but one of 23 manor homes owned by de Pulteney at the time of his death. Penshurst seems to have had a particular pride of place. Sir John spared no expense in improving the manor, and his magnificent Great Hall (c. 1341), unaltered to this day, is still referred to as one of the grandest in the world.

Although de Pulteney had received a license to crenelate in 1341, he had no good reason to do so. Protective walls were added during the French invasion scares of 1377, and a subsequent owner — Sir John Devereux — received a second license to crenelate in 1393. The next major phase of construction did not occur until the Duke of Bedford took ownership in 1413. Brother to Henry V and regent for the king's young heir, Bedford took the only significant steps toward fortifying the estate, adding the towers and increasing the height of the walls. Still, Penshurst Place remained a welcoming residence of unparalleled comfort; clearly none of its owners seriously envisioned the role of "fortress" for this *grande dame*.

Penshurst Place continued to play a supporting role in history throughout the Tudor era. It was briefly owned by Edward Stafford, Duke of Buckingham, the arrogant High Constable of England who was arrested and tried for high treason in 1521, under orders from Cardinal Wolsey. Its lush grounds provided the occasional romantic respite for Henry VIII while he wooed Anne Boleyn. In 1552, Edward VI granted the elegant manor to his steward, Sir William Sidney, first Lord Penshurst; it has remained the Sidney family home ever since. Sir William's son, Henry Sidney, added the two graceful main wings in the 1560s.

More than many of England's stately homes, Penshurst Place retains a host of medieval features. The set piece is, of course, de Pulteney's Great Hall, a.k.a. the Barons Hall. Note the magnificent 60-foot-high chestnut hammerbeam ceiling and the carved minstrels' gallery. Throughout, you will note exceptional furnishings, tapestries and art from the 1400s through the 1600s. The Sidney family crypt displays a vast collection of armor and weapons, and even the on-site toy museum offers several whimsical playthings from the Middle and Tudor Ages. Be sure to stroll through the gardens. One dates from 1346; the second, a rare example of formal Tudor landscaping (most were destroyed during the Georgian period), was praised by Ben Jonson in his poem "To Penshurst."

❖❖

SIR JOHN DE PULTENEY (1290–1349)

Whether or not he was the richest merchant of his time, de Pulteney sure spent money as if he were! In addition to the 23 manor homes he owned throughout England, de Pulteney owned an impressive number of commercial properties in London and made sizeable donations to various religious foundations. His London enterprises are of particular interest. John de Pulteney endowed the Chantry of Corpus Christi in St. Lawrence Church, Candlewick Street, and a smaller, but significant, chantry at St. Paul's Cathedral. He also funded the construction of All Hallows, in Lower Thames Street.

His two London homes were lavish enough to be sought, upon his death, by leading aristocrats of the time. Coldharbour, near Dowgate, became the London residence of the Earls of Salisbury, and later was home to George, Duke of

Clarence—the ill-fated brother of Edward IV. Pulteney Inn was the London home of the Black Prince and his stepson the Earl of Exeter. The combination of de Pulteney's aristocratic tastes, inherited wealth and savvy business ventures made him unique among the merchant class—one of the few who successfully straddled London's economic and social castes.

❖❖

THE SIDNEYS OF PENSHURST PLACE

Of all the numerous names and titles associated with Penshurst Place, we find the most interesting to be Sir Henry Sidney, his wife, Lady Mary, and their first son, Philip. Sir Henry was the son of Sir William Sidney, tutor and household steward to Edward VI. In 1552, the young king expressed his affection for his faithful servant by awarding Sir William Penshurst Place. Unfortunately, Sir William did not live long enough to fully enjoy life at Penshurst, and the property soon passed on to his son, Sir Henry.

Like his father before him, Henry Sidney was close to the Crown; he was honored as a Knight of the Garter in 1564. However, the title came with no financial consideration, and—as all good Tudor groupies know—life as a favored courtier in that day and age could be very costly. Sir Henry found himself the owner of one of England's grandest estates and, as a result, deeply in debt. However, his financial embarrassments did not prevent him from erecting a handsome new entrance tower at Penshurst, an expression of gratitude for the king's generous gift to his father.

In all other ways, Sir Henry seems to have been a conservative man; indeed, his common sense and cautious nature allowed him and his family to survive, unscathed, one of the most vicious political intrigues of the day. Sir Henry's wife, Lady Mary, was a Dudley. Her father was the Duke of Northumberland, her brother was Guildford Dudley, and her sister-in-law *(three guesses!)* was none other than Lady Jane Grey, the reluctant "Nine Days Queen." These three kin of Lady Mary would be convicted as traitors in the plot to usurp the throne from Mary Tudor; all three would die on the executioner's block. *(Of course, Lady Mary's **other** brother, Robert Dudley, Earl of Leicester, was Elizabeth I's rumored lover, "Sweet Robin" . . . but that's another story for another book!)*

Clearly, Henry and Mary Sidney were leaving nothing to chance. When their first son was born in 1554 (the same year as Jane and Guildford went to the block), the couple earned major brownie points with the queen by naming the child after Mary's husband, Philip II of Spain. They gilded the lily by having Mary's consort stand as godfather to their child. To this day, the Sidney family still names each firstborn son Philip *(although we assume it's okay for them to rest easy now).*

Young Philip Sidney is one of those rare historical figures whose name has remained unsullied with time. A talented poet, whose work still ranks at the forefront of Elizabethan literature, he was, in the family tradition, a favorite at court. He was also a skilled statesman and in 1585 was appointed Governor of Flushing in the Netherlands. Unfortunately, the role would bring about his untimely death. In 1586, while defending the Dutch against Spain *(we wonder what his godfather thought about that!)*, Sir Philip was wounded by musket fire. Even in the shadow of death, his noble bearing did not fail him; it was reported that as he reached for his water bottle, his attention was drawn to a comrade who was in equally dire straits. Sidney handed his water bottle to the dying soldier, with the immortal words "Thy necessity is yet greater than mine." Sir Philip died one month later at the age of 31. He was accorded the honor of a state funeral at St. Paul's Cathedral, setting a precedent to be repeated only for Admiral Nelson and Sir Winston Churchill. Sir Philip's helmet is proudly displayed at Penshurst Place.

❖ ❖

✝ While you're in the area . . . Chiddingstone

>>>

Short on historical events, but long on atmosphere, the nearby hamlet of Chiddingstone is well worth your time. There is even a footpath connecting Penshurst Place with Chiddingstone, for the hale and hearty amateur historian! Chiddingstone is a largely unspoiled Tudor neighborhood and a good choice for midday refreshment. The village traces its ancestry to 814 CE, when it was deeded in a land grant to one of the earliest Archbishops of Canterbury; the connection to the See of Canterbury still remains. The village store was once owned by Anne Boleyn's father, and Henry VIII's widow, Katherine Parr, was once married to a Chiddingstone resident, Sir Edward Burgh. Chiddingstone is so well preserved that locals claim there are only two "new" buildings in the entire village: the 20th-century village hall and rectory. Be that as it may, the streetscape remains little changed from the way it must have looked in the 15th century.

While in Chiddingstone, look for the ancient church of **St. Mary's**. It was built well before its first official mention in 1486—possibly early in the 13th century, based on excavations on the property. We particularly enjoyed the amusing collection of stone faces that run along the top of the yellow-brown church's west tower *(now's the time to pull out those binoculars we advised you to bring!)*. Look closely: you'll find one has two heads, another sports two noses, two mouths and three eyes, and several are making rude faces in the direction of the village.

• •

☞ Did you know?

Did that "castle" on the outskirts of Chiddingstone catch your eye? April Fools! Chiddingstone Castle is not a "castle" at all, but a mock-Gothic creation of Henry Streatfield, erected in 1805 on the site of the Streatfield ancestral home. Yes, there was once a medieval manor home upon this site, but nothing remains. Although occasionally open to the public, Chiddingstone Castle is chockablock with oddities and artifacts from Japan, Egypt and Jacobite England. Not our cup of tea, and presumably not yours!

• •

ANCIENT INNS AND EATERIES

~ The Cottages at Ightham Mote
Ivy Hatch
Sevenoaks
01732-810378

Charming half-timbered cottages, believed to have been built in 1475, on the grounds of a beautiful moated medieval manor home. See the entry on Ightham Mote.

~ Old Cloth Hall
Cranbrook
01580-712220

If it was good enough for Elizabeth, it's good enough for us! A notoriously finicky eater, the queen quite enjoyed her lunch here in 1573. If you're an overnight guest in this beautiful home—parts of which date back 500 years—you'll be treated like royalty.

~ Grasshopper Inn and Country Club
Moorhouse
Westerham Road (A25)
Westerham
01959-563136
13th-century inn that also functions as a country club. The restaurant and bar are open for morning coffee, lunch, dinner and bar snacks.

~ Tudor Village
Hever Castle
Call the Hever Castle information line for details
Although the accommodations are not genuinely Tudor, we are intrigued that you can actually spend the night here. You will have to tap into your hidden talents as a social director—the rooms are available exclusively for groups of 10 or more—but it may well be worth the effort. No luxury has been spared in the 25 guest rooms, and the private dining room will stage a Tudor banquet for your party, complete with strolling minstrels and period music.

~ King Henry VIII Inn
Hever
01732-862457
Appropriately decorated with portraits of the famous Tudor lovebirds and displaying copies of their most intimate correspondence. Open lunch only, Tuesday–Saturday. We like this one. It's worth a drop-by. Located right next door to the castle, it's a comfy, cozy pub with good food and beverages.

~ The Castle Inn
Chiddingstone
Edenbridge
01892-870247
Built in 1420, this restaurant—like all of Chiddingstone—has an air of genteel antiquity about it. A handsome open kitchen

lets you watch the preparation of traditional English roasts and game. The wine list is impressive, and the lounge offers a pleasant way to sit and relax with Chiddingstone residents. Open for morning coffee, lunch, afternoon tea, dinner and snacks year-round.

❖❖

A CURE FOR WHAT AILS THEE

Whether it's jet lag, the stress of meeting the publisher's deadline, or the after-effects of a particularly, er . . . "merrie" . . . night out in London, we've been known to suffer from our fair share of crashing headaches and rolling stomachs. Curious as to how our foremothers may have coped with such complaints, we delved into tomes of medieval domestic wisdom and came up with the following herbal "simples"—which seemed not-quite-simple-enough for someone in truly dire straits!

~ For migraines
In your cauldron of water place half a dish of barley and one handful each of vervain, betony and other herbs that might be good for the head *(preferably legal)*. Boil well and when the herbs are well steeped, wrap them in a clean cloth and lay them upon the sickened brow.

~ For stomach complaints
Take one pound of cumin and bray it with a mortar *(don't ask us where you'll find the strength to do this)*. Add a hearty quantity of good, stale ale and bring it to a boil, skimming the foam from the surface from time to time. When it is well steeped, remove it from the fire, strain it through a clean linen cloth and drink the lukewarm "liquor." The hot sediment from the boiled cumin should be put into a linen bag shaped like a heart, and laid upon the malcontent stomach. *(If you ask us, blackberry brandy and a hot water bottle would suffice!)*
❖❖

CONTENTS

TRIP 5

Maidstone

Airs and Graces

o title this trip "Maidstone" is somewhat misleading, we admit. In reality, you will be spending very little time on your tour actually in the town of Maidstone — in fact, if you have determined that you cannot, or care not, to see the Archbishop's Palace, you'll probably do well to avoid the busy town altogether. Still, all of the other interesting sites on this trip sport a "Maidstone" address, so "Maidstone" it is.

Some advice about planning this particular trip: although Maidstone proper and Leeds Castle are both accessible from London by rail, each of the smaller outlying sites needs to be reached by car. You could arrange for a car and driver from Maidstone, or you could pre-book a taxi from the train station at Leeds. However, if you are going to bear that expense, we think you'd be better off hiring a car and driver from London and combining the Maidstone sites with another trip in Kent. For instance, we visited Faversham in the morning and the Maidstone sites in the afternoon. You might prefer to combine two trips where train travel is not convenient — Sevenoaks is one suggestion.

Regardless of how you get there — get there! Leeds Castle will fill your fairy-tale fantasies, and you'll be delighted by some of the lesser-known sites as well. We were!

✠ Maidstone Town Centre Tourist Information Centre

The Gatehouse
Palace Gardens
Mill Street
Maidstone

>>

PHONE
01622-602169

LOCATED
A20 to the M20, junction 5 and follow information signs to Mill Street

TRAVEL
Trains depart London for Maidstone East Station; travel time is approximately 1 hour.

ADMISSION
Free of charge

>>

There are two information centers in the town of Maidstone. If you plan to visit the Archbishop's Palace, this is the more convenient one.

~

✠ Archbishop's Palace

Mill Street
Maidstone

>>

PHONE
01622-663006

OPEN
10:30 a.m.–5:00 p.m. daily, year-round

Note: This is one of the most popular wedding venues in England, as well as a busy meeting/conference center. You MUST phone ahead to determine access on the day of your visit.

ADMISSION
Free of charge

CONVENIENCES
The Solar Restaurant and Tea Room serves light meals when weddings and meetings are not in progress.

>>

From the outside, the Archbishop's Palace is a site to behold — grand, gracious and medieval. Built in the 14th century, this was yet another of the Archbishop of Canterbury's residences, and one would have to assume among the most sumptuous. Only recently renovated and opened to the public, the palace features several well-restored rooms, which suffer, in our opinion, from a rather "institutional" aura *(there seems to be a steady stream of event bookings, requiring one to navigate banquet tables, wedding balloons and auditorium seating)*. An adjacent apothecary garden is open on Wednesday afternoons from May through August.

While you're in Maidstone . . .

~ Trywhitt-Drake Museum of Carriages
The ancient stables of the Archbishop's Palace are located directly opposite the palace grounds on Mill Street. Unfortunately, the only attraction from our era is the exterior of the building itself. Should you want to explore in depth, the museum is open 10:00 a.m.–4:30 p.m. during the summer season.

~ Maidstone Museum and Bentlif Art Gallery
Located on St. Faith's Street, this museum sports a broad spectrum of displays on topics as diverse as Victorian Children and Japanese Art. Although the museum makes much of its "Elizabethan" roots, essentially only the foundations of the building date from that era. There are several mock-Tudor wings, and a brief description of the property's architectural evolution. If you go, go for the other attractions. Phone 01622-754497 for details.

~ Wool House
Maybe you'll have better luck than we did in your attempt to gain access to Wool House. This 15th-century half-timbered

house was once used for the cleaning of wool. Although owned by the National Trust, it is essentially a private property, and you must write in advance for an appointment to tour (summer access only). Application may be made to Tenant, Wool House, Wells Street, Loose, Maidstone, Kent ME15 OEH.

~

⊥ Leeds Castle
Maidstone

>>

PHONE
01622-765400

LOCATED
4 miles east of Maidstone, accessible from the A20 or the M20, junction 8

TRAVEL
Leeds is a quick, easy and *popular* trip from London. There are many bus and charter-car tours available, and you can pick up details at the London Transport Centre and most tourist information offices. British Rail offers an inclusive train/transfer/admission ticket for travel from Victoria Station. With this purchase, a designated bus will take you to and from Bearstead Station, the closest depot to Leeds Castle. Travel time from London is approximately 1¼ hours.

OPEN
10:00 a.m.–5:00 p.m. daily, March–October
10:00 a.m.–3:00 p.m. daily, November–February

Note: Leeds Castle operates a conference facility and does, upon occasion, close for major business functions. To avoid disappointment, be sure to call ahead and verify opening hours.

ADMISSION
£9.50 Adults
£6.00 Children
£8.50 Seniors
Family ticket available

>>

Considered by many to be the loveliest castle in all of Britain, Leeds came by its breathtaking beauty relatively late in life *(as middle-aged amateur historians, we take heart in that fact).* Much of what *appears* to be medieval about the castle is, in fact, the result of 19th- and 20th-century "improvements" to the property, made in what could reasonably be termed medieval-*style* design. With its pristine landscaping, tasteful period furnishings and peculiar collection of Middle Age memorabilia (including a very odd collection of medieval dog collars!), one can barely believe that this Disneyesque setting was once one of the most foreboding fortresses in southeast England. Its lively tourist trade can give Leeds the feeling of "McCastle," but there is plenty to amuse the amateur historian for a few pleasant hours.

Like the ugly duckling transformed into a delicate swan, the castle that shines in the waters of Leeds reflects an amazing transformation. One thousand years ago, when the first fortress was built on this site, defense mattered far more than glamour ... although the strategic setting, which spans two small islands in the River Len, lends itself equally to both. Still, all indications are that the first building on the property was more frightening than fanciful.

It is believed that the first stern wooden structure was erected in 857 during the reign of King Ethelbert of Kent by a courtier named Leede. The well-positioned fortress captured the attention of William the Conqueror; he granted Leede's Manor (cited in the *Domesday Book*) to one Hamon de Crevecoeur, whose son built the castle's first stone keep and gatehouse. Only the cellar and the stonework from this original Gloriette Tower remain.

Leeds Castle stayed in the de Crevecoeur family for many generations. In 1139, the site was a focal point for an armed battle between King Stephen and his cousin Empress Matilda, both of whom claimed the crown of England. Led by Matilda's base-born brother Robert, Earl of Gloucester, forces loyal to the empress briefly held Leeds before it fell, under siege, to Stephen. The castle fell into royal hands a second time during the reign of Henry III, when Robert de Crevecoeur joined the revolt led by Simon de Montfort. The king seized the castle, awarding it to his new Sheriff of Kent and Warden of the Cinque Ports, Roger de Leybourne. It is to de Leybourne that Leeds's spectacular water defenses (created by damming the River Len) are credited. De Leybourne died while on Crusade with King Henry's son Edward; in 1278, de Leybourne's son William conveyed the castle to his father's esteemed comrade, then King Edward I, and his queen Eleanor of Castile.

Leeds has cultivated a reputation as the "ladies' castle," the Castle of Queens, and Eleanor of Castile was the first of many royal women to harbor a deep affection for the site. Leeds was a favorite residence of Eleanor and Edward I, and a grand-scale renovation of the property took place during their reign. Perhaps the most significant addition was the lovely chapel in the Gloriette Tower, a chapel that would be closely linked with Eleanor. Upon her death, Edward ordered that perpetual prayer be offered in this chapel for the soul of his beloved consort; four canons and a clerk celebrated daily Mass in Eleanor's memory throughout the reigns of the next four monarchs, each of whom reconfirmed the chantry. *(One cannot help wondering how Edward's second queen, Margaret, must have felt with all the chants and prayers evoking the name of her predecessor . . . for Edward gave Leeds to Margaret as a wedding present. The newlyweds even spent their honeymoon there!)*

The third queen associated with Leeds was the wife of Edward II—the "She-Wolf"—although her links to the castle were rather less romantic than those of her mother-in-law. Edward had presented the castle to one of his "very good friends," Lord Bartholomew de Baldesmere. In 1321, the noble unwisely refused to give shelter to the volatile Queen Isabella, who instantly sought revenge. *(Do we detect a trend here? See our entry on Arundel Castle for a strikingly familiar story.)* Leeds was captured under siege and de Baldesmere was beheaded. By 1327, King Edward had suffered an even worse fate *(don't ask)*, and the merry widow took up residence with her lover, Roger Mortimer, Earl of March—until forced by her son Edward III to retire at Castle Rising. The third Edward promptly set about improving the fortification and upgrading the royal apartments at Leeds.

A very young queen, Anne of Bohemia, next received the gift of Leeds. Her husband, Richard II, dearly loved the castle and commissioned the master craftsman Henry Yevele—whose portfolio includes Westminster Hall and Canterbury Cathedral—to add his special touch to Leeds. So pleased was the king with the results that he came to prefer Leeds over most other royal residences. Unfortunately, the days he had to enjoy its pleasures were numbered. Richard was deposed, losing his crown to his cousin Henry Bolingbroke. This usurper and his second wife, Joan of Navarre, sought relief from plague-ridden London at Leeds during the 1403 epidemic. In keeping with tradition, the castle was given to Queen Joan—and in keeping with an even grimmer tradition, her time at the castle was all too short. During the reign of her stepson Henry V, Joan was charged with witchcraft and confined to Pevensey Castle.

Leeds was then awarded to Henry V's bride, Katherine of Valois. Some years later, the widowed Katherine would retreat to Leeds Castle, there to fall in love with—and secretly marry—her Clerk of the Wardrobe, Owen Tudor. Again, tenure at Leeds proved to be ill-fated. Their secret made known and deemed traitorous, the dowager queen and her commoner husband were taken prisoner. Could anyone have guessed that their son Edmund Tudor would eventually sire the future King Henry VII? The seeds of the Tudor dynasty had been planted at Leeds.

Although no other queen would come to own Leeds, Henry VIII took a personal interest in the castle and made a virtual hobby out of improving it. With Henry's deep pockets and love of luxury, Leeds made its final glide from fortress to palace. The mighty defensive structure remained intact, but throughout the royal residences Henry brought beauty and light, adding large, sun-splashed windows and erecting the graceful Maiden's Tower, home to Katherine of Aragon's ladies-in-waiting . . . one of whom happened to be the winsome, wily Anne Boleyn.

Henry was the last royal owner of Leeds. The king bestowed

the castle on his Lord Deputy of Ireland, Sir Anthony St. Leger. And, if the future of Leeds would henceforth be less dramatic, so would it be less colorful. Indeed, Leeds continued to evolve from a royal palace cloaked in an air of intrigue to a stately manor home veiled in the demeanor of respectability. Ironically, recent generations have gone to great lengths to *medievalize* this respectable estate back to its "Gothic" roots.

Finding traces of the medieval and Tudor eras at Leeds takes some perseverance. Whether wandering the 500-acre estate or meandering through the sprawling castle buildings, you'll find your attention diverted by landscaping and furnishings from the 17th through the 19th centuries. Even what appears to be medieval is often not the genuine article. Our inventory includes some original stonework in the curtain wall (although the wall was foreshortened in the 19th century to afford an unimpeded view of the lake); bow windows from 1512 and a rare *Adoration of the Magi* tapestry from the 14th century in the Banqueting Hall; a medieval carved ceiling, an ancient oak bed and an aumbry cupboard for storing church vessels in the Queen's Bedroom; and oak furnishings and tapestries from the Tudor era in the Maids of Honor Room. You'll also find a 1527 missal belonging to Katherine of Aragon.

In short, decide early on to enjoy Leeds for its serenity and beauty and take your pursuit of history a little less seriously. Now's the time to remember the words: *amateur* historian.

You'll be happier for it.

~~

✝ Aylesford Priory
Aylesford
Maidstone

>>

PHONE
01622-717272

LOCATED
Off A229, junction 6 or M20, junction 5

OPEN
  Daylight hours daily, year-round

ADMISSION
  Free of charge

CONVENIENCES
  Tearoom and gift shop

>>

In 1240, the Earl of Cornwall returned from the Holy Land with some rather unusual souvenirs: a bevy of hermits. Exactly who these hermits were, or what attracted the Earl of Cornwall to them *(and vice versa!)*, is information we've, admittedly, not quite grasped. What we *do* know is that they established themselves here, on the banks of the River Medway, and founded what has come to be known as Aylesford Priory (a.k.a. the Friars). Nothing remains of their medieval church, but there are several other medieval buildings on the priory grounds, including the Guest's Hall, which at one time could be entered by boat from the river. Aylesford is currently owned by Carmelite nuns; one of their chapels contains the relics of the first prior of Aylesford, Simon Stock.

St. Leonard's Tower
West Malling
Maidstone

>>
PHONE
  None

LOCATED
  South of West Malling, on an unclassified road west of the A228

OPEN
  Exterior only, accessible during daylight hours daily, year-round

ADMISSION
  Free of charge

>>

This diminutive Norman keep is believed to have been constructed in 1080 by Bishop Gundulf, the prolific builder who masterminded Rochester Cathedral and portions of Rochester Castle. Unfortunately, the interior of St. Leonard's is inaccessible; you must content yourself with poking around outside, or save your admiration of Gundulf for your visit to Rochester!

〰️

✝ Boughton Monchelsea Place
Boughton Monchelsea
Maidstone

>>>

PHONE
01622-743120

LOCATED
On the B2163, 5½ miles from M20, junction 8 or 4½ miles from Maidstone via the A229

OPEN
9:00 a.m.–8:00 p.m. by appointment Monday–Friday, year-round

ADMISSION
£2.75 Adults
£1.50 Children

>>>

The sedate elegance of Boughton Monchelsea Place belies its rather turbulent beginnings. This Tudor manor home was built by Sir Robert Rudson in 1567. Rudson's father had been Lord Mayor of London, and the family was well regarded, until Sir Robert made the unfortunate decision to involve himself with Sir Thomas Wyatt in rebellion against Queen Mary. In retribution, the Crown seized Boughton Monchelsea; eventually, Mary did sell it back to Rudson, but at a tidy profit, you can be sure.

Lovely as it is, Boughton Monchelsea offers little of its Tudor heritage. The interiors—if you have planned ahead to secure an appointment—are primarily Victorian. The grounds are quite handsome—they overlook a private deer park—and the facade of the home is certainly impressive. However, with limited access, and few vestiges from "our" era, we wouldn't recommend you go to extraordinary lengths to include this stop on your itinerary.

Stoneacre

Otham

Maidstone

>>>

PHONE
   01622-862871

LOCATED
   3 miles southeast of Maidstone, in a narrow lane at the north end of Otham village; don't hesitate to ask a local for directions!

OPEN
   2:00–6:00 p.m. Wednesday–Sunday, April– October

ADMISSION
   £2.60 Adults
   £1.30 Children
   Family ticket available

>>>

With so many castles, abbeys, cathedrals and grand manor homes, it's refreshing—and rare!—to catch a glimpse of how "normal" people may have lived in Tudor times. Stoneacre gives you that chance. This 15th-century half-timbered house was a yeoman's home . . . okay, not exactly the *lumpen proletariat*, but hardly up there with the "swells" either! The owners have been very careful to cull furnishings for Stoneacre evocative of its origins. The original Great Hall is particularly interesting, and the re-created cottage garden will delight anyone with a passion for flowers and herbs. Charming!

✝ Sutton Valance Keep
Sutton Valance Village
Maidstone

>>>

PHONE
01732-870872

LOCATED
Off the A274 on the east side of the village; you may need to ask directions in town

OPEN
Daylight hours daily, year-round

ADMISSION
Free of charge

>>>

Originally built in the 1000s, this modest keep once stood guard on the main route from Maidstone to Rye; there is some speculation that it may have served as a tollbooth as well, this being a lucrative trade route in ancient times. Its usefulness was relatively short-lived, however; although technically it was owned by Simon de Montfort, it was not one of the rebel baron's primary outposts. After de Montfort's defeat at Evesham in 1265, the keep was awarded to Henry III's supporter William de Valance. The property remained abandoned, however, and has stood in ruins for nearly 800 years.

• •
☞ Did you know?

The keep at Sutton Valance may have an underwhelming history, but the town itself has a rather significant past. A Roman cemetery and Saxon battlefield in the vicinity attest to its ancient roots. After the Conquest, it was granted to William I's half brother Odo of Bayeux. *(Is there a square acre in Kent that was NOT granted to Odo?)* Although the village was originally called Town Sutton, the name was changed when William de Valance took ownership of the small castle in 1265. A major force in England's broadcloth trade, the town attracted a large number of Flemish weavers in 1331, when Edward III put a stop to the export of unwashed wool. One of the village's most successful cloth merchants was William Lambe; he became master of London's Clothworkers Company in 1531, and used a portion of his sizeable income to found Sutton Valance Free School, which operates to this day.

• •

ANCIENT INNS AND EATERIES

~ Tanyard
Wierton Hill, Boughton, Monchelsea
01622-744705
Once upon a time, this charming B&B was a medieval tannery. Quiet, pastoral setting and renowned breakfasts. Five bedrooms and one suite.

~ Maplehurst Mill
Frittenden (about 13 miles from Maidstone)
01580-852203
Since 1309, this has been a mill site—you can still fall asleep to the gentle sounds of the millrace waters. Accommodations are in the handsomely restored mill, while candlelight meals are enjoyed in the ancient miller's home. Five bedrooms, swimming pool.

~ Ringlestone Inn
Ringlestone Hamlet, near Harrietsham, Maidstone
01323-870218
16th-century inn and restaurant. Noted for its English pies cooked to order from local produce. Also features English wines and liqueurs. Open for morning coffee, lunch, tea and dinner.

~ The George Inn
44 The Street
Newnham, near Sittingbourne
01795-890237
16th-century pub and restaurant. Entertainment includes live jazz, live 1960s music, quiz nights and murder mystery nights. Open for morning coffee, lunch, tea, dinner and bar snacks.

CONTENTS

TRIP 6

Lamberhurst

Spirits and Spiritual

hen the mood for a peaceful, low-octane tour strikes—albeit one with spooky overtones—this is the trip to take. The drive* through the countryside is beautiful, and the sites are varied and compelling. Tonbridge Castle has a fascinating history and creative displays that are bound to intrigue children. Although Bayham Abbey is a ruin, do not let this deter you. These ruins are extensive and are, by far, the most evocative, "spiritual" ruins we have visited. And with Scotney Castle you'll double your pleasure: a medieval castle and a Tudor manor home co-exist in perfect harmony on this lovely site.

If you're on the ball, you've noticed that three of the Lamberhurst sites are listed in "Kent" and one is listed in "Sussex." Very good! Lamberhurst sits on the border between the two shires. Bayham Abbey earns its Sussex address by virtue of being just slightly west of town. For your touring convenience, we have grouped all of the Lamberhurst sites together.

Tip!

If you plan to combine the sites on this tour in one visit, do not plan your trip for Monday or Tuesday—Scotney Castle is closed at the beginning of the week.

---

*The sites on this trip are not easily accessible by rail. We recommend this as a car trip.

✝ Tonbridge Castle
Castle Street
Tonbridge

>>

PHONE
01732-770929

LOCATED
300 yards north of the Medway Bridge at Tonbridge town center, off High Street

TRAVEL
Trains run frequently from Charing Cross and Waterloo Stations.

OPEN
9:00 a.m.–5:00 p.m. Monday–Saturday, April–September
10:30 a.m.–5:00 p.m. Sunday, April–September
9:00 a.m.–4:00 p.m. Monday–Saturday, October–March
10:30 a.m.–4:00 p.m. Sunday, October–March

ADMISSION
£3.80 Adults
£1.90 Concessions
Family ticket available

CONVENIENCES
Gift shop and tourism center

>>

If you like Madame Tussaud's in London, you are going to love Tonbridge Castle. Life-size wax figures are scattered throughout the castle remains in scenes that re-create slices of life from the early Middle Ages—the heyday of Tonbridge Castle. An audio tour puts the scenes into perspective with vivid descriptions of the activities on display. We warn you, though, all is not fun and games at Tonbridge Castle. There is a spooky air about this dark and ancient structure that raised the hair on the backs of our necks and served as an alarming reminder that the gatehouse and wall chambers through which you are walking once were the scenes of bitterly fought battles in which blood flowed and men died. In fact, we were tempted to write this whole site as a *Ghost Alert!*

As typical with the first sites selected to be Norman strong-holds after the Battle of Hastings, Tonbridge, on the bank of the River Medway, had long been a strategic defensive point. The Saxons had already been here. William the Conqueror was quick to recognize the site's importance and awarded it to his loyal supporter Richard Fitz Gilbert as one of the spoils of war following the Battle of Hastings. A Norman baron, Fitz Gilbert had left behind his castle of Bri-onne to follow his duke and seek his fortune in England. His gamble was well rewarded. In addition to being awarded Tonbridge, Fitz Gilbert was given significant estates in Suffolk at Clare; hence derived the family name "de Clare" that was to resound through most of the major events of the medieval age.

Fitz Gilbert first constructed a wooden motte and bailey castle on the site. The motte he constructed, at about 60 feet high, is still one of Tonbridge's most impressive features. The castle, however, didn't last long. After the death of the Conqueror, Fitz Gilbert chose the wrong side in the civil war that

* *

Did you know?

If you think that Richard Fitz Gilbert was grateful for the largesse bestowed upon him by William the Conqueror, think again. The men who followed Duke William from Normandy to England did not do so out of the goodness of their hearts or commitment to a political cause. Their only cause was to fill their pockets. Legend has it that before he left Normandy, Fitz Gilbert used a rope to measure the dimensions of his lands at Brionne. When he was awarded Tonbridge, he used that same rope to compare the two estates. Apparently, Tonbridge came up somewhat short—much to Fitz Gilbert's fury! Theory has it that only after Fitz Gilbert complained about the size of the Tonbridge estate was the Conqueror moved to pacify his belligerent baron with the additional land grant centered at Clare.

* *

resulted from the challenge of the right of the Conqueror's son William Rufus to inherit the throne of England. Fitz Gilbert chose to back Odo, Bishop of Bayeux and Earl of Kent, in his support of the claim of the Conqueror's eldest son, Robert, Duke of Normandy. William Rufus was incensed by this betrayal and laid siege to Tonbridge in 1088. It only took him two days to capture the castle and burn it and the town surrounding it. Fitz Gilbert then retired to a monastery. He died three years later.

But his son, the first Gilbert de Clare, was able to keep the Tonbridge lands in the family by becoming fast friends with William Rufus. In fact, he was one of the huntsmen with William when the mysterious arrow that killed the king was fired in New Forest in 1100. It was this Gilbert de Clare who began construction of a stone castle at Tonbridge. The remains of the curtain wall you see today were part of that structure.

Tonbridge stayed in the hands of the de Clare family for another 200-plus years and the family continued to grow in wealth and power, despite the propensity of its owners to fall into conflict with the reigning monarch. Roger de Clare and his son, another Gilbert, did it again in 1215. As two of the pro-moters and guardians of Magna Carta, they fell afoul of King John. John set siege to Ton-bridge just five months after he signed Magna Carta in June 1215, captured it and held it until his death the following year. The castle was returned to the de Clare family by the council that governed England during the minority of Henry III.

• •
☞ Did you know?

Although the historical record is clear that William the Conqueror did give Tonbridge to Richard Fitz Gilbert, the See of Canterbury challenged his right to do so. For hundreds of years, the archbishops of Canterbury claimed that the see was the rightful owner of the property. One particu-larly colorful confrontation between the Church and the de Clares oc-curred when Thomas à Becket was archbishop. He sent a message to Roger de Clare, demanding that the earl (by this time the family held the title Earl of Hertford; Roger was the second one) pay homage to him, rather than to King Henry II, for the lands. Roger—not to mention Henry! —was infuriated by the order. The story is that, in a fit of temper, the earl forced Becket's messenger to eat his words, literally—parchment and seal both.
• •

The castle was "modernized" in the latter half of the 13th century by yet another Gilbert de Clare, this one known as the "Red Earl" because of the color of his hair and complexion. (The family now held the title of the Earl of Gloucester and this de Clare was the third—and the most notorious.) The Red Earl built a mammoth gatehouse that served both defensive and housing purposes. The five-story structure contained guardrooms, living quarters and an enormous Great Hall that was once used to stage a grand banquet for Edward I and his queen Eleanor of Castile. This impressive—and somewhat frightening—building is what you tour today when you visit Tonbridge. When you walk into the middle of the gatehouse, look up at what was once the Great Hall level and pay special attention to the carved stone heads that frame the fireplace and windows. They supposedly represent the Red Earl, his wife and his parents.

The castle finally passed out of the hands of the de Clares when the last Gilbert de Clare, son of the Red Earl, was killed at the Battle of Bannockburn in 1314. Tonbridge then became part of the holdings of the Staffords, the dukes of Buckingham. This powerful family was not much interested in this relatively small castle; they had much more impressive homes scattered all over England. They allowed Tonbridge to gradually fall into disrepair.

◇◇◇

GILBERT DE CLARE, THIRD EARL OF GLOUCESTER (1243–1295)

Gilbert de Clare was just 19 years old when his father died in 1262 and he became the third Earl of Gloucester and one of the most powerful lords in England. It didn't take him long to make his mark on the world stage. With a head of flaming red hair—and a temper to match—de Clare early on was labeled the "Red Earl." He also had an ego and an attitude consistent with his fiery nickname. The problem was that his flame never burned consistently in one direction for very long and often blew back to scorch him.

The Red Earl came into his inheritance at an uneasy time in English history. Unhappy with Henry III's lackadaisical governance, many of the barons, led by Simon de Montfort, Earl of Leicester, were attempting to force the king to abide by a division of power between the monarch and the lords that was set out in the Provisions of Oxford. Needless to say, Henry was forcefully resisting this effort.

Afire with a reformer's zeal, the Red Earl joined forces with de Montfort and threw himself wholeheartedly into the campaign for change. That quickly brought the king's wrath down on him. In 1264, Henry and his son Prince Edward captured Tonbridge Castle, took the earl's wife prisoner and burned the town. That was the last victory Henry himself won in this war. Next came the Battle of Lewes in May 1264, where an army led by de Montfort and de Clare (who had just been knighted by de Montfort) scored a resounding victory over the royalist forces.

The de Montfort/de Clare partnership did not long enjoy the fruits of this victory, however. Neither man was of a temperament that enjoyed sharing the limelight or saw compromise as a virtue. Just one year after the Battle of Lewes, the Red Earl broke faith with de Montfort. He helped Prince Edward escape confinement and lent his forces to a relentless drive to wrest power from de Montfort. They achieved their objective in August 1265 when the Earl of Leicester was killed during the slaughter that was the Battle of Evesham.

De Clare's alliance with Edward was no easier than the one with de Montfort had been. Perhaps out of a guilty conscience for his own betrayal of the cause of reform, the Red Earl became the champion of the barons who had supported de Montfort. Claiming that Henry and Edward had treated these mutinous lords too harshly, de Clare took up arms again to try to force forgiveness — not to mention the return of the lands and property of the disenfranchised rebels. He was successful . . . to a degree. Henry and Edward compromised by agreeing to allow the former rebels to buy back their lands. But the price for this agreement was high. The Red Earl had once again proven himself untrustworthy and had lost the confidence of his king and prince. As surety for the earl's future good behavior, Henry and Edward demanded that de Clare surrender Tonbridge Castle or his eldest daughter to royal control for three years. (*This was considered an equal trade?*) De Clare chose to surrender the castle.

All was forgiven and forgotten between the earl and the prince upon the death of Henry III in 1272. When Edward returned from Crusade for his coronation, he was met in Dover by the Red Earl, who escorted him back to Tonbridge for a week of lavish celebration. The bond between the two men was further strengthened when Edward arranged a marriage between his daughter Joan of Acre and the earl — a unique solution to Edward's problem of keeping the treacherous earl under control. Apparently, it worked. The Red Earl staged no more rebellions against his king and father-in-law.

❖ ❖

✝ Bayham Abbey
Lamberhurst

>>>

PHONE
01892-890381

LOCATED
Off the B2169, 1¾ miles west of Lamberhurst

OPEN
10:00 a.m.–6:00 p.m. daily, April–September
10:00 a.m.–5:00 p.m. daily, October
10:00 a.m.–4:00 p.m. Saturday and Sunday, November–March

ADMISSION
£2.20 Adults
£1.10 Children
£1.60 Seniors

>>>

Bayham Abbey was founded in 1208 by the Premonstratensian monks, also known as "White Canons." It remained active until 1536 when, during the Dissolution of the Monasteries, it was parceled off to royal favorites, before eventually lapsing into disrepair. (Actually, Cardinal Wolsey had attempted to dissolve Bayham, along with 22 other monasteries, in 1525, with the intention of using the proceeds from the properties to fund his new college at Oxford. Riots by the local citizenry caused him to quickly rethink his suppression of Bayham!) In the 18th century, the evocative ruins, which grace the banks of the River Teise, were incorporated into the landscape plan of a large Georgian home; they are now part of a romantic park owned by English Heritage.

Although relatively small compared to other British abbey

• •

☞ Did you know?

The distinctive golden-yellow stone used to construct the Bayham Abbey church is a sandstone indigenous to Tunbridge Wells. It is considered to be the finest and most easily carved stone in England. It is also remarkably erosion-resistant, which is why the intricate Bayham carvings are so well preserved.

• •

ruins, Bayham has several charming features to make your visit worthwhile. This house apparently never enjoyed the munificence of a single wealthy patron, as some White Canon abbeys did. Yet clearly the monks of Bayham Abbey fully intended to make their house as beautiful as possible, and they were able to generate the resources to do so. Indeed, the abbey was also known as "Beaulieu," meaning beautiful (not to be confused with its better-known compatriot of the same name in Hampshire).

• •
☞ Did you know?

A sizeable portion of the building funds for Bayham Abbey came from a rather unlikely source: nearby **Michelham Priory**. In 1229, the newly formed Michelham Priory was given the gift of a church at Halisham. Thirty years later, the canons at Bayham took umbrage over the transaction and engaged in a prolonged legal battle to have the church deeded to them. It took another 30 years to reach a decision—during which time Bayham enjoyed the proceeds from Halisham. Bayham was ultimately awarded the property on a technicality, and although compensated for a portion of its expenses, Michelham Priory was virtually ruined by the cost of the defense.
• •

It is believed that during the fervor of religious building generated by Henry III's activities at Westminster, work began on a spectacular new choir and lavish presbytery at Bayham. The stonework is of the highest quality, and the detailed carvings in the abbey walls (c. 1260) were so painstakingly executed that they have withstood the ravages of time particularly well—it is worth the effort to carefully admire them.

The most complete structure still standing at Bayham is the gatehouse on the shores of the well-stocked lake. Major portions of the church and the canons' residence make up the balance of the interesting ruins. One whimsical note is the unusual sight of a tree sprouting from the rubble of an altar, which gives this very Christian setting a Druid-like touch.

Ghost Alert!

It will come as no surprise that the spirits who frequent the Bayham ruins are peaceful souls. When the moon is bright and the clock strikes midnight, a procession of White Canons has been sighted en route to the abbey chapel. Faint traces of incense, chanting and the distant peal of bells are said to accompany the prayerful monks.

❖❖❖

THE PREMONSTRATENSIAN MONKS

Commonly known as the White Canons *(with a name like "premonstraten-sian," they needed a nickname!)*, this French-based order of monks arrived in England from Prémontré in 1142. They were relatively moderate as religious orders went—not as cloistered as the harsh Cistercians nor as worldly as the Augustinians, although they did follow a narrow interpretation of the monastic rule outlined by St. Augustine of Hippo. Although they recognized the role of the church in society, they did not engage in church ministry, nor were they active proponents of charitable community work. Theirs was a life devoted primarily to contemplative prayer and self-denial. They were strict vegetarians, lived off the fruits of the land, and inflicted upon themselves the deliberate discomfort of garments overrun with fleas and mites.

For the most part, the White Canons chose remote locations for their abbeys and priories, where they could be left in relative peace while enjoying ample acreage for their farming activities. Their pious, self-denying lifestyle led many secular persons to believe that the White Canons' prayers of intercession were somehow more powerful, more pleasing to the Almighty. As a result, the monks were fortunate enough to attract the sponsorship of wealthy, influential patrons throughout the Middle Ages. Still, the White Canons would never be considered "rich," as many Benedictine, or even Cistercian, orders were. Indeed, Bayham Abbey was eventually forced to merge with two other Premonstratensian houses—Otham in Sussex and Brockley in Kent—in order to avoid financial ruin.

❖❖❖

THE DISSOLUTION OF THE MONASTERIES

When King Henry VIII broke with Rome in 1533 in order to take a second wife, he went on to proclaim himself Head of the Church of England. This was not a title blithely granted by a citizenry that had always taken its Roman Catholic identity seriously. Henry soon realized that a firm hand would be needed to enforce his self-appointed authority. Partly to exercise control and partly to divert the riches of the Church into his depleted coffers, Henry embarked upon a ruthless attack on all religious orders. Within four short years, over 800 British monasteries were closed, their stately buildings and fertile lands reverted to the Crown or given as tokens of appreciation to the king's "yes-men."

The Dissolution of the Monasteries symbolizes the end of England's Middle Ages. An entire way of life was abolished, almost overnight. This was a multiple loss—physical, spiritual and social. Many of the country's most striking medieval buildings were torn down and in their place rose ostentatious mansions, more often than not built from recycled monastery stone. Of greater impact was the loss of social services provided by the monks. The monastic houses were refuges for society's outcasts—the sick, the poor, the elderly. Who would tend to these people now? There was a great cultural loss as well . . . no more worldly travelers seeking a night's comfortable lodging in exchange for news and lore gleaned from foreign lands . . . no more flourishing societies of scholars and writers drawn to monastic halls for informal debate.

In time, a slow, nonchalant rebuilding of social institutions and houses of worship would evolve. A case of "too little, too late," these newer foundations would never command the central role that monasteries had served in English society.

❖❖❖

✝ Scotney Castle
Lamberhurst/Tunbridge Wells

>>

PHONE
01892-891081

LOCATED
1 mile south of the village of Lamberhurst; follow signs from A21.

OPEN
11:00 a.m.–6:00 p.m. Wednesday–Friday, May–September
2:00–6:00 p.m. Saturday and Sunday, May–September
Noon–6:00 p.m. Bank Holiday Mondays
Closed October–April

ADMISSION
£4.20 Adults
£2.10 Children
Family ticket available

>>

A medieval "twofer"? Well, not exactly. Although there *are* two "castles" at Scotney, only one is medieval. It was commissioned by Roger de Ashburnham, Conservator of the Peace for Kent and Sussex, in response to the violent French raids of 1377. All that is left of the medieval castle are the ruins of Ashburnham Tower, one of the castle's original four round bastions. There are also vestiges of a brick Elizabethan home, part of which encompasses the medieval hall range.

For 300 years, Scotney was home to the Catholic Darrell family, who made history late in Elizabeth's reign for successfully harboring a Jesuit priest on the property. Although Scotney was scoured high and low in 1598, the good father remained undetected; when the furor died down, he went on to become the provincial head of the Jesuit order in England.

The remains of the medieval castle were thoughtfully preserved in the mid-1800s as an integral part of the landscaping for the "second" Scotney Castle. Indeed, it is the lovely moated setting and spectacular gardens of this fine country estate that will capture your attention. If it's summertime, you'll be able to see the inside of the ruined tower with its unusual "priest-hole," which allowed the hideaway to have some semblance of communication with the outside world. The rest of the year, you can walk the grounds and revel in the ambiance of the romantic scenery: a pleasant stopover en route to many of the other nearby medieval and Tudor sites, such as Bayham Abbey.

Pattyndenne Manor
Goodhurst

>>>

PHONE
   01580-211361

LOCATED
   West side of B2709, 10 miles east of Tunbridge Wells and 1 mile south of Goodhurst

OPEN
   By prior appointment only to groups of 20–55 people
ADMISSION
   Group rates only
   £4.50 Adults
   £3.20 Children
>>>

Unless you're part of a tour or a lecture series, or unless you are particularly persuasive at rallying large groups of perfect strangers to accompany you on your excursions, you probably won't have much success gaining access to Pattyndenne. That's a shame, because this is one of the most intricate uses of timbering you'll ever find. The house was used by Henry VIII as a hunting lodge—given Pattyndenne's off-the-beaten-path location, it's easy to imagine why! The owners of this private home do a superlative job of pointing out all of the architectural nuances and—as an added treat—give you a peek at the *(haunted!)* 13th-century prison.

ANCIENT INNS AND EATERIES
~ Royden Hall
   Tonbridge
   01622-812121

With Tonbridge's close proximity to Rochester and its many attractions, you may want to consider spending a night out of London in this area. The town of Tonbridge is not the most beautiful English village, but there is one charming—and suitably ancient—hotel on the outskirts of town that offers magnificent views of the Weald. Royden Hall is a fine Tudor manor home with large paneled rooms, beautiful landscaping and several charming outbuildings.

◇◇◇

BED, BREAKFAST, BAWDS AND BEER

Throughout our travels, we've come across numerous ancient inns—that is to say, modern inns in ancient buildings. Few of the "Ancient Inns and Eateries" listed in our book have served the wayfaring traveler since the Middle Ages. More typically, the home of a medieval merchant or Tudor esquire has been recently restored by a hospitable family to serve up a hearty dose of atmosphere along with the traditional English fry-up. The vast majority of ancient B&Bs were put out of business ages ago . . . and the reason has less to do with lack of business than with lack of morals.

To the medieval traveler, B&B would have been much more likely to suggest "brothel and bawdy house" or "booze and brawls" than the charming "bed and breakfast" today's tourist might envision. Most urban inns and eateries grew as amenities for neighboring bath houses, or "stews," where naked men and women could frolic cheek-by-jowl in steaming water . . . your basic medieval hot-tub party. Should all that bathing whet the appetite for additional merriment, the adjacent inn and eatery could supply a "bed" (or matted rushes), some ale, and a meal. Even hostels operating with the express purpose of sheltering the devout on pilgrimage were not above making an extra farthing or two by supplying a willing wench to warm the weary traveler. *(The exception, we would like to assume, were the hospices run by monks on abbey grounds—then again, the Bishop of Winchester all but pimped for his streetwalking "Winchester Geese," so who knows?)*

If one tired of liquor and illicit love, other forms of entertainment surrounded medieval inns. Bear-baiting, acrobats and jugglers, animal acts and, eventually, "legitimate" theater jostled for the spare pennies of transients out on the town. Not too different from most 21st-century tourist zones—but not the scenario to stoke a smile on the frosty faces of the Puritans. These paragons of purity proved themselves to be the ultimate party-poopers. From bath houses to brothels, beer halls and eventually the Bard's boards, vast numbers of businesses were forced to close, virtually overnight. Curtailed merriment, coupled with Protestantism's disapproval of excessive adoration of saints and a widespread fear of the plague, caused 16th-century tourism—religious and secular—to tank.

Few ancient inns managed to stand for long. Hastily built of less-than-top-grade materials, they easily succumbed to fire and the ravages of time. Today the amateur historian looking for a "medieval" night's rest will while away the evening in a half-timbered homestead—the "stewing" provided by a private jacuzzi and the beer proffered by a perfectly respectable hostess.

That's progress for you.

◇◇◇

CONTENTS

Faversham

Mostly Medieval

iny pockets of well-preserved history abound in Kent, but we have a certain soft spot for the ancient port town of Faversham. Faversham markets itself as the "Medieval Gem of Kent," and we have to agree.

Why *(you may ask)*, when there's no castle to awe you, no cathedral to inspire you? Maybe it's the fine collection of timber-framed houses, pristine in their plaster and whitewash. Perhaps it is the peculiar touch of a guildhall-on-stilts, beneath which local traders still hawk their wares. Or maybe it's the touch of intrigue lent by Arden House in Abbey Street, site of the infamous murder of Thomas Arden in 1551—the house, after all, was built from the remains of the Faversham Abbey gatehouse. Ah ha! That's the ticket: it was at Faversham Abbey, in 1154, that King Stephen was laid to rest. Sadly, nothing remains of the abbey, but plenty of Stephen lingers on—in *our* hearts, at least.

Whether you, like us, are fanatical about medieval monarchs or are simply anxious to steep yourself in as-close-to-authentic-as-possible ancient atmosphere, come to Faversham. You won't be sorry.

Tip!

Although we would enjoy Faversham any day of the week, we recommend you plan your visit for Saturday. This will allow you to see the Faversham market in full swing *and* visit Maison Dieu, on the outskirts of town, which is open only on weekends.

Tip!

If your travels find you in the vicinity of Faversham during early July, lucky you! The first three weekends of July are devoted to Faversham's "Open House" program, when many of the privately owned ancient properties are open for a rare public view. Check with the Fleur de Lis Heritage Centre for details.

~~

✝ Fleur de Lis Heritage Centre
13 Preston Street
Faversham

>>>

PHONE
01795-534542

WEBSITE
www.faversham.org

LOCATED
50 miles southeast of London via the M2 or A2

TRAVEL
Trains depart Victoria Station approximately every 30 minutes; travel time is 75 minutes.

OPEN
10:00 a.m.–4:00 p.m. daily, year-round
10:00 a.m.–1:00 p.m. Sunday, year-round

ADMISSION
£2.00 Adults
£1.00 Children

>>>

Faversham is a village that takes its history very seriously—and seems to have a ton of fun in the process! Nowhere is that combination more in evidence than at the Fleur de Lis Heritage Centre. This is not your typical tourist information center. Here you'll find a treasure trove of insights into the people, places and events of ancient Faversham, as well as a wealth of suggestions of how to make your visit more rewarding. We spent nearly an hour poking through maps, local lore and schedules of upcoming events... and then popped back at the end of our visit, armed with questions, which the friendly staff clearly enjoyed answering.

In addition to travel and touring tips, the center runs a charming heritage museum. If you're particularly interested in all things "Kent"—perhaps the history really grabs you, or you have ancestors who hailed from this county—then you owe it to yourself to visit the award-winning Fleur de Lis Museum. Thoughtfully crafted from a 15th-century coaching inn, the museum has some fine exhibits on a wide variety of Faversham/Kent-related topics. *(But what really excited us was the bookstore. How many books can one person have on Kent? Don't ask!)*

☞ **Did you know?**

Conspirators plotting the demise of Thomas Arden hatched their scheme over libations at the Fleur de Lis— back when it was a coaching inn and alehouse. A plaque above the door at the Centre attests to the fact.

✝ Faversham Open-Air Market
Marketplace
Faversham

PHONE
None

OPEN
Tuesday, Friday and Saturday

ADMISSION
Free of charge—*which means more money to spend on goodies!*

If you visit no other open-air market on your trip to England, this is the one *not to miss*. The market takes place beneath the pillared arches, or "stilts," of the Faversham guildhall; portions of the building date from 1574. The market itself is the oldest of its kind in Kent, having been established in 1086. Colorful, bustling and ever so tempting, the market will make you want to linger as long as the weather and your wallet permit! Strike up a conversation with some of the vendors—as we said, Faversham takes its history *seriously,* and everyone from the cheese merchant to the butcher can add a worthwhile footnote to the city's history.

Tip!

Many of Faversham's shops close early on Thursdays—yet another reason to schedule your visit for Tuesday, Friday or Saturday.

∿

✝ St. Mary of Charity
Church Street
Faversham

>>

PHONE
01795-532595

OPEN
8:00 a.m.–5:00 p.m. daily, year-round
Limited touring during worship

WORSHIP
Holy Communion: 8:00 a.m. Sunday
   10:30 a.m. Wednesday
Service: 10:00 and 11:30 a.m. Sunday
Choral Evensong: 6:30 p.m. Sunday
Evening Prayer (said): 5:30 p.m. Tuesday–Friday

ADMISSION
Donation requested

>>

Faversham may not boast a cathedral, but St. Mary of Charity comes very close in size—the only bigger churches in Kent are Canterbury and Rochester cathedrals. The parish church is readily identified by its graceful flying spire (c. 1794). Vestiges of its 1070 Norman origins may still be seen, despite Victorian remodeling. Of particular interest are the grotesque misericords beneath the quire, a fine collection of medieval and Tudor memorials and the elegant double-aisled transept, which provides sweeping interior vistas. We were captivated by the muted colors and evocative images of the medieval frescoed pillar, which dates from the 14th century. *(We found the sheep grazing in the churchyard to be rather unusual as well!)*

◆◆◆◆◆◆◆◆◆◆◆◆◆◆◆◆◆◆◆◆◆◆◆◆◆

☞ Did you know?
The Trinity Chapel (a.k.a. the Lady Chapel) at St. Mary Charity bears a plaque in memory of King Stephen. Church tradition holds that upon demolition of Faversham Abbey, the remains of Stephen and his family were transferred to this chapel—rather than being tossed into the creek, as history claims. We would like to believe this legend, even though there is no documented proof.

◆◆◆◆◆◆◆◆◆◆◆◆◆◆◆◆◆◆◆◆◆◆◆◆◆

✝ Arden House
Abbey Place
Faversham

>>>

Arden House is privately owned and is open to the public only during Faversham's "Open House" program in July. Check with the Fleur de Lis Heritage Centre for specific dates and times. It is worth your while, however, to stroll past the lovely house—there are several plaques to read and bits and pieces of Faversham Abbey to spot.

>>>

When you stand and look at this charming English residence, it's hard to fathom its sordid past. This 16th-century home was the scene of the terrible murder of one Thomas Arden in 1551. The most notorious homicide of the Tudor era, the crime had all the elements necessary to capture the public imagination: sex, violence and greed. Thomas Arden was murdered at home by his wife and her lover—her servant!—aided and abetted by other household staff, as well as by some of the Arden neighbors. *(One can't help but wonder what type of person could rally so many willing participants in his demise!)* The tragedy inspired the play *Arden of Feversham*, significant for being the first play in the English canon to use a contemporary event for its plot. The play is still part of the staged classical repertory in the UK. The house itself is believed to be the only setting of an Elizabethan play that remains intact. *(We'll have to check our Shakespeare and get back to you on that one.)*

* * * * * * * * * * * * * * * * * * *
☞ Did you know?

The gatehouse to Faversham Abbey is incorporated into Arden House's Tudor architecture. Thomas Arden was employed by the Crown to sell off the abbey's holdings during the Dissolution. In 1540, he purchased the gatehouse—which in its time had hosted such luminaries as Cardinal Wolsey—along with a load of rubble from destroyed abbey buildings, and used these as the set pieces for his domestic haven. Little did he know he would be constructing a den of iniquity!
* * * * * * * * * * * * * * * * * * *

☩ A lost treasure . . .
Faversham Abbey

≫≫

Faversham was originally founded as a Cluniac priory, but a generous endowment by King Stephen allowed the abbey to break away from the tight control of its mother order. Although Stephen maintained several other religious institutions, it was Faversham Abbey that he held closest in affection. When Stephen died on October 25, 1154, he was laid to rest here, alongside his wife, Maud, and his son Eustace.

Unfortunately, the royal

* * * * * * * * * * * * * * * * * * *
☞ Did you know?

Faversham boasts over 475 historic "listed" buildings, many of which are medieval or Tudor. It also features the longest historically preserved street in England, the country's oldest gunpowder mill *and* the country's oldest brewery. *(To which we say, "Cheers!")*
* * * * * * * * * * * * * * * * * * *

family did not, as they say, "rest in peace." For reasons too parochial to detail, the abbey was engaged in continual power struggles with the townfolk of Faversham. This was one abbey not particularly mourned by the locals when the Dissolution brought about its demise. Still, it seems particularly harsh that the bodies of Stephen, Maud and Eustace were tossed into Faversham Creek — or so the story goes. By 1671, the abbey had been completely razed; all that remains is a small section of the gatehouse, incorporated into Arden House.

• •

☞ Did you know?

In 1541, a boatload of rubble from Faversham Abbey was shipped to Calais to help shore up the defenses.

• •

✚ Davington Priory Church (a.k.a. Church of St. Mary Magdalene)
Davington Hill
Faversham

PHONE

   01795-533272

OPEN

   At random hours, or for worship

WORSHIP

   8:30 and 10:30 a.m. Sunday
   9:30 a.m. Tuesday
   9:15 a.m. Friday

Although there is not a tremendous amount to actually *see* here, at least take the time to stroll past this stark 12th-century church. Davington was founded by Fulk of Newnham in 1153 as a nunnery. Strangely, it survived the Dissolution due to the fact that the last nun-in-residence had up and died, beating Henry to the punch. The surviving church tower is Norman, and from the stone lantern gate you can enjoy winsome views of the town.

✝ While you're in Faversham . . .
Faversham Stone Chapel

>>

Located in an open field alongside the A2, 2 miles west of Faversham, you'll come across a . . . well, another pile of old stones, known to all who care to ask as the "Faversham Stone Chapel." No, it isn't medieval, nor is it Tudor. It is, however, the only "for certain" British example of a Roman temple converted during Roman rule to a Christian church. Remains of the small, square mausoleum may not thrill you, but, hey!—far be it from us to leave any old stone unturned!

• •
☞ Did you know?

Theater gossip is a cottage industry—and was 500 years ago, too! Playwright Christopher Marlowe's father was a native of Ospringe. Dutiful son that he was, Chris was a frequent visitor to the Faversham area . . . which gave rise, at the time, to speculation that he might have had a hand in the writing of *Arden of Feversham*.
• •

〜

✝ ## Maison Dieu
Ospringe
Faversham

>>

PHONE
01795-534542

LOCATED
On the A2 in Ospringe, ½ mile west of Faversham

OPEN
2:00–5:00 p.m. Saturday and Sunday, April–October

ADMISSION
£1.00 Adults
80p Children
80p Seniors

>>

The amateur historian has few chances to glimpse ancient "public" institutions—churches and guildhalls aside. Maison Dieu (Norman French for "God's House") is your chance to see what an early version of a Marriott might have looked like. Although the present timber-framed building dates from the 1500s, Maison Dieu was actually founded by Henry III in 1234. The property served as a combination hospital/inn for pilgrims en route from Dover to the shrine of St. Thomas à Becket in Canterbury. It originally consisted of a rectory for the priests who managed the hospital, a chapel, pilgrims' dormitories, a ward for the ill, and separate, sumptuous royal lodgings, known as "Camera Regis" or King's Rooms. There was also a Lazar house for lepers, a farm to keep the larders stocked—and a cemetery for the unfortunates for whom Maison Dieu's "TLC" simply wasn't enough.

◆ ◆

☞ Did you know?

One of the best educated rulers of her time, Elizabeth understood the importance of formal schooling for girls. On July 14, 1576, she founded Faversham's Free Grammar School of Elizabeth, Queen of England. The original schoolroom is open to the public on the first three Saturdays in July as part of Faversham's "Open House" program.

◆ ◆

Maison Dieu has several interesting exhibits on the role of hospice from ancient to modern times. We were particularly engaged by the roster of royalty who took advantage of the Camera Regis—nearly every monarch and his consort, from Henry III to Edward IV. The visits of Henry V were particularly poignant: he stopped en route to London after his victory at Agincourt . . . and too few years later, again en route to London, for burial at Westminster.

✝ Reculver Tower and Roman Fort

Herne Bay

>>

PHONE

01227-740676

LOCATED

3 miles east of Herne Bay, on the beach at Reculver

OPEN

Daylight hours daily, year-round

ADMISSION

Free of charge

>>

For over 800 years, these massive Norman towers, located at the mouth of the Thames estuary, have served as an important coastal landmark for Britain's shipping industry. The towers are the remnants of a 12th-century church, which was erected amid the remains of a Roman fort, c. 210 CE. Both the fort and the tower are in ruins—your tour will be limited to the site's external features.

It is believed that Reculver was one of Augustine's first stops upon arriving in Britain; this was a primary seat in the domains of the Saxon king, Ethelbert. The Norman towers replaced an early Saxon minster, built within the confines of the fort. Shards of an exquisite Saxon cross found on this site bear testimony to Reculver's very early Christian roots

Ghost Alert!

Reculver may be associated with early Christianity, but it saw its fair share of pagan rituals. Human sacrifice, including the offering of infants to the gods, is known to have been practiced here. The eerie wail of a baby is said to haunt the Roman fort to this day.

ANCIENT INNS AND EATERIES

~ Shelly's
Faversham
01795-531570
This 16th-century edifice in Market Place is now home to one of the town's most popular restaurants.

~ Sun Inn
Faversham
01795-535098
Step back into the 1500s in this friendly local pub. Its Faversham-brewed beer is a "must-try."

~ The Phoenix Tavern
98–99 Abbey Street
Faversham
01795-532757
Thai food in a medieval setting—who says history isn't spicy?

~ Barnsfield
Fostal, Hernhill
Faversham
01795-536514
16th-century country B&B on 4 acres just outside of town.

~ White Horse
The Street
Boughton
Faversham
01227-751343
15th-century coaching inn.

~ Leaveland Court
Leaveland
Faversham
01233-740596
15th-century farmhouse; heated outdoor swimming pool.

CONTENTS

Canterbury

Getting Oriented

e recommend that you devote the better part of a day to touring Canterbury. Few other towns in England have as many historic sites for the medieval enthusiast to enjoy. These sites, however, are spread throughout the city. Although Canterbury is not large, navigating your way along narrow, unevenly paved streets while dodging throngs of tourists can be trying. (*Unless you've already visited Canterbury, you have no idea just how crowded the town is!*) This overview will help orient you and, if your time in Canterbury is limited, help you "pick and choose" among the attractions.

Unless you have a burning passion to attend service at Canterbury Cathedral, we suggest you do not visit Canterbury on a Sunday. Many of the museums are closed; the cathedral, on the other hand, is even more crowded than usual on the Sabbath.

If you are planning to visit most of the medieval sites in Canterbury, consider purchasing a **Canterbury Museums Combination Ticket**, which provides reduced-price entry to **Canterbury Heritage Museum**, **West Gate Museum**, and the **Roman Museum**. On our most recent visit, this combination ticket was available at a rate of £4.00 per adult.

✝ Canterbury

LOCATED

58 miles southeast of London and accessible by either the M2 or A2

TRAVEL

If you plan to arrive by car, be advised that parking within the city walls is severely curtailed. We recommend you avoid parking in the town center altogether, and opt for the outlying Park & Ride lots, just to the north and south of town on the A28. Frequent bus service will shuttle you to and from your automobile.

Trains leave at least hourly from Victoria Station; be sure to board the right car—if you have any doubts, ask!—as the train to Canterbury splits en route; travel time is about 90 minutes.

>>

STRIKING OUT ON FOOT: PILGRIM-STYLE

Before grumbling about how much walking you're about to do, bear this thought in mind—Canterbury was England's premier pilgrim destination for centuries. It goes without saying that not only did these fervent men and women traverse the length and breadth of Canterbury on foot, they traversed the length and breadth of *England,* sometimes walking for months on end, for the very privilege of being in the spiritual presence of St. Thomas à Becket. Yes, you'll put some miles on your "sensible shoes," but at least when the day is over, some sort of *vehicle*— other than your own two feet—will whisk you back to London, or wherever your evening plans may take you. Your soles may protest a bit, but your soul, we assure you, will give thanks!

Leaving Canterbury East Station, cross the footbridge that spans the A2 and turn right at the ancient **Canterbury City Walls**. Dating from the 13th and 14th centuries, these bastions were built atop Canterbury's Roman foundations. Continue along these walls to the bus station and turn left—the tower that you'll see on your right is all that remains of **St. George's Church**, where the Elizabethan playwright Christopher Marlowe was baptized in 1564. Look for St. George's Street—it will turn into High Street—then turn left onto St. Margaret's Street. Here you'll find the tremendously helpful **Canterbury Visitor Information Centre**, as well as an animated display depicting Chaucer's renowned *Canterbury Tales*.

Head back to St. Margaret's Street and approach **Canterbury Cathedral** via Mercery Lane. This was the traditional pilgrim's route to the cathedral. During the Middle Ages, Mercery Lane was lined with stalls selling healing waters from **Becket's Well**, as well as other relics from lesser saints. At the end of Mercery Lane, you'll find **Butter Market**, Canterbury's ancient trade center. Just opposite the market is **Christ Church Gate**, the main entrance to the cathedral since 1557. See if you can spot the Tudor "rose and crown," as well as Becket's shield, among the gatehouse carvings.

In addition to the many sites you will want to explore in the cathedral close, there are several other religious attractions in Canterbury: behind the cathedral, just outside the Roman wall, is **St. Augustine's Abbey**. Although essentially a ruin, it features the tombs of several Saxon saints and kings. **St. Martin's Church**, another Saxon church, dates from the reign of King Ethelbert; to find St. Martin's, walk behind the abbey, turn left on Monastery Street, left again on Longport, then make one last left, just past the jail.

From St. Martin's Church, return to the main part of town by way of Longport and Church Streets until you come to Burgate. Walk up Burgate and turn left into Butchery Lane. There you will find the **Roman Museum**, which incorporates the remains of an excavated villa and re-creates life in Roman Canterbury.

Leaving the museum, wend your way along High Street— you'll pass **Queen Elizabeth's Guest Chamber**, where Gloriana entertained her French suitor, the Duke of Alençon (it's now Queen Elizabeth's Restaurant). Also in High Street is the 12th-century **Eastbridge Hospital of St. Thomas**. High Street will become St. Peter's Street; at the end of it, you'll come to **Westgate**, the 14th-century gateway to Canterbury, now a museum with spectacular views of the town and surrounding countryside. Also in St. Peter's Street are the half-timbered Tudor cottages known as the **Weavers' Houses**.

From Westgate, return along St. Peter's Street and turn right into Stour Street. Here you'll find the 14th-century **Poor Priests' Hospital**, now home of the **Canterbury Heritage Museum**. Just off Stour Street, look for **Greyfriars Church**, the oldest Franciscan building in all of Britain.

Follow your map of Canterbury back to the train station, by way of Castle Street. At the end of the street, you'll see the ruins of an 11th-century **Norman Castle**. Cross Castle Street and turn left at the city walls that you passed initially, taking the overpass back to the train station.

⁕

✝ Canterbury Visitor Information Centre
34 St. Margaret's Street

>>>
PHONE
   01227-766567
ADMISSION
   Free of charge
>>>

We recommend you make this your first stop in Canterbury. You'll find infinite information on all of Canterbury's historic sites, as well as current events, such as concerts, plays and pageants. You can exchange currency, buy stamps and pick up several different maps to aid in your getting around town.

Ghost Alert!

Although we haven't personally engaged in this pasttime, we have it on very good authority that the **Ghosts Tour of Canterbury** is great fun. The after-dark tour takes you through the medieval byways of town, and is led by well-trained official Ghost Tour guides. Tickets may be purchased at the Visitor Information Centre, which is also the tour's meeting site. Unfortunately, this tour is only available on summer weekend evenings. (*We wonder: do ghosts hibernate?*)

HISTORIC CANTERBURY

Canterbury, the medieval city on the River Stour, is arguably the historic and cultural capital of Kent. In addition, Canterbury plays a pivotal role in England's religious life—not only is this the ecclesiastical capital of the United Kingdom, but its cathedral is the mother church of the Anglican Communion and Episcopal denominations, worldwide.

Actually, the history of Canterbury is far older than its "medieval" label would have you presume. Signs of a settlement were found by Julius Caesar's troops in 54 BCE, although the Romans chose not to occupy Canterbury until much later. The ancient walls that surrounded the Roman village of *Durovernum Cantiacorum* date from the late 2nd century; they form the foundation for Canterbury's later medieval walls. Portions of an amphitheater, villa, forum and various temples have all been found in Canterbury—you'll see remnants of the Roman past as you tour the town.

Like all of Britain's Roman settlements, Canterbury was abandoned in the 5th century, when Roman legions were called back to their mother country to defend the failing empire. They left behind a sophisticated infrastructure of waterworks, roadways and public buildings, which rapidly fell to decay; within fairly short order, Canterbury was little more than a ghost town. It wasn't until the first Danish invaders set up camp on the outskirts of town that Canterbury began to revive. By the 6th century, it had regained its status as a lucrative trade center and capital of the Kentish kingdom.

The rebirth of British Christianity propelled Canterbury to national and, eventually, international prominence. Previous attempts to convert England to Catholicism had been moderately successful as early as the Roman occupation. But, like its Roman inhabitants, all traces of Christian worship had vanished from the island by the mid-5th century. That would change when the first Catholic queen arrived on English shores in 589. Bertha was a Frankish princess, convent-educated in France before marrying the Anglo-Saxon King Ethelbert of Kent. She continued practicing the religion of her childhood while residing at court in Canterbury. Queen Bertha and her priest were permitted to practice their faith in private, and would leave Canterbury through the **Queningate** to worship in the small chapel of St. Martin's, just outside the city walls. Here Bertha officially welcomed St. Augustine and his fellow missionaries, sent by Pope Gregory in 597. Apparently the delegation was persuasive enough to convert King Ethelbert; the king and his entire Anglo-Saxon court were baptized by Augustine on Whitsunday 597.

By the turn of the century, Canterbury was solidly Christian. Construction was well under way on an impressive cathedral inside the town walls. Just beyond the walls, a major abbey provided the full range of monastic spiritual and physical succor,

◇◇◇

ST. AUGUSTINE (D. 604)

The first Archbishop of Canterbury, Augustine was chosen by Pope Gregory to lead the papal delegation to England, with the express purpose of converting the heathen Anglo-Saxon island. Augustine had been an exemplary Benedictine monk in Gregory's monastery of St. Andrews in Rome and had proven himself both diligent and devout. In 596, he was named prior of St. Andrews; by 597, he had been selected to head the delegation to the foreign land.

Augustine did not let His Holiness down. He was warmly welcomed upon his arrival by Queen Bertha of Kent and within the year had converted her husband, Ethelbert, and his entire Anglo-Saxon court. By 604, Augustine had converted a second English king, Sebert of Essex, and established thriving bishoprics at Canterbury, Rochester and London. The monastery and school Augustine founded at Canterbury fast became one of the most influential centers of learning in the Western world.

◇◇◇

an internationally renowned library and scriptorium, plus a burial ground for Saxon kings—and future saints. These two religious foundations, Christ Church Cathedral and St. Augustine's Abbey, would dominate Canterbury's cultural and civic life until the Dissolution of the Monasteries—a period of nearly 1,000 years.

Clearly, Christianity was the dominant theme in Canterbury—just how much *more* of a story it would become, no one could have guessed. Few towns in England are so focused on a single historical event. Yet the murder of Thomas à Becket on December 29, 1170, was, for Canterbury, *the* defining moment. The town may have been the official home of Christendom in Britain for the past 500 years, but with the death and subsequent canonization of Becket, Canterbury became the country's leading "tourist" destination. Granted, those tourists were pilgrims on a mission of religious fervor, but Canterbury still outstripped London, as well as Dover and York, in the number of transients passing along its streets throughout the Middle Ages. The entire demeanor of the town altered to accommodate the transient population, with inns, taverns, hospices, markets and souvenir stalls vying with one another for the travelers' coin. As you stroll through Canterbury today, you will see that many of these buildings have withstood the test of time. However hastily they may have been constructed, an unusual number of medieval buildings have survived fire, World War II bombings and misguided attempts at "modernization."

Stunning as it is to imagine that Becket's shrine was demolished under orders of Henry VIII, it is even more telling that the destruction of the shrine did little to stem the tide of devout who continued to journey to Canterbury throughout the Tudor era, and beyond. For 900 years, Canterbury has never waned as a popular pilgrim destination; today it ranks with Lourdes and Santiago de Compostela as one of the Christian world's most revered religious sites. Whether you're driven to visit Canterbury by a love of history or spiritual devotion, you will find a wealth of attractions far exceeding your expectations.

✝ Canterbury Cathedral (a.k.a. Cathedral Church of Christ)

>>>

PHONE

01227-762862

OPEN

9:00 a.m.–7:00 p.m. daily, April–October

9:00 a.m.–5:00 p.m. daily, November–March

Note: There is limited or no touring during church service and no guided tours on Sunday.

WORSHIP

Holy Communion: 8:00 a.m. Sunday

Matins: 9:30 a.m. Sunday

Sung Eucharist: 11:00 a.m. Sunday

Choral Evensong: 3:15 p.m. Sunday

Evensong: 6:30 p.m. Sunday

Weekdays: Check cathedral calendar for details, or call for information.

ADMISSION

£3.00 Adults

£2.00 Children

CONVENIENCES

Gift shop and bookstore; permission to take interior photographs must be obtained at the Welcome Centre.

>>>

ARCHITECTURAL HISTORY: 602–1200

Within three years of his arrival in England, St. Augustine re-consecrated an existing church building, close by the city wall, laying the groundwork for Canterbury's first cathedral dedicated to Christ. A second building was added 150 years later by Archbishop Cuthbert. It served as a baptistry and burial grounds for the cathedral's archbishops. Both of these ancient buildings were badly damaged during the Danish invasion of 1011 and were burned to the ground during the Norman Conquest in 1066.

True to William the Conqueror's master plan, a Norman

archbishop was quickly confirmed to the See of Canterbury; Archbishop Lanfranc—whose investiture had to be conducted in a makeshift building close to the Saxon ruins—proved to be a fortunate choice as head of the church at Canterbury. Almost immediately, he set about reconstructing the cathedral in a grand style that would underscore the city's newly earned religious supremacy over the larger northern town of York. Traces of Lanfranc's Romanesque church, which was consecrated in October 1077, can still be seen as you tour the cathedral's west front.

Further enhancements were undertaken by Lanfranc's brilliant successor, Archbishop Anselm. The eastern transept stairway towers, the treasury and the crypt were all commissioned by Anselm, as was the Chapel of the Holy Innocents and a massive, light-filled quire with seven new altars. These renovations were consecrated in 1130. By 1174, they, too, had succumbed to extensive damage by fire. However, vestiges from this era are plentiful; the southeast staircase tower and the wall painting in St. Gabriel's Chapel are two examples of Anselm's fine work.

In 1175, master builder William Sens began work on a complete reconstruction of the quire. His artistic vision and exacting attention to detail made him a true innovator in church architecture and placed Canterbury at the forefront of world-renowned houses of worship. Tragically, while working on the east transept vault, Sens fell from the scaffolding and was permanently impaired. His work was completed by "William the Englishman," whose artistic talents are best seen in the Trinity and Corona Chapels. The quire, as you experience it today, was completed in 1184, the combined work of two of the most talented Gothic architects of the 12th century.

CATHEDRAL QUICK TOUR

Canterbury Cathedral is more than awe-inspiring. For the first-time visitor, it can be downright daunting! There is so much to absorb, both inside the cathedral and as you stroll around the close. To help make your visit a bit more manageable—and, therefore we hope, more *enjoyable*—we have provided you with two brief overviews of Canterbury Cathedral. The first is a walking tour around the cathedral "close," or grounds. Weather permitting, this 30-minute jaunt will provide you with a sense of the cathedral's expansion over time. The second is a quick walking tour of the medieval and Tudor highlights *inside* the cathedral; it should take between an hour and an hour and a half, depending on how much time you allot for features that postdate the medieval and Tudor eras. In addition to our overviews, many helpful guidebooks are available at the cathedral's information kiosks, as is a free-of-charge floor plan, which will make our interior quick tour all the easier.

~ A stroll around the cathedral close

As you enter the grounds of Canterbury Cathedral through Christ Church Gate, you will note that there are three distinct complexes of buildings: the cathedral itself, the ruins and intact buildings of Christ Church Priory, and the Archbishop's Palace. Focus your attention, first, on the cathedral *(hard to miss —we don't need to describe it to you!)*. You are now looking at the **Southwest Porch**. The two graceful towers that accent this western end of the cathedral are known as the **Arundel Tower** (farthest from the entrance) and **St. Dunstan Tower**, which serves as the cathedral's bell tower. The 300-foot-high central tower was the original bell tower; this is **Bell Harry Tower**, which dates from around 1500. To the east is the highly decorative Romanesque **St. Anselm Tower**.

••••••••••••••••••••••
☞ **Did you know?**

The official entrance to Canterbury Cathedral is via Christ Church Gate. The gate was commissioned by Henry VII to commemorate the marriage of his son Prince Arthur to the Spanish Infanta, Katherine of Aragon. We find this ironic, since it was this very marriage that Katherine's second husband—Henry VIII—used as the "excuse" to divorce her . . . a divorce that ultimately led to the creation of the Church of England, over which Canterbury Cathedral reigns supreme.
••••••••••••••••••••••

Built and improved upon over several centuries, Canterbury

Cathedral is a showcase for many different architectural styles. As you stroll along the south side of the cathedral, these various designs provide clues to the building's history. Here's what to look for: The pointed arches along the nave are Gothic (late 14th century/Yevele). Rounded arches are signature features of Norman architecture (also known as *Romanesque*), and you'll find these on the exterior of the quire (12th century, and the oldest portion of the building/Lafranc and Anselm). **Trinity Chapel** mixes Gothic and Norman styles, which mark the 13th century, a period of transitional design (Sens and William the Englishman).

At the far end of the cathedral, you will come to the circular **Corona Chapel**. Don't be fooled by its rather modern demeanor; Corona Chapel was built at the same time as Trinity Chapel. Both were intended to house relics associated with St. Thomas.

Rounding the Corona Chapel, you will enter the enclave of **Christ Church Priory**. In its day, this was one of the wealthiest and most influential Benedictine monasteries in Britain (St. Augustine was not, as one might assume, an Augustinian; he was, in fact, a Benedictine). Facing you are the ruins of the **Monks' Infirmary**. To their right is the Norman **Infirmary Chapel**. Wend your way through the ruins and enter the **Infirmary Cloister**. The park-like area just beyond the arcade was once the infirmary's medicinal herb garden (*Cadfael fans, take note!*).

Bear right, and venture down **Dark Entry**, the reputedly haunted "alley" that will bring you to the decidedly less ominous **Green Court**. This handsome lawn is bordered by buildings with striking red tile roofs. Originally the monastery's domestic quarters, they now form part of the **King's School** campus. Take particular note of the yellow stone building diagonally to your left—here you'll find the architecturally significant **Norman Staircase**, considered to be the finest of its kind. The fact that the staircase is "under-roof" is one of its unusual features. The stairs once led to the prestigious **North Hall** inn for prosperous lay pilgrims; the building is now part of King's School, and access to the staircase is restricted.

Brave the shadowy confines of Dark Entry once again. Bear right through the infirmary cloister and stop for a moment in the manicured courtyard. The rubble to your left is the remains of the **Monks' Dormitory**; behind you is the small **Prior Wilbert's Water Tower**, which was part of the sophisticated 12th-century water purification system for the cloister.

Return to the cloister and continue on past the **Chapter House** to the 14th-century **Great Cloister**. Believed to be the fourth building on this site, the Great Cloister is noted for its intricate fan vaulting, decorated with the coats of arms of families who funded the building's construction. Access to the Chapter House is restricted, but it is worth noting that this was where the monastery's official business—including the election of priors and archbishops—took place. If you do happen to wrangle your way inside, examine the ceiling; you will find a carved boss believed to depict Henry Yevele, designer of the cathedral's nave. The Chapter House roof dates from the 15th century; the stained glass is, alas, Victorian.

Exit the cloister from the opposite end, and head west. On your right, you will pass the gates of the **Archbishop's Palace**, which is not open to the public. Complete your stroll by walking past the cathedral's **Great West Door** and returning to your starting point, the Southwest Porch. You should now be ready and raring to begin your tour of the interior of Canterbury Cathedral.

☞ Did you know?

King's School is the oldest public school in England, and certainly one of the most prestigious. It traces its lineage to the 13th century, when it was founded as the Archbishop's Almonry School. Henry VIII confirmed the school as part of the cathedral's foundation in 1541, requiring that education be provided for 50 financially strapped scholars each year. The name "King's School" dates from the 19th century. Among the many famous graduates of King's was the Elizabethan dramatist and poet Christopher Marlowe.

~ Insights on the interior

Enter the cathedral by way of the Southwest Porch. You are now in the **Nave**, the main body of the church — during the Middle Ages, this would have been the *only* public area of the cathedral. If you have already explored medieval and Tudor London, you may have been lucky enough to enjoy the stunning architecture of Westminster Hall. This nave was designed by the same architect, Henry Yevele, perhaps the leading builder of his era. Work on the nave began in 1377 and took nearly 30 years to complete. This Perpendicular Gothic-style building replaced an earlier Romanesque nave, which history credits as being nearly as magnificent as the present one.

Pause for a moment to appreciate the **Great West Window** at the rear of the nave. The lower panels of the window feature some of the oldest stained glass in Europe — 13 of the major figures on the bottom two rows date from the early 13th century.

Proceed now along the north aisle of the nave; the medieval shrines and chantry chapels that once lined this side of the nave have long since disappeared, and most — but not all — of the memorials in this sec tion of the cathedral postdate our period.* If you are pressed for time *(or lack the interest),* bypass them and head directly to the

Did you know?

From the late 1500s until the early 1900s, the Archbishop of Canterbury resided exclusively at his London residence, Lambeth Palace. It wasn't until the Archbishop's Palace was renovated in the early 20th century that the archbishops returned to Canterbury for primary residence.

*Note: There is a tremendous amount to see and appreciate in Canterbury Cathedral, much of which postdates the medieval and Tudor period of history. We do not mean to imply that you should give these "modern" attractions short shrift. However, since our area of "amateur expertise" does not extend beyond 1600 (nor, quite honestly, does our interest), we have not included the more recent features on our tour. The official guided tour will give you insights into the cathedral's history from the 17th through the 20th century, if you are inclined to experience this important building in its entirety.

Martyrdom Chapel in the northwest transept. Here Thomas à Becket was murdered by four of Henry II's overzealous knights on December 29, 1170. The spot where the saint was felled is marked by a modern version of the **Altar of the Sword's Point**; the original medieval altar was distinguished with two of the cathedral's many St. Thomas relics. Despite many centuries of renovations, the floor where Becket fell has remained unaltered.

❖❖❖

ST. THOMAS À BECKET (1118–1170)

Perhaps no name is as closely associated with a particular city as Becket's name is with Canterbury. Were it not for the martyrdom and subsequent canonization of this controversial archbishop and political powerhouse, Canterbury would probably have been just another of the Western "cathedral towns," rather than flourishing as a pilgrim's mecca for nearly a thousand years.

Ironically, it was the City of London that Becket held in closer affinity; London was his hometown, the site of his early education, the town in which he began his rise in power, the center around which his controversial life at court revolved. Indeed, throughout the Middle Ages, London was also a pilgrim site closely linked with the miracles and powers of intercession credited to St. Thomas.

Thomas Becket was born on December 21, 1118, in London's Cheapside (incidentally, the "à" before "Becket" was a conceit added later in life). His father, Gilbert, was a wealthy merchant and onetime Sheriff of London. His mother, Matilda, was a devout Catholic, who no doubt instilled in young Thomas the deep convictions that would eventually influence the later years of his career. Even when you consider his somewhat privileged upbringing, Thomas was exceptionally well educated, first at Merton in Surrey and later at the leading schools of Paris. He returned to England in 1140 and, at the age of 22, found his first professional mentor, Theobald, Archbishop of Canterbury. Under his sponsorship, Becket went on to study both canon and civil law, before being promoted to Archdeacon of Canterbury. His strong administrative skills and his overarching interest in the politics of the day prompted Theobald to recommend Becket, in 1154, to the newly crowned King of England, young Henry of Anjou.

Henry II and Thomas Becket struck up a close, trusting, and mutually respectful relationship. Becket was widely regarded as the king's closest advisor, serving as diplomat, administrator and personal confidant. Both men were major personalities: strong, decisive and passionate, with a shared zest for living "fine and fast." To outside observers, it must have seemed a match made, if not in heaven, at least in the most blessed of earthly realms.

It was, therefore, the most natural of choices in 1162 when Henry appointed Becket to succeed his mentor, Theobald, as Archbishop of Canterbury. Yes, there was the small problem that Thomas was, from the Church's standpoint, only a clerk in the minor orders; he was hurriedly ordained a priest on June 2, consecrated as bishop on June 3, and enthroned as archbishop just after lunch the same day. Once Henry II wanted something done, waiting was never an option!

Henry's fondest hope was that his close friend Thomas would assist in extending the Crown's authority over the Church, specifically on the issues of taxation and disposal of Church property. Surprisingly, Becket—largely seen as Henry's "yes-man" until this point in time—had a sudden change of heart. Taking his duties as archbishop far more seriously than anyone would have guessed, Becket took a hard and fast stand in favor of an independent, autonomous Church—protected, but never to be interfered with, by the monarch. He was particularly immovable on the issue of how clergy could be tried and punished under the law. Needless to say, Henry—who was equally implacable in his zeal to reform England's archaic legal system—was bitterly disappointed. And, in true Plantagenet style, rage followed closely on sorrow's heels. So acrimonious did the debate between king and archbishop become, that within two years of being elevated to the prestigious and powerful See of Canterbury, Becket fled to France in self-imposed exile.

By 1170, a tenuous peace was fostered between the two old friends. Becket cautiously returned to Canterbury amid great fanfare from the citizens of Kent. Then he rather *incautiously* excommunicated a handful of Henry's closest allies, including the Archbishop of York. For Henry, that was the last straw. Never one to mince words, the infuriated king ranted to all in earshot, "Will no one rid me of this turbulent priest?"

Unfortunately, four ambitious knights found such a challenge an irresistible chance to get on Henry's good side. Richard Brito, Hugh de Moreville, Reginald Fitz Urse and William de Tracy set out at once for Canterbury, where they pursued Becket into the cathedral and murdered him on consecrated ground in the church's nave. Never one to mince words himself, Becket spat the rather coarse salutation "You pimp!" at one of his assailants, just seconds before his decapitation.

Word of the foul deed traveled quickly through the streets of Canterbury, where Becket was particularly beloved. Within hours, throngs of mourners braved a sudden and violent thunderstorm to flock to the cathedral and pay their final respects. Two days later, the first of a series of Becket-linked miracles took place—you'll see many of these wondrous events depicted in the Miracle Windows of Trinity Chapel. In 1173, just three years after the assassination, Pope Alexander III canonized St. Thomas à Becket.

Henry's "Thomas troubles" were far from over, however. No sooner was the news of Becket's death heralded than waves of protest against the king began, first from the common people, then from the Church and, ultimately, from his own inner circle. In July 1174, attempting to make amends, Henry donned a hair shirt, walked barefoot through the streets of Canterbury, was flogged by priory monks, and processed on his knees down the long cathedral nave to the shrine of St. Thomas. There he publicly begged forgiveness and asked St. Thomas's spiritual intercession for God's mercy. The humiliation of the king is illustrated in a stained-glass window on the north side of Trinity Chapel. Although the public furor died down after this act of contrition, Henry II went to his grave tainted by this scandalous incident.

❖ ❖

To the right of the altar, you will find a stairway leading to the **Crypt**, the oldest part of the cathedral. Here you will find a small museum displaying some of the cathedral's treasury—the valuable vessels, plate and vestments from ages past. Unfortunately, the museum is not open during the winter months. Although Carole may vehemently disagree, undercrofts can be quite beautiful; certainly this is one of the loveliest you'll see . . . even if the dim light makes actually "seeing" it a tad difficult. The supporting columns that bear the weight of the cathedral are exquisitely carved, with intricate capitals that warrant appreciation. The center of the crypt is graced by the chapel of **Our Lady of the Undercroft**, with its glorious painted ceiling. The chapel was endowed in the 1360s as a chantry by Edward the Black Prince, in gratitude for being granted papal dispensation to marry his cousin Joan, the "Fair Maid of Kent." Joan Plantagenet's face is carved in one of the bosses of the crypt's vaulted ceiling.

You should exit on the south side of the crypt, cross the transept, and mount the few stairs to the **Quire**. As you ascend, take a moment to linger in front of the quire screen and look up. To us, this is one of Canterbury's finest features: the stunning fan-vaulted ceiling of the **Bell Harry Tower**, named for Prior Henry Eastry, who donated one of the original cathedral bells. We could look at it for ages—if it didn't make us dizzy to think of the towering *(and probably shaky)* scaffolding required for the medieval masons and artisans to render this magnificent work of art, so high above the cathedral's floor! The Bell Harry Tower is the only major portion of the cathedral, aside from Christ Church Gate, to be constructed between the reign of Henry VII and his son's Dissolution of the Monasteries.

Also of interest is the **Quire Screen**, commissioned for the cathedral in 1405. Amateur historians will want to spend a while identifying the various monarchs whose statues adorn the screen. *(Okay, we'll let you in on the secret! From left to right, they are Richard II, Henry V, Ethelbert of Kent, St. Edward the Confessor, Henry IV and Henry VI. We do not know the reason behind this peculiar chronology, but so be it.)* This quire dates from 1174, when fire destroyed the church's original quire. As you wander through the quire, your attention most likely will be drawn to the lovely stained-glass windows that adorn the north aisle. The windows were commissioned over a period of years by various archbishops of Canterbury; the cathedral has handouts that explain the stories illustrated by these windows. Among the many interesting effigies in the north quire aisle is the tomb of Cardinal Thomas Bourchier, a mainstay

* *

☛ Did you know?

During the Middle Ages, the quire was separated from the nave by the quire screen. Mass was hidden from public view; participants could hear—but not see—the celebration of the Eucharist . . . and despite the "hearing," little was actually understood, for the Mass was conducted in Latin. This practice of obscuring the Mass from the congregation was abandoned by the Church of England during the Reformation.

* *

of the Yorkist cause during the Wars of the Roses. Bourchier crowned King Edward IV in 1461, and is a justly prominent figure in Shakespeare's *Richard III*.

You will also, no doubt, be drawn to one of the cathedral's

most lavish monuments, in memory of Archbishop Henry Chichele. Chichele was a passionate supporter of Henry V, and had the honor of welcoming his hero to Canterbury as the victorious king made his way back to London from Agincourt. Chichele also had the sadder honor of receiving Henry's body at Dover after his untimely death in France. It is interesting to note that although Chichele did not die until 1443, he commissioned his own tomb nearly 20 years prior to his death. Not one to leave things to chance, he also endowed a foundation at Oxford, the College of All Souls, on the condition that its members continue the upkeep on the extravagant, gilded memorial at Canterbury . . . and so they do, every 50 years.

The 12th-century reconstruction of the cathedral provided the opportunity to extend the quire in order to encompass the shrine for St. Thomas. Until the Reformation, the shrine was located just behind the main altar in the **Trinity Chapel**.

> **☞ Did you know?**
>
> Although never crowned, King John's first wife, Isabella of Gloucester, a.k.a. Hawise, was buried in Canterbury Cathedral. Their marriage ended in annulment well before her death in 1217; however, she and John remained friends throughout her life. Another interesting aside concerns a different daughter-in-law of Henry II: Berengaria, wife of Richard the Lionheart. Although history has condemned her as the "queen who never stepped foot inside England," Berengaria was on hand for several state occasions during the reign of John. One such occasion was the translation of Becket's bones to Trinity Chapel in 1220, which Berengaria was present to witness.

Even if Becket had not been associated with so many miracles, nor credited with such potent powers of intercession, his shrine would have been likely to attract throngs of visitors based on its beauty alone. This was one of the most lavishly bejeweled shrines in Christendom, crafted of gold and silver and studded with precious stones. Its destruction by Henry VIII was not only sacrilegious; it was wanton vandalism of art as well.

Although the medieval shrine is no longer part of Trinity Chapel, there are vestiges from that era literally at your feet.

The intricate mosaic, **Opus Alexandrium**, and the large round tiles on the floor were laid when St. Thomas's relics were conveyed to the chapel in 1220. The rather uncomfortable-looking stone throne, or *Kathedra*, is known as **St. Augustine's Chair**; since the 13th century, it has been used for the enthronement of the archbishops of Canterbury, much as St. Edward's throne is used by the monarch at Westminster Abbey.

You have now come upon the attractions that are certain to make any amateur historian's heart beat a bit faster: the **Royal Tombs**, which command pride of place on both sides of Becket's shrine. On the north side is the **Tomb of Henry IV** (d. 1413) and his second wife, the unpopular Joan of Navarre (d. 1437). Their impressive effigies lie beneath an elaborate canopy, adorned with their coats of arms. Henry's chantry **Chapel of Edward the Confessor** is just across the aisle. On the chapel's opposite side is the **Tomb of Edward the Black Prince**, first son of Edward III and father of Richard II. A replica of his striking black armor, from which he earned his nickname, is on display near Edward's tomb (his original accouterments are to be found in the south quire aisle).

♦♦♦♦♦♦♦♦♦♦♦♦♦♦♦♦♦♦♦♦
☞ Did you know?
Oh, those fanciful Victorians! Who else would look upon the glorious golden effigy of the Black Prince and decide that it did, indeed, need to be painted *black*? For years, the latten effigy was stifled under a thick coat of ebony paint. In the 1930s, less sentimental minds prevailed, and the prince's effigy was restored to its gilded splendor.
♦♦♦♦♦♦♦♦♦♦♦♦♦♦♦♦♦♦♦♦

◇◇◇

EDWARD THE BLACK PRINCE (1330–1376)

The eldest son of Edward III, Edward the Black Prince was known in his own time as Edward of Woodstock. He earned his sobriquet posthumously, a reference to the startling ebony-colored armor that he wore on the battlefield (*although the French would probably argue that it was his post-battle cruelty that earned him his dark reputation!*).

As befitting the heir-apparent to the throne of England, Edward began adding titles to his royal résumé at a very early age. By three, he was Earl of Chester.

At age seven, he was titled Duke of Cornwall, distinguishing him as England's first duke. In 1343, he was officially recognized as Prince of Wales, although he would never set foot in that country. Such impressive honors came with an equally impressive income—next to England's second duke, Henry Grosmont of Lancaster, Edward was the wealthiest peer in the land.

In his day, Edward III had been known as one of the great military geniuses of the times; his son the Black Prince showed every promise of following in his father's mighty footsteps. The prince distinguished himself early on, winning a devastating victory at age 16 over the French at Crécy. He continued to pound his way through the early years of the Hundred Years War, capturing King John II of France at Poitiers when he was 26 years old. In 1362, he was appointed Prince of Aquitaine and temporarily turned his attention from fighting to governing. Battle was in his blood, however, and by 1367, he found himself defending Pedro the Cruel in his fight to maintain the throne of Castile. During this Spanish campaign, Edward contracted the infection that would render him incapable first of riding, then of walking. He died of complications from this illness on June 8, 1376, after spending his last five years as an invalid in England.

Edward married relatively late in life, and when he did so his choice raised more than a few eyebrows. Lovely as she was, Joan, the "Fair Maid of Kent," was Edward's twice-widowed cousin. Edward was not marrying for political reasons, however; in this instance, public opinion mattered little. This was a love match, about which Edward was so serious that he doggedly sought and obtained the papal dispensation necessary in order to marry close kin. Edward and Joan enjoyed a happy marriage, and their eldest son, Richard, would go on to claim the throne that premature death denied his father.

As a young boy, Edward of Woodstock had been educated at Canterbury. The cathedral always held a special place in Edward's heart. When the pope agreed to his marriage, the prince endowed a chantry chapel in the crypt of the cathedral to express his gratitude. It was his desire to be buried in this chapel so closely linked with Joan. The monks of Canterbury overrode his request. In their minds, it was far more befitting that a prince of such stature be buried as close to possible to the cathedral's favorite son, St. Thomas. Edward was buried in the Trinity Chapel at Canterbury, his armor and shield proudly displayed over the magnificent latten effigy commissioned by his wife, Joan.

❖❖

Proceed around the south end of the quire and descend into the south aisle of the nave. You will find monuments to many 14th- and 15th-century archbishops of Canterbury in this section of the cathedral. Look for the ancient *(and somewhat worse for wear)* effigy of Prior Henry Eastry (d. 1331); for 46 years, Eastry served as prior of the cathedral's monastic foundation. He has the added distinction of being the only prior buried in a full tomb within the main cathedral. The next major feature from the medieval era can be seen in the **Warrior Chapel (a.k.a. St. Michael's Chapel).** The funerary monument of Margaret Holland (d. 1439) is one of the most elaborate you'll see outside of Westminster Abbey. She is buried with her husbands, John Beaufort, Earl of Somerset, and Thomas, Duke of Clarence, second son of Henry IV.

This concludes your visit to Canterbury Cathedral; you will find yourself just outside the gift shop, where you can stock up on suitable medieval-style mementos. *(We have more "Black Prince" bookmarks between us than we care to admit!)*

• •

☞ Did you know?

Although most medieval monarchs are buried at Westminster Abbey, Henry IV specifically requested burial at Canterbury. There are two ironies in that request. First, Henry actually died while at prayer in Westminster Abbey. Second, he is buried in the same chapel as Edward the Black Prince, the father of Richard II whose crown Henry usurped in 1399. *(We wonder whether or not Edward has let his nephew Henry "rest in peace.")*

• •

Also while you're in Canterbury . . .

✝ St. Augustine's Abbey
   Longport

>>>

PHONE
   01227-767345

LOCATED
   In the town of Canterbury, ¼ mile from the cathedral close

OPEN
   10:00 a.m.–6:00 p.m. daily, April–September
   10:00 a.m.–5:00 p.m. daily, October
   10:00 a.m.–4:00 p.m. daily, November–March

ADMISSION
   £2.50 Adults
   £1.30 Children
   £1.90 Seniors
>>

Founded by St. Augustine in 598, the abbey is certainly one of the earliest existing Christian sites in Britain. This was the original headquarters of Augustine's monks, the first missionaries sent as part of Pope Gregory's papal delegation from Rome. The original church was entirely rebuilt just after the Norman Conquest, and local lore claims that the Bayeux Tapestry may have been created in the abbey's outstanding light-filled library. Located just outside the ancient wall, the abbey is essentially a ruin, but it does contain tombs of numerous Saxon saints and kings. A recently opened museum displays several artifacts from the abbey's 1,000-year history, and state-of-the-art computer graphics do a convincing job of depicting the building's original splendor.

• •
☞ Did you know?
At the time of the Reformation, the monastic buildings of St. Augustine's were destroyed and a royal residence was built among the ruins. It was used by Henry VIII and his wife Anne of Cleves *(we assume not simultaneously!)*, as well as by Elizabeth and Charles I.
• •

You may notice that some of the ancient buildings on the abbey grounds appear to be teeming with young people; these are now residences for the King's School, England's oldest public school.

〜

✝ St. Martin's Church
North Holmes Street

>>

Widely believed to be England's oldest "still-in-use" parish church *(although, it seems to us, we've heard that claim numer-*

ous times before!), St. Martin's dates to the Roman era. The church played an important role in Britain's Christian life, for it was here, in 597 CE, that King Ethelbert's Catholic wife, Queen Bertha, first welcomed the papal delegation, headed by St. Augustine. In fact, Bertha named the church after St. Martin, Bishop of Tours, France, where the queen had spent her childhood. Christian worship has continued uninterrupted at St. Martin's for over 1,400 years.

〰

✝ Roman Museum
Butchery Lane

≫≫

PHONE
    01227-785575

OPEN
    10:00 a.m.–5:00 p.m. Monday–Saturday, June–October
    1:30–5:00 p.m. Sunday, June–October
    10:00 a.m.–4:00 p.m. Monday–Saturday, November–May
    Closed Sunday, November–May

ADMISSION
    £2.40 Adults
    £1.20 Children

≫≫

This is a particularly well conceived museum. Its subterranean location houses the remains of a 100 CE Roman villa, a reconstructed Roman marketplace, silver and glassware excavated from the site, and an interactive program that lets you "take part" in an archeological study. This museum is particularly child-friendly.

✝ Eastbridge Hospital of St. Thomas
High Street

>>
PHONE
   01227-476168

OPEN
   10:00 a.m.–5:00 p.m. Monday–Saturday, year-round
   11:00 a.m.–5:00 p.m. Sunday, year-round

ADMISSION
   Free of charge
>>

This 12th-century pilgrims' hospice provides a welcome moment of peace, apart from the hustle and bustle of Canterbury's busier attractions. Poor or sick pilgrims would have slept on rushes in the undercroft; the upper level refectory and chapel were used for communal meals and prayer.

∿

✝ West Gate Museum
St. Peter's Street

>>
PHONE
   01227-452747

OPEN
   11:00 a.m.–12:30 p.m. and 1:30–3:30 p.m. Monday–Saturday,
   year-round
   Closed Sunday

   Note: If you are keen to see this attraction, please note the limited opening hours and plan accordingly.

ADMISSION
   £1.00 Adults
   50p Children
>>

Are you up for some exercise? Wend your way along the very narrow circular staircase *(not for the claustrophobic!)* to the heights of Canterbury's medieval city gate. The view of the cathedral from here is worth those aching thigh muscles. Back inside, there are prison cells and guard chambers to visit; the collection of armor dates from the Cromwellian civil war.

The Weavers' Houses
St. Peter's Street

>>

Today they are shops, filled with curios and souvenirs. However, this cluster of half-timbered Tudor cottages once provided refuge to Flemish Huguenot weavers escaping persecution on the Continent.

Canterbury Heritage Museum
Stour Street

>>
PHONE
   01227-452747

OPEN
   10.30 a.m.–5.00 p.m. Monday–Saturday, June–October
   1:30–5:00 p.m. Sunday, June–October
   10:30 a.m.–5:00 p.m. Monday–Saturday, November–May
   Closed Sunday, November–May

ADMISSION
   £2.40 Adults
   £1.20 Children
>>

Housed in a handsome 14th-century riverside building, this museum's award-winning displays interpret Canterbury's rich history, including Roman occupation and—of course!—the murder of Thomas à Becket. This was originally the Poor Priests' House, established shortly after Becket's death for priests who were either too old or too ill to continue their pastoral duties.

~~

✝ Greyfriars
Off Stour Street

>>>

Greyfriars has the distinction of being the oldest Franciscan building in Britain. Of unusual design, it straddles the River Stour.

~~

✝ Canterbury Tales
St. Margaret's Street

>>>
PHONE
   01227-479227
OPEN
   9:30 a.m.–5:30 p.m. daily, March–June, September and October
   9:00 a.m.–6:00 p.m. daily, July and August
   10:00 a.m.–4:30 p.m. daily, November–February
ADMISSION
   £5.90 Adults
   £4.90 Children
>>>

If you loved Madame Tussaud's in London, you might well enjoy this animated one-hour pilgrim's journey to the shrine of St. Thomas à Becket. Audio—and olfactory—effects add to the sense of, er, "realism." Children love it.

✝ Norman Castle
Castle Street

>>

This mammoth keep was built shortly after the Norman Conquest; estimates range between 1070 and 1094. Unlike many castles in Kent, this one has seen more than its share of historical events. In 1216, it was captured by Louis, Dauphin of France. In 1381, the local insurgent Wat Tyler seized the castle during the Peasants' Revolt, and in the 17th century, it surrendered to parliament during the Civil War. (*Did this place have a run of weak castellans, or what?*) During the times when it was *not* in enemy hands, the castle was often used as a prison. On a grim note, it was here that many of the town's Protestants met their fiery deaths during the reign of Mary Tudor.

ANCIENT INNS AND EATERIES

The following restaurants and hotels are in historic buildings located within Canterbury proper.

~ Alberry's Wine Bar
St. Margaret's Street
01227-452378

A portion of the Roman amphitheater is exposed in this *very popular* subterranean bar.

~ Cathedral Gate Pizzaland
Butter Market

The building dates from 1437; the bill of fare is totally 21st-century.

~ Liberty Tea Room
Burgate

The Bull Inn was a 15th-century pilgrims' hostel; today, it houses a famous London accessories shop and a popular first-story tearoom.

~ Queen Elizabeth Restaurant
High Street

This exceptional 15th-century building is where Elizabeth dallied with her French suitor, the Duke of Alençon.

~ Simple Simon's
Church Lane
01227-762355

True to its 14th-century heritage, this restaurant invokes the atmosphere of a bustling medieval hall—the large open fire is a welcome attraction on raw, damp days. The fare is hearty, and meat pies are a specialty. The main restaurant serves dinner only; the separate pub serves lunch.

~ Weavers Coffee Shop
St. Peter's Street

Riverside medieval building with gabled windows and light fare.

~ Anchor House
25 North Lane
01227-768105

Four rooms in a 14th-century coaching inn; exposed-beam restaurant open to non-hotel guests.

~ Cathedral Gate Hotel
36 Burgate
01227-464381

Twenty-four rooms in a 1438 building overlooking the cathedral.

~ The Country Hotel
High Street
01227-766266

Seventy-three rooms, including 13 "theme" rooms (e.g., *Tudor*) in Canterbury's only Michelin-star hotel, c. 1588; Sully's Restaurant, in the hotel, is considered outstanding.

~ Greyfriars House
   6 *Stour Street*
   01227-456255
Six rooms in the recently restored 11th-century monastery gate-house.

~ House of St. Agnes
   71 *St. Dunstan's Street*
   01227-472185
Nine rooms in a historic Tudor building.

CONTENTS

Dover

The Key to England

he proximity of Dover to the coast of France — just 17 miles separate them — guaranteed from the beginning of history that the natural port located here would be a busy trade center and a strategic focal point for the defense and conquest of England. The hustle and bustle of commerce, as well as the tides of war, have defined the history of Dover from as early as Celtic times and continue to do so today.

Described by the medieval chronicler Matthew Paris as "the key to England," Dover was the main point of embarkation to and from the Continent throughout the Middle and Tudor Ages. The comings and goings of kings and queens, the high nobility and princes of the Church, and the elaborate ceremonies and preparations that accompanied their departures and arrivals were commonplace events.

Control of the port at Dover was so critical that the castle was a focal point of almost every struggle for the English crown. Tales of long-lasting sieges, transfer through treachery and bloody battles make up the history of the castle.

So important was Dover that medieval governments took great pains to ensure the city's prosperity so that defenses would not be neglected. They went so far as to pass a law in 1465 that made Dover the only legal point of embarkation for Calais, reinforcing Dover's position as the crown jewel of the Cinque (pronounced "sink") Ports. Watling Street, the road that linked

London and Dover, remained one of the busiest in England throughout the Middle Ages.

Today, the great castle, built by Henry II, which sits on top of Dover's white cliffs, is a marvel of medieval and Tudor history. And while a devoted medieval enthusiast can easily spend most of a day poking into all the treasures of this site, anyone looking for a little diversionary history can find it by combining a trip to Dover Castle with visits to a Roman painted house in the town of Dover and side trips to two of Henry VIII's nearby defensive "gun forts," Deal and Walmer Castles. You can also salt your trip with quick peeks at the Dover Town Hall, once a medieval hospital, a few smaller castles and manor homes dotted around the countryside and the lovely parish church of Hythe (another of the Cinque Ports) with its bloodcurdling crypt containing 2,000 medieval skulls. This is the farthest out of London of our "day trips"—it takes about two hours to get to Dover. But, trust us, the journey is well worth it. The castle is terrific, even if the town of Dover doesn't do the best job of promoting its other medieval sites, and Deal is a gem.

❖❖

THE CINQUE PORTS

The Cinque Ports were a Norman creation meant to bolster the defenses of the southeast coast of England. Five cities—Hastings, Dover, Hythe, Sandwich and Romney—were designated Cinque Ports and granted special tax advantages and other privileges in return for providing men and ships when called upon by the monarch.

Throughout the Middle Ages, these port cities played a critical role in the defense of England, but their importance declined beginning in the 14th century as the receding coastline and silted-up river mouths made several of the harbors unusable. Only Dover remains a major port, although ceremonial roles are still preserved for the Cinque Ports in affairs of state. For example, the Cinque Port Barons still have places of honor reserved for them during coronation ceremonies at Westminster Abbey and a Lord Warden of the Cinque Ports is still appointed and installed in office in an elaborate pageant held in Dover.

Today, these towns have turned their attention to attracting a tourism crowd focused on more modern attractions (*think boardwalks, cotton candy and cheesy tourism trinkets)*, but traces of their rich medieval heritage can still be found if you are determined and persevere. Major sites in Dover, Hastings and Hythe are covered through entries in this book. You can also find in Dover the ruins of St. James the Apostle Church, the Norman parish church founded on the site of a Saxon church, where the courts of the Cinque Ports met until 1851. There is not much left in New Romney from our period that we can find *(which is why we didn't write about it)*. Nor does Sandwich offer a lot other than its medieval network of streets and alleys lined with picturesque timber-framed houses, an extensively renovated Elizabethan guildhall with a small museum and remnants of the town wall. However, it is a charming town located just 10 miles from Dover if you are looking for reasons to extend your visit to the southeast coast of England.

❖❖

✝ Dover Tourist Information Centre
Townwall Street
Dover

»»

PHONE
  01304-205108

E-MAIL
  tic@doveruk.com

LOCATED
  Off the A2

TRAVEL
  Regular train service leaves from Charing Cross or Victoria Station. Travel time is 1½ hours.

»»

We've made the Tourist Information Centre the first entry in this "trip" for the sake of consistency, but we'll tell you right up front that it is not really worth the effort of going there. It is poorly stocked with literature and we found the staff to have very little knowledge about the medieval and Tudor history of Dover. They were much more interested in promoting trips to Calais. Calais is not a bad place to go, especially for an enthusiast of medieval and Tudor history, but it doesn't work as a day trip from London. We'll explore Calais in another book. We suggest that you skip the information center and head straight to the castle. That's much more fun.

〰

✝ Dover Castle
Dover

≫≫≫

PHONE
   01304-211067

LOCATED
   East of Dover, easily accessible from the M20 or A2; the castle is just over 1 mile from the Dover Priory Station.

OPEN
   10:00 a.m.–6:00 p.m. daily, April–September
   10:00 a.m.–5:00 p.m. daily, October
   10:00 a.m.–4:00 p.m. daily, November–March

ADMISSION
   £7.00 Adults
   £3.50 Children
   £5.20 Seniors
   Family ticket available

CONVENIENCES
   Restaurant and gift shop

TIP!
   Because of the extremely well done exhibits and displays at Dover Castle, this is a great trip if you have children in tow.

≫≫≫

Rich in history and awesome in size and scope, Dover Castle warms the cockles of the heart of any passionate amateur historian of the Middle Ages. The main features of the castle are essentially the same as they were in the 13th century (although the battlements are shorter), so it is easy to conjure up the lords and ladies, knights and retainers, churchmen and servants who would have crowded the bailey, walked the high walls and wandered through the Great Hall of the central keep. There is much to see and do at Dover Castle, so if you are like us and absolutely must poke into every nook and cranny of such a rich medieval site, you should plan to spend a good chunk of a day at Dover Castle.

But if you are crunched for time and limited to a quick "breeze through," here are the sights you want to be sure to seek out.

The oldest remains on the castle grounds are a beautifully preserved Saxon church built around 1000 that incorporated a Roman lighthouse as its bell tower. The church was reconstructed in the 18th century and approximately the top 20 feet of the Roman tower were rebuilt; otherwise, the structure is original and has many fascinating Roman, Saxon and medieval features.

The central keep with its Great Hall, royal chambers and stunning private chapel (c. 1188) named for Thomas à Becket is a "not-to-be-missed" attraction. When you pass through the wooden forebuilding that guards the entrance to the keep, be sure to look for the medieval graffiti among the more modern scratchings on the walls of the lower chapel.

Other features dating from medieval times are the **Constable's Gateway** (one of the most formidable gatehouses we've ever seen), a spine-tingling labyrinth of ancient tunnels, Henry III's Great Hall (1240) and, of course, the walls, towers and gatehouses. Scattered throughout the castle grounds are examples of medieval and Tudor armaments and weaponry.

Dover Castle's critical role in the bloody struggles for England's throne that dominated medieval history is dramatized in a multimedia presentation reenacting the defense of the castle against a French invasion force in 1216. The Tudor history of the castle is brought to life through displays depicting the household staff preparing the keep in anticipation of Henry VIII's arrival. Scenes of the times are re-created in the watching chamber, presence chamber and royal bedchamber. There is also an introductory film to the castle.

THE CASTLE'S HISTORY

However much the Norman kings and their descendants appreciated the strategic importance of Dover, they were not the first to recognize it. Dover was fortified as early as the Iron Age. When you visit it, you will see why. Here, just 17 miles separate England from France. There is also a natural harbor formed by the River Dour in the middle of a 13-mile-long chalk cliff.

The Celts were the first to take advantage of the strategic position of the rugged hill on the harbor's northeast edge. They built a large fort, surrounded by high earthen ramparts on top of the hill. Since then, the hilltop has been continually fortified.

The strength of Dover's defensive position is highlighted by the fact that even Julius Caesar passed it by when he came to conquer England. Saying "it was clearly no place to attempt a landing," Caesar sailed on to a friendlier-looking site about 7 miles north. But the Romans did not long neglect Dover and soon returned to build a strong sea fort, flanked by two "pharos" (lighthouses), on the hilltop. And when the Romans left, the Saxons moved right in. Eventually, they built a fortified town —a "burgh"—on top of the hill and provided for the salvation of its citizens by building the church of **St. Mary-in-Castro** in about 1000. To provide a bell tower for their church, the Saxons incorporated one of the Roman "pharos." The church, which was rebuilt in the 1880s, and its tower stand today on the grounds of Dover Castle.

◆ ◆

☞ Did you know?

Records of the castle from 1223 reveal that one sergeant and one guard were directed to keep a light burning at all times in the church of St. Mary. The light is still kept burning today.

◆ ◆

Ghost Alert!

Plenty of ghosts from all eras are said to haunt Dover Castle, but for our particular interests, you might want to keep a sharp eye out when visiting St. Mary-in-Castro. A Roman soldier and a hooded monk supposedly haunt the "pharos."

Nor did William the Conqueror miss the strategic importance of this site. The third castle built by the Normans in England was at Dover. William's half brother, Odo, Bishop of Bayeux, supervised the construction of a "prefab" structure assembled from parts brought from Normandy. This was the first castle constructed after the Battle of Hastings as part of William's strategy to fortify the southeast coast and provide a line of retreat should that become necessary. One of the 13th-century gates to the castle, **Peveral's Gate**, is possibly named after the first Norman constable of Dover Castle, William Peveral.

The imposing keep you see today at Dover was built by Henry II in the 1180s. It was the last of the gigantic square stone keeps built in England. Henry wanted to build a vast fortification that could command and protect Dover's critical harbor no matter how strong the enemy might be. He had to move the entire ancient Saxon burgh of Dover to accomplish his objective.

The result of Henry's efforts was an incredibly massive, fiercely formidable castle, the like of which had never been seen before. The central keep was 80 feet tall with walls on each side 100 feet long and 20 feet thick. Two curtain walls surrounded the keep and inner bailey. The high outer wall was equipped with 30 towers. The inner wall, built even higher than the outer one so defenders could shoot arrows at any invaders who managed to breach the outer wall, had 14 towers. The tops of these towers were chopped off to make room for gun emplacements in one of the endless "updatings" of the castle to accommodate new defense strategies, so they are somewhat diminished from their medieval state but still very impressive.

The frightening defenses of Dover didn't stop Prince Louis,

• •

☞ **Did you know?**

King Stephen (reigned 1135–1154), whose reign marked one of the most turbulent and violent periods in English history, died at Dover Castle on October 25, 1154, during a conference with the Count of Flanders. According to the contemporary chronicler Henry of Huntingdon, "He was buried in Faversham Abbey beside his wife and son, having reigned unhappily and with great labor for 19 years."

• •

though, when he led a force from France in 1216 at the invitation of the English barons who were rebelling against King John. Borrowing Caesar's trick, Louis shrewdly landed elsewhere on the southeast coast, quickly subdued all the surrounding area and then laid siege to Dover Castle. Led by Hubert de Burgh, John's justiciar, a mere 140 knights managed to hold the castle against the might of Louis's army. Eventually, however, the French forces were able to find the castle's one vulnerability—an area of high ground outside the castle's north gate where they could avoid downward fire from the defenders on the walls. The French managed to breach the wall by undermining this gate and letting it collapse into the tunnel, but they never were able to get past the inner wall. De Burgh's meager force pushed Louis's troops back through the breach and the French lost their taste for trying to crack open such a strong nut. It is this battle for the castle that

* *

☞ Did you know?

The towers of medieval castles were designed to accommodate the needs of archers, who played a critical role in castle defense. Their importance increased as use of the crossbow became widespread in the 12th century. But not everyone was happy with this development in warfare. The nobility and the Church were particularly upset because the crossbow threatened the feudal order. It was such a powerful weapon that an arrow fired from a crossbow could penetrate the armor of a knight, thereby giving any run-of-the-mill peasant the ability to kill anyone in the nobility. The Church tried to ban the crossbow in 1139, but the efforts were futile. It remained a preeminent weapon of castle warfare throughout the Middle Ages.

* *

is dramatized today in an extremely well done multimedia presentation.

De Burgh did not forget the lesson learned by the near victory of the French invaders. Soon after Henry III inherited the throne, de Burgh set about repairing the damage and further strengthening Dover's defenses. He closed off the old north gate and built defensive structures beyond it to block the high ground from future besiegers. He also linked the outer defenses with the tunnels, the maze of underground passages that have proven so useful for England's defense through the ages. De

Burgh constructed the Constable's Gateway (1220) to replace the north gate and made sure it was defensible by equipping it with six overlapping towers. The Constable's Gateway still serves as the residence of the deputy constable of Dover Castle. But de Burgh did not stop there; he went on to extend the castle's outer wall and towers all the way to the cliff's edge. No way was he ever going to risk again an invasion force toppling this all-important strategic strongpoint.

• •

☞ Did you know?

William Longchamp, Bishop of Ely and justiciar in England during Richard the Lionheart's sojourn as a crusader, took refuge in Dover Castle in October 1191. Longchamp, who was very loyal to Richard but tone-deaf politically, had made great enemies of most of the leading barons in England during Richard's absence. Richard's brother John, the future King John, did not hesitate to take advantage of this conflict to promote his own ambitions and clear a path to the throne. Because of pressure brought by John and the barons, the bishop was forced to yield his offices and give his brothers as hostages. He attempted to protect himself and leave the country by escaping from Dover Castle dressed as a woman. The disguise must have been terrific because Longchamp was discovered only when an amorous fisherman got too carried away by lust and attempted to kiss the bishop. Apparently, the whole episode tickled John's funny bone because, in an uncharacteristically kind gesture, he let Longchamp leave the country and go into exile in France.

• •

❖ ❖

HUBERT DE BURGH (D. 1243)

Trust not those cunning waters of his eyes,
for villainy is not without such rheum;
and he, long traded in it, makes it seem
like rivers of remorse and innocency.
—William Shakespeare, *King John*

Hero or villain? Historians have long puzzled over which term best describes Hubert de Burgh, one of the most powerful—and intriguing—political figures of the 13th century. A self-made man who rose to power through loyalty to King John, de Burgh has a historical record full of contradictions.

He was greatly respected for his redoubtable military skills and seems to have earned a justifiable reputation for honor—at least when it involved loyalty to his feudal lord. He was one of the longest-serving of the early medieval justiciars, holding that office from 1215 to 1232, and a strong proponent of Magna Carta, seeing that it was reissued three times during his tenure as justiciar. Yet he apparently was not tremendously well liked by his peers and was viewed as avaricious, rapacious and self-serving. He was unable to build lasting political coalitions and made enemies of some of the other powerful leaders of the time, most notably Peter des Roches, Bishop of Winchester.

One of the most mysterious—and perhaps best-known—legends surrounding de Burgh is his role in the disappearance of Prince Arthur of Brittany, King John's nephew and rival for the throne of England. The story—made famous by Shakespeare in his play *King John*—is that de Burgh, who was awarded custody of the prince after he was captured in battle in 1202, refused to carry out John's order to mutilate Arthur. Allegedly, John ordered that Arthur be blinded and castrated. The idea, apparently, was that such mutilations would make Arthur a much less attractive candidate for the throne. The truth is that no one knows what happened to Arthur; he was simply never seen again after sometime in 1203. Rumors abounded that he was dead and that he had been killed by John himself in a drunken rage, but the truth of what happened and what role, if any, de Burgh played in the prince's disappearance is lost to the mists of history.

De Burgh's rivalry with the cunning Bishop of Winchester ultimately led to the justiciar's downfall. Des Roches played upon the insecurity, wavering loyalties and overweening pride of the young, immature Henry III to undermine the king's confidence in de Burgh and have him stripped of lands and titles in 1232. Des Roches's own fall from grace in 1234 brought about a partial restoration of de Burgh's property, but he never regained the power he had wielded in the final years of John's reign and during the years of Henry's minority reign.

◇◇

De Burgh's efforts paid off for John's daughter and Henry III's sister, Eleanor de Montfort, wife of Simon de Montfort, Earl of Leicester. Following Simon's death at the Battle of Evesham (August 1265) and the resulting collapse of the barons' rebellion against Henry III, Eleanor—supported only by a small band of household knights—managed to hold the castle against the royal forces for two months while she negotiated terms that ensured the survival of herself, her daughter, her younger sons and their retainers.

After 1500, when the use of gunpowder lessened the value of castle defenses, Dover declined in importance. But through the ages, any time England confronted the threat of invasion, Dover has been revived as a critical military outpost.

Today, the castle that you see is basically the one constructed by Henry II and bolstered by de Burgh with modifications for the defensive needs that arose whenever an invasion threat was perceived. Barracks were added around the base of Henry's great keep in 1744 when French Jacobites were considered to pose an invasion threat and the medieval buildings

* *

☞ **Did you know?**

One future king of England spent time at Dover Castle as a prisoner. Prince Edward, the future Edward I, was held captive at Dover after the Battle of Lewes in May 1264 during which the baronial forces led by Simon de Montfort resoundingly defeated the army of King Henry III.

* *

there were destroyed. Now those barracks house a regimental museum, restaurant and archeological exhibit.

❖ ❖

HENRY II (1133–1189; REIGNED 1154–1189)

Arguably one of the greatest of the Norman monarchs, Henry II was a remarkable man who led an even more remarkable life. An able military commander, an astute politician and a brilliant strategist, Henry brought the Norman empire to the apex of its power and reach, controlling all of England and most of what is now France and spreading Norman influence into Scotland, Wales and Ireland. At the pinnacle of his strength, Henry stood high above all other kings, but he lost everything at the end of his life, dying alone, bereft of family and friends, mourned only by one illegitimate son.

Henry inherited the throne of England from Stephen of Blois, who had usurped it from Henry's mother, Matilda, the daughter of Henry I. Matilda and Stephen fought a bloody civil war for 14 years, from 1139 to 1153, before the conflict finally ended with the war-weary magnates of England forcing an agreement on both sides. The agreement called for Stephen to remain king for the rest of his life and for Henry to assume the crown upon Stephen's death.

When Stephen died in 1154, Henry set about repairing the damage that 14 years of civil war had done to the country. He healed the rifts that had divided the baronage, reformed the civil justice system, restored order and security to the land and established a peace that allowed England to grow prosperous again.

But life was not so peaceful in Henry's private affairs. In 1152, he had married the fiery Eleanor of Aquitaine, the greatest heiress in France, whose landholdings doubled the scope of Henry's influence on the Continent. At first, the marriage seemed to be a great success. The couple appeared to be well matched in political skill and ability—Eleanor often acted as Henry's deputy when he visited various parts of their vast domain—and their private life seemed satisfactory. They had eight children together, five sons and three daughters. But Henry was a notorious womanizer and both Eleanor and Henry were of volatile temperament. (He was infamous for rolling on the floor and chewing the straw when in a fury.) No one knows for sure what caused the breakdown of their marriage, but the results were dramatic.

Eleanor encouraged the eldest three of their four surviving sons, the "Young King" Henry, Richard the Lionheart, Geoffrey of Brittany and the future King John, to rebel against their father. The young "eaglets," as Henry II called them, were chafing at the bit for greater power and autonomy in the lands their father had ceded to them and were more than happy to yield to their mother's urgings.

Their first attempt at rebellion in 1173 ended in disaster. Henry moved with his customary speed and efficiency to squash the incipient rebellion, managing also to capture Eleanor, who was then kept in close confinement until Henry's death in 1189. The second attempt was more successful and was aborted only with the untimely death of the "Young King" in 1183. But it didn't stop there.

Richard, now heir to the throne, joined with Philip of France in 1188 to wage war on a now old and sick Henry II. After conquering Normandy and Maine, Richard and Philip forced a humiliating peace upon Henry at Ballon in France on July 5, 1189. Henry was carried from the negotiating site in a litter and taken to his castle at Chinon, where he learned that his youngest—and favorite—son, John, had joined Richard's rebellion. This final betrayal was more than Henry could stand. He lapsed into delirium and died the next day, attended only by his illegitimate son Geoffrey. (It was common in medieval times to use the same name for both legitimate and illegitimate offspring; hence, Henry had two sons named "Geoffrey.")

As Henry's funeral cortege traveled from Chinon to Fontevrault Abbey where he was to be buried, it was met by a remorseful Richard. But Henry took one last revenge for Richard's betrayal. The medieval chronicler Ralph of Diceto, dean of St. Paul's Cathedral from c. 1180 to 1201, reported that "at his [Richard's] coming blood began to flow forthwith from the dead king's nostrils as if his spirit was moved with indignation." *(And so it should have been.)*

❖ ❖

While you're in Dover ...

✝ Roman Painted House
New Street
Dover

>>

PHONE
   01304-203279

LOCATED
   Just east of York Street in the town of Dover

OPEN
   10:00 a.m.–5:00 p.m. daily except Monday, April–September
   Closed October–March except for pre-booked parties

ADMISSION
   £2.00 Adults
   80p Children
   80p Seniors

>>

When it comes to "laying the foundation" for just how ancient a role Dover played in English history, stop by the Roman Painted House. Excavated in the 1970s, this fascinating site was built around 200 CE as a "hotel" for Roman officials traveling back and forth to the motherland. The wall paintings are well preserved and you can see vestiges of the ahead-of-its-time central heating system, as well as the wall of the Roman fort that, rather inconveniently, cut through a wall of the hostel. A small museum built around the house explains the work of local archeologists.

✝ Dover Museum
Market Square
Dover

>>>

PHONE
01304-201066

WEBSITE
www.dovermuseum.co.uk

OPEN
10:00 a.m.–6:00 p.m. daily, year-round

ADMISSION
£1.75 Adults
95p Children
95p Seniors

>>>

This small museum's major claim to fame is a boat from the Bronze Age, way before our period, but kind of intriguing if you are into prehistoric items. There's not much here of interest to medieval and Tudor enthusiasts except a 1598 portrait of Elizabeth I and a few static displays describing Dover's medieval history. This is the only place in Dover where we found any information about the town's other medieval sites and what we did find was sketchy at best. Nor was the staff very knowledgeable. If you want to explore any other medieval sites in Dover, you will be on your own with only us *Amateur Historians* to guide you.

> **☞ Did you know?**
>
> An Augustinian priory dedicated to St. Martin was founded in Dover in 1130 by Archbishop of Canterbury Corbeil. The priory survived until the Dissolution of the Monasteries, when Henry VIII confiscated the lands and buildings and converted the property into a farm. The gatehouse, refectory and guest hall of the old priory are still in use as part of Dover College. They are not open to the public.

✝ Dover Town Hall (a.k.a. Maison Dieu)

Biggin Street
Dover

>>

PHONE
01304-201200

E-MAIL
tourism@doveruk.com

OPEN
9:00 a.m.–4:30 p.m. Monday–Saturday, year-round

ADMISSION
Free of charge

>>

Maison Dieu was founded in 1203 by Hubert de Burgh as a hostel for pilgrims and a place to care for the sick and the poor. It was staffed by the Augustinian monks from Dover Priory. An impressive building with a sweeping Great Hall, Maison Dieu was a favorite resting point for English kings; John stayed here in 1213, Edward II in 1307 and Richard II in 1396. Henry VIII claimed the building in 1544 and used it as a brew-house, bakery and stable. Eventually the building was sold to the Corporation of Dover to serve as a civic center. It was restored in 1859 and is now used as a town hall, hosting a wide variety of civic events. The day we visited, ballroom dancing lessons were being conducted in a side chamber off the hall. The hall itself, with its soaring ceiling and wall decorations of coats of arms of major nobles of the Middle Ages, still evokes the spirits of the knights, nobles and monks who once inhabited this place.

Also while you're in the area . . .

Two of Henry VIII's famous coastal forts, Deal and Walmer, are within an easy distance of Dover. If time allows, it makes every bit of sense to include them in this visit.

✝ Deal Castle
Victoria Road
Deal

>>

PHONE
  01483-252000

LOCATED
  On the A258, southwest of the town center of Deal

OPEN
  10:00 a.m.–6:00 p.m. daily, April–September
  10:00 a.m.–5:00 p.m. daily, October
  10:00 a.m.–4:00 p.m. Wednesday–Sunday, November–March

ADMISSION
  £3.10 Adults
  £1.60 Children
  £2.30 Seniors

CONVENIENCES
  Gift shop

>>

• •
☞ Did you know?
When Anne of Cleves arrived in England to become the fourth wife of Henry VIII, she landed at Deal at 5 a.m. on December 27, 1539. She spent the day resting at Henry's newly built castle of Deal before being escorted to Dover by the Duke and Duchess of Suffolk and the Bishop of Chichester.
• •

• •
☞ Did you know?
When viewed from the air, Deal Castle takes on the distinctive sexfoil pattern of the Tudor rose.
• •

This may well be one of the most unusual and best-preserved castles you'll ever see. A series of six low, seemingly concentric circles, Deal Castle seems almost extraterrestrial in nature. Henry VIII's huge, round bastions were meant to create the most menacing demeanor possible and surely they succeeded. Completed in 1540, this is the largest of the famous Henrican "gun forts" built to protect England's coast when invasion from Continental forces seemed a distinct possibility. At the time, an impressive 119 "guns," or cannons, comprised the major part of Deal's garrison.

Like most of the coastal forts, Deal saw little military action. Indeed, its closest call to defense during the Tudor era was when the Spanish Armada — at the time all but defeated — sailed past the Deal shoreline.

Exploring Deal is an extraordinary experience. The coastal views from the bastions are glorious and a welcome relief after meandering through Deal's seemingly endless dark labyrinths and huge, daunting basement. The information center at Deal is well conceived; interactive displays and clever exhibits make the history of Deal, the Cinque Ports and Henry's military strategy come alive.

☞ Did you know?

Before Walmer became the official residence of the Warden of the Cinque Ports, that honor belonged to Dover. Henry III began the practice of combining the appointment of the warden with that of the Constable of Dover Castle as a means of strengthening royal control over the somewhat unruly cities. Seven hundred years later, the reigning monarch still follows that custom.

✝ Walmer Castle
Deal

PHONE
01304-364288

LOCATED
South of Walmer on the A258, or junction 13 off the M20; alternatively, take the M2 and exit at Deal; follow signs.

OPEN
10:00 a.m.–6:00 p.m. daily, April–September
10:00 a.m.–5:00 p.m. daily, October
10:00 a.m.–4:00 p.m. Wednesday–Sunday, November–March
Closed January and February

ADMISSION
£4.50 Adults
£2.30 Children

CONVENIENCES
Tearoom and gift shop

Another of Henry VIII's coastal defensive castles, Walmer has been the official residence of the Wardens of the Cinque Ports since 1709. Therefore, it is much more of a stately home than a castle and a great many of the trappings are Victorian rather than Tudor. Still, if you are seriously into Tudor history and particularly interested in defensive forts, it's worth a quick trip around the grounds.

~~

✝ Saltwood Castle
Near Hythe

>>

Note: Saltwood Castle is a private home and is not open to the public. You may catch a peek from the footpath along the castle walls, but please be mindful of the residents' privacy.

>>

So why did we tease you by putting in an entry that you simply *cannot visit?* Well, it's that old Becket thing again. The history of Saltwood Castle is just too interesting to overlook.

Saltwood stands guard—at least visually—over the Cinque Port of Hythe. From 1026, the property was part of the extensive real estate portfolio of the archbishops of Canterbury, although it was occupied and managed by subtenants. During the civil war between Stephen and Matilda, Henry de Essex, Constable of England and Lord Warden of the Cinque Ports, built the current castle. Unfortunately, in 1163, de Essex lost whatever honors he'd accumulated; he was accused of turning tail during a skirmish with the Welsh, a cowardly action that resulted in the royal standard falling into Welsh hands.

At this point, the castle's future should have been determined by the archbishop of Canterbury. Unfortunately, relations between the archbishop, Thomas à Becket, and the monarch, Henry II, were, shall we say, dicey. Henry seized the castle and awarded it to Becket's bitter enemy Ranulf de Broc. To weave an even more sinister story, it is supposedly at Saltwood that Becket's four assassins met to plot his murder before traveling to Canterbury to implement their foul deed. Technically, the plan for Becket's demise was drafted in his own castle . . .

It was a repentant Henry who returned Saltwood to the care and keeping of Canterbury's archbishops. The castle was renovated into a seaside retreat for men in this high-pressure *(and high-risk)* job. In 1382, Archbishop William Courtney elected to use Saltwood as his primary residence and began an extensive "home-improvement" plan, which included improving the castle's defenses—one would assume against the continued specter of French invasion. The fortified gatehouse was designed by master architect Henry Yevele.

The last archbishop affiliated with Saltwood was Thomas Cranmer; ever able to sense which way the political wind would blow, he gifted the castle to Henry VIII on the advent of the Reformation.

~~

✝ Lympne Castle
Near Hythe

>>

PHONE
    01303-267571

LOCATED
    3 miles northwest of Hythe off the B2067

OPEN
    10:30 a.m.–5:30 p.m. Monday–Thursday, May–September

ADMISSION
    £2.00 Adults
    50p Children

>>

This is not the most exciting castle in Kent, but if you have a burning ambition to "see 'em all," here's another one for your roster. Lympne's ancestry has Roman, Saxon and Norman roots; the castle you see today was built in 1360. More appropriately seen as a fortified home, the "castle" consists of two squat towers flanking a large Great Hall. During the Middle

Ages, the property was owned by the archdeacons of Canterbury, clearly less concerned with military prowess than with income-producing real estate. The most impressive feature of Lympne, in our minds, is the view—on a clear day you can look straight across to France!

~

✝ St. Leonard's Church
Church Road
Hythe

>>

PHONE

01303-263739

LOCATED

A259 through the center of Hythe

OPEN

10:30 a.m.–noon and 2:30–4:00 p.m. Monday–Saturday, May–September

2:30–4:00 p.m. Sunday, May–September

Note: Special arrangements can be made for groups wanting a tour October–April by booking ahead with two weeks' notice.

ADMISSION

50p Adults
10p Children

>>

This whole site is a major *Ghost Alert!* If this place ain't haunted, then we don't know what is! The lovely parish church of St. Leonard's was built in 1080 and has a beautiful 12th-century nave and many other features of great interest to medieval and Tudor enthusiasts. However, the big attraction here— and one of the most macabre we've ever encountered—is the crypt's medieval ossuary, where 2,000 skulls and 8,000 thigh-bones stand neatly arranged like spice jars on a cook's rack. Accumulated between 1230 and 1500, they are believed to have been assembled as a "tourist" attraction for Canterbury-bound pilgrims. There must be something to be said for that, since donations to the crypt still represent a large portion of the church's annual income.

⚡

✝ Godinton House
Godinton Park
Ashford

>>

PHONE
01233-620773

E-MAIL
ghpt@godinton.fsnet.co.uk

LOCATED
Off the A20, 2 miles northwest of Ashford, on Godinton Lane

TRAVEL
Trains depart London from both Charing Cross and Victoria Stations for Ashford; taxi service is available from Ashford Station.

OPEN
2:00–5:30 p.m. Friday–Sunday, April–October

ADMISSION
£5.00 Adults
£2.00 Children

>>>

For those interested in the archetypical British stately home, you'd be hard-pressed to find one more spectacular than Godinton House. Not only does it combine elements from both the medieval and the Tudor periods, but the parkland setting is glorious. Formal, walled Italian gardens contrast becomingly with the expanse of wildflowers beyond.

ANCIENT INNS AND EATERIES
~ The Crown Inn
Finglesham, near Deal
01304-612555
16th-century restaurant with oak beams, flagstones and inglenook fireplace; serving lunch and dinner daily.

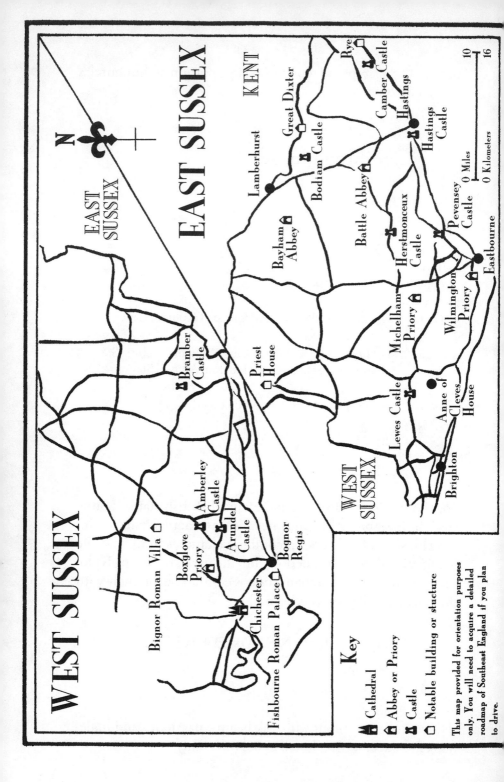

WEST SUSSEX

EAST SUSSEX

EAST SUSSEX

WEST SUSSEX

KENT

N

Bignor Roman Villa

Boxglove Priory

Amberley Castle

Arundel Castle

Fishbourne Roman Palace

Chichester

Bognor Regis

Bramber Castle

Priest House

Bayham Abbey

Lamberhurst

Great Dixter

Bodiam Castle

Rye

Camber Castle

Hastings

Hastings Castle

Battle Abbey

Herstmonceux Castle

Pevensey Castle

Eastbourne

Michelham Priory

Wilmington Priory

Lewes Castle

Anne of Cleves House

Brighton

0 Miles   10

0 Kilometers   16

Key

🏛 Cathedral

⛪ Abbey or Priory

♜ Castle

⌂ Notable building or structure

This map provided for orientation purposes only. You will need to acquire a detailed roadmap of Southeast England if you plan to drive.

Sussex

◇   ◇   ◇

CONTENTS

Rye

Pocket Full of Rye

f you're looking to saturate yourself in medieval atmosphere, minus some of its grimmer, grimier aspects, you'd be hard-pressed to find a more conducive spot than the ancient town of Rye. Indeed, Rye has it all . . . a striking castle (or part of one!), an awe-inspiring church, some of the best-preserved medieval residences in all of England, and a romantic setting, to boot. Plan to allocate the better part of the day to enjoying the village of Rye, or, choose to spend a night out of London in one of Rye's painstakingly restored historic inns.

Although Rye may seem thoroughly relaxed in the 21st century, its history is anything but. The seaside has now receded 2 miles into the distance, but Rye was once one of England's Cinque Ports, chartered by the Crown in the 11th century for the purposes of defending the coastline from French invaders and pirate marauders. In return for their vigilance, the citizens of Rye enjoyed a number of royal perks, including exemption from national taxes and the privilege of retaining any profits realized by their courts of justice. In addition, the Crown would typically "ignore" the profitable pastime of smuggling, which tended to add a handsome sum to the pockets of some of the village's less honorable residents. Rye endured a particularly violent French raid in 1377. When you consider the devastation the town suffered in the process, the fact that so much of its medieval heritage has remained unharmed seems all the more impressive.

✝ Rye Tourist Centre
Strand Quay
Rye

>>>

PHONE
   01797-226696

LOCATED
   63 miles southeast of London; take the A21 to Filmwell, then travel
   the A268 to Rye; you may also approach Rye from Hastings or Dover
   on the A259.

TRAVEL
   Trains run from both Charing Cross and Victoria Stations; you must
   change trains at Ashford. Total travel time is just under 2 hours.

>>>

✝ St. Mary the Virgin Church
Lion Street at Church Square
Rye

>>>

OPEN
   Daylight hours daily, year-round

   Note: The clock tower is not always accessible.

>>>

Perhaps the best place to start your tour of Rye is from the clock
tower at St. Mary the Virgin Church, founded in 1150. This
church clock (c. 1500s) has the distinction of being the oldest in
England still functioning with its original clockworks. If you are
truly daring, you can brave the narrow, winding staircase to the
top of the clock tower, brace yourself against the sea breezes,
and enjoy a lovely view of the red-roofed medieval village. The
coastline, 2 miles away, is a spectacular backdrop. In the bell
room, you'll find the clock's 18-foot pendulum and an interesting narrative on the church bells—seized by the French in 1377,
and recaptured in a retaliatory raid on Normandy in 1378.
    Upon your retreat, spend a moment catching your breath

inside the ancient church itself; the stained-glass windows are magnificent and there are numerous memorials from our period to enjoy.

～

Other medieval sites in Rye . . .

✝ Rye Land Gate
Cinque Ports Street
Rye

>>

If you've left your car in the public car park, you may have already noticed the vestiges of the ancient city wall that once surrounded Rye. If you've arrived by train, turn left on Cinque Ports Street to find your destination. The Land Gate is the only remaining gate of the three built in 1340. It originally housed the winch for operating Rye's drawbridge.

～

✝ Augustine Friary
(a.k.a. the Monastery)
Conduit Hill
Rye

>>

The citizens of Rye may have defended their nation against French invaders, but their sympathies were roused by the persecution of the Huguenots in the 1500s. The Monastery, which dates from 1340, was a popular sanctuary for Huguenot refugees; details can be read inside the potter's shop that now occupies the building.

✝ Ypres Tower and Rye Museum

Gun Garden

Rye

>>>

OPEN

10:30 a.m.–1:00 p.m. and 2:15–5:30 p.m. daily, April–October

Note: On our most recent visit, Ypres was closed for repair.

>>>

Ypres (pronounced "Wipers") Tower was built under orders from Henry III in 1249 as part of Rye's defensive system. By 1430, it had lost its military importance and become the home of John de Ypres, for whom it is named. By 1513, the city of Rye had repurchased the tower for use as the town jail—a role it filled until the mid-1800s. Ypres Tower now houses the Rye Museum, where you may peruse a variety of artifacts pertaining to Rye's colorful past.

∿

✝ Mermaid Street

>>>

Arguably the best-preserved medieval byway in all of Britain, Mermaid Street has stood virtually unchanged for centuries. The cobblestoned street sweeps down from the highest point of the city, and its bevy of tiny passages lined with picturesque cottages invites your exploration. You'll find ancient storefronts chock-full to bursting with modern trinkets, and plenty of historic tearooms and inns, including the famous Mermaid Inn (c. 1156), where you can enjoy a pleasant repast while soaking up the *(greatly sanitized!)* residential atmosphere of medieval Rye.

While you're in Rye . . .

✝ Great Dixter House

Northiam

Rye

>>

PHONE

01797-252878

E-MAIL

greatdixter@compuserve.com

LOCATED

Take the A21 to A28 at Filmwell; take the A28 approximately 10 miles to the village of Northiam; follow signs to Great Dixter.

TRAVEL

Trains depart Charing Cross for Hastings; from Hastings, take a taxi or the 400 bus to Great Dixter in Northiam. Total travel time is approximately 1 hour 45 minutes.

OPEN

2:00–5:00 p.m. Tuesday–Sunday, April–October

ADMISSION

£6.00 Adults

£1.50 Children

>>

Despite the fact that Great Dixter was built in 1460 and boasts one of the largest timber-framed halls in England, the real attraction here is the Christopher Lloyd landscaping. Ponds, meadows, unusual topiaries and exotic flowers make Great Dixter a visual delight. The home was restored in 1910; you must take the guided tour if you want a peek inside.

∿

✝ Winchelsea

>>

The village of Winchelsea dates back to the Roman era, although all vestiges of that ancient settlement were long gone by the time the great storm of 1287 struck. So devastating was that tempest that the entire village of Old Winchelsea was submerged, and so it stayed until Edward I began work on his ambitious hilltop "new town." This is one of the few medieval "planned communities." A very large, awe-inspiring parish church served as the hub from which sprang a grid of sensibly designed streets, with plenty of room for future growth—all encompassed by a fortified town wall.

Unfortunately, it wasn't as fortified as it needed to be. In 1377, as the Hundred Years War reached a violent crescendo, Winchelsea was ransacked by the French. The parish church –cum–town center was largely destroyed (it's now roughly half the size it once was), and the master plan for Winchelsea's continuing development was laid to ruin. Additional raids by the French, coupled with the rapidly receding sea, sealed Winchelsea's fate.

* *

☞ Did you know?

Murderess, Adulteress, Queen and— Religious Icon? The parish church of **St. Thomas** in Winchelsea sports a carving of Isabella, the "She-Wolf of France," Edward II's unfortunate choice for a bride. It can be spotted above the church's east door. A companion carving of King Edward depicts him with a particularly pained expression. Inside the church, you will find well-worn carvings of Edward I and his second wife, Margaret of France. The couple was married in 1218 by Robert of Winchelsea, Archbishop of Canterbury. Look for them above the ancient tomb of Gervase Alard.

* *

Today, Winchelsea is partly a village and partly a walled meadow. Three of the original town gates—Strand Gate, Pipewell Gate and Newgate—are still standing, although in various degrees of ruin. The distance between them illustrates the intended scope of Edward's new town. Pipewell Gate was rebuilt after French raids in 1380; it is by this structure that you'll find the only remaining portion of the medieval city wall.

✝ Camber Castle
Near Rye

>>>

PHONE

01797-223862

LOCATED

1 mile south of Rye off the harbor road, across the fields from A259

OPEN

Information Centre: 2:00–5:00 p.m. Saturday, July–October
Exterior: Since Camber Castle is a ruin, the exterior is accessible daily during daylight hours.

ADMISSION

£2.00 Adults
£1.00 Children
£1.50 Seniors

>>>

Severely limited open hours (summer Saturdays only) make Camber Castle unusually difficult to visit, particularly if you're looking for "official" insights and information. Still, if you're particularly interested in coastal defense, or in the reign of Henry VIII, you might find it worth your while to seek out Camber, if only to poke around its ruined shell on your own.

Generally regarded as one of the finest among Henry's many coastal "gun forts," Camber was built early in Henry's rule (1512) to help protect Rye Harbor from the very real threat of French invasion—a distinct possibility throughout Henry's reign. Like many of Henry's later forts, Camber boasts a strong circular tower, specifically designed to withstand cannon fire. A series of rounded bastions lent the tower close protection. In 1539, as the possibility of a papal-sponsored Catholic invasion loomed ever nearer, Henry added Camber's mighty curtain wall, punctuated by numerous gun platforms. For the next three years, a series of renovations allowed Henry to fine-tune his military architecture, making Camber, in some ways, virtually match the other coastal castles, Walmer and Deal.

Despite all of the thought, preparation and extraordinary expense that went into creating an impenetrable coastal fortress, Camber saw virtually no military action. By the end of the Tudor era, the sea had receded some 2 miles, reducing Camber to a sort of inland dinosaur. Although Charles I ordered its demolition, it is time and tide—or, in this case, merely time—that has reduced Camber to rubble.

ANCIENT INNS AND EATERIES

Be forewarned—Rye is definitely an upscale town. All that atmosphere does not come cheap! While there are "bargains" to be had in both room and board, you can assume that the greater the historical ambience, the higher the price tag. If you're staying overnight, it's worth noting that evening attire at most Rye restaurants tends toward the dressy side. Still, Rye has a reputation for great restaurants, and you can expect to dine well for your dollar.

~ The Flushing Inn
Market Street
01797-223292
Seafood is the star attraction at this charming 15th-century hostelry.

~ Fletcher's House
Lion Street
01797-223101
One of Rye's oldest medieval homes, with a reputation for innovative cooking. Our innkeeper highly recommended this spot.

~ The George Hotel
High Street
01797-222114
Centrally located on High Street, the George has operated as a coaching inn and hotel since 1575. The full-service restaurant is open to the public.

~ King Charles II
High Street
01797-224954

Yes, we know Charles wasn't a medieval monarch, but this beautifully timbered inn dates from 1420. The guest rooms are handsomely appointed with antiques.

~ The Mermaid Inn
Mermaid Street
01797-223065

This very old half-timbered pirate's hideaway looks like it might topple right into Mermaid Street! We enjoyed a lovely dinner here, one of Rye's most romantic settings, while the wait staff told stories of the resident ghosts. The atmosphere at lunch is more casual. The Mermaid also has overnight accommodations.

~ The Strand House
Winchelsea
01797-226276

One of Winchelsea's oldest houses, dating from the 15th century, is now a charming B&B.

CONTENTS

Pevensey, Hastings & Battle

The Start of the Story

hile this makes for a daunting one-day trip out of London, and truly is most comfortable and enjoyable split into two days, we have grouped these sites because of their linked history. Pevensey, Hastings and Battle are where it all begins, as those of you who are steeped in the lore of early English medieval history are well aware. It was at Pevensey that William, Duke of Normandy, landed in September 1066 when he came to England with a force of some 7,000 men to press his claim to the English throne. He quickly acted to secure his landing by moving onto Hastings, which offered a stronger defensive position. From there, he initiated raids on the surrounding countryside to tempt King Harold south and force a definitive battle. As we all know, William's strategy was successful. Within three weeks of his landing at Pevensey, William confronted Harold at the Battle of Hastings, resoundingly defeated the Saxons and thus changed the course of English history and earned the sobriquet "William the Conqueror."

There are some caveats to this trip. Although the history is fascinating, some of the actual sites are less than compelling. Pevensey is interesting and has extensive ruins, but it stands alone in the countryside and is accessible only by car. Hastings leaves much to be desired; the town does a very poor job of promoting its medieval and Tudor heritage. Battle Abbey also is a ruin, but the remains are substantial and ongoing renovation and excavation continue to reveal more and more of the site's rich history.

~

Pevensey Castle
Pevensey

>>>

PHONE
01323-762604

LOCATED
Off the A259, between Eastbourne and Bexhill

OPEN
10:00 a.m.–6:00 p.m. daily, April–October
10:00 a.m.–4:00 p.m. Wednesday–Sunday, November–March

ADMISSION
£2.50 Adults
£1.30 Children
£1.90 Seniors

>>>

Pevensey was where it all began. It was here that William the Conqueror landed with his invasion force on September 28, 1066, to claim the throne of England, which he swore Edward the Confessor had bequeathed to him. One of the oldest historical sites in England, Pevensey once was a formidable defensive point, used by both the Romans and the Saxons before the Normans occupied it. Standing high on a hill, isolated on a narrow peninsula with limited land access and a sweeping view of the English Channel spread before it, Pevensey became a pivotal point in the civil wars that raged across England under Norman hegemony. An almost impregnable fortress, Pevensey never fell to assault, although the garrison was starved out through siege several times in the castle's turbulent history. Today, the sea has receded and the walls are crumbling, but you can still get a sense of the critical role this castle played in the politics of medieval times.

The strategic importance of the site is demonstrated by the fact that the Romans first built a defensive fort, named Anderida, here in the 3rd century. When the Romans hightailed it out of England, the fort became a hideaway for nomadic natives. The *Anglo-Saxon Chronicles* records that these poor souls were slaughtered where they slept by invading Saxons in 491. After the Conqueror landed, one of the first things he did was convert the ancient fort into a motte and bailey castle, leading some scholars to label Pevensey as the first Norman castle in England.

Control of Pevensey was granted, after the Battle of Hastings, to William's half brother Robert, Count of Mortain. Unfortunately for William Rufus (the Conqueror's second son and heir to the English crown), Uncle Robert sided with Robert, Duke of Normandy (the Conqueror's eldest son), when the brothers Rufus and Robert began fighting over their inheritances. The Count of Mortain and his brother Odo, Bishop of Bayeux, held Pevensey firmly for nephew Robert and the castle fell to Rufus only after prolonged siege.

Siege again brought about the surrender of Pevensey Castle when Gilbert, Earl of Pembroke, held it against King Stephen of Blois in 1147. The technique failed, though, to bring about the fall of the castle when possession was again disputed during the barons' revolt against Henry III. After the Battle of Lewes on May 14, 1264, when the forces of Simon de Montfort broke the royalist army, the battered survivors fled to Pevensey for safety. The castle was then under the control of Peter of Savoy, Earl of Richmond, the uncle of Queen Eleanor of Provence. The earl

> **☞ Did you know?**
>
> Following Harold's defeat at the Battle of Hastings, Pevensey became one of four sites in England where the Normans built a stone keep inside a Roman fort. Of these four castles, Burgh and Walton have been lost to time, Pevensey is a ruin and only Portchester retains the full glory of its Norman keep and original Roman walls.

had greatly expanded the already formidable castle's defenses, building a 12-foot-thick and 25-foot-high curtain wall and strong bastion towers, encircling 10 acres of castle grounds. His foresight proved providential. De Montfort's son (also Simon) laid siege to the castle; secure behind the earl's fortifications, Henry's supporters held firm for nearly a year. The younger Simon was forced to break off the siege in the spring of 1265.

These intimidating defenses were not enough to prevent a fourth, and final, siege of Pevensey. After Henry Bolingbroke challenged Richard II's right to the throne and claimed the crown for himself in 1399, supporters of the king laid siege to Pevensey. The castle was then a Lancastrian holding (control having been assigned to Bolingbroke's father, John of Gaunt, in 1372) and had been left in the capable hands of Lady Joan Pelham, wife of the castle constable, Sir John Pelham, who had already joined Bolingbroke's forces in the field. Lady Pelham successfully defended the castle and after Richard was deposed, Bolingbroke—now Henry IV—granted the honor of Pevensey to Sir John.

♦♦♦♦♦♦♦♦♦♦♦♦♦♦♦♦♦♦♦♦♦♦♦

☞ Did you know?

For the "honor" of serving as castellan of Pevensey, poor Sir John paid a heavy price. He had to serve as gaoler to James I, King of Scots, who was captured in 1406, and Queen Joan of Navarre, the second wife of Henry IV, after she was accused of practicing witchcraft during the reign of her stepson Henry V.

♦♦♦♦♦♦♦♦♦♦♦♦♦♦♦♦♦♦♦♦♦♦♦

Ghost Alert!

If, during your visit to Pevensey, you happen to encounter a "pale lady," don't be alarmed. It is just Lady Pelham, still walking the outer walls of the castle, directing the defense against the royal forces.

Pevensey declined in importance as a strategic outpost as the sea began to recede. With money always tight in the royal exchequer, the castle was pretty much left to rot away. It had ceased to be occupied by the time the Tudors acceded to the throne. Its defensive importance was recognized again in the late 1500s when gun emplacements were added to help guard the southeast coast against invasion by the Spanish Armada.

What you see today are the remains of the ancient Roman wall and the bastions that once surrounded the fort and were later incorporated into the defensive structure of the Norman keep built by the Count of Mortain. There also are remains of unidentified medieval buildings in the inner bailey, a 13th-century gatehouse with dungeons at the bottom and, of course, the impressive curtain wall built by Peter of Savoy.

Mixed in with these medieval and Tudor treasures are remnants of history from World War II. Once again during that war, the strategic defensive importance of Pevensey was recognized and the crumbling castle was pressed into service as an observation and command center. The structures built then to meet that purpose—a new blockhouse and tower—were made to look like ancient ruins in order to fool the Germans.

• •

☞ Did you know?

A master at the game of using symbolism to fuel political spin, William the Conqueror left England the way he had come, via Pevensey. In March 1067, just three months after being crowned King of England and six months after first landing on the coast, William felt secure enough on his new throne to return to Normandy to check on his domains there. He left his half brother Odo, Bishop of Bayeux, and a trusted lieutenant, William Fitz Osbern, as regents in charge of his new domain. William had the ships for the return voyage fitted with white sails to denote victory and peace. He departed on calm seas with an impressive entourage, leaving behind a subdued, but not yet fully conquered, kingdom.

• •

Living quarters for the military personnel posted to Pevensey were created in the existing medieval towers and machine gun emplacements were built on top of the curtain wall. These have all been left in place as another important historical footnote. This means that even though a structure at Pevensey may *look* medieval, it doesn't necessarily date from that period.

❖❖

WILLIAM THE CONQUEROR (1028–1087; REIGNED 1066–1087)

William the Conqueror is a towering historical figure and justifiably so. His ambition to rule a kingdom changed the course of Western civilization, imposing Continental customs and religious and social orders on Anglo-Saxon England and engaging England in Continental affairs as it had never been before. *(Isn't it amazing what greed and ambition can do?)*

The inauspicious circumstances of William's birth and his perilous youth gave no hint of the grand role he was to play in setting the direction of the second millennium. He was born in Falaise, Normandy, in 1028, the fruit of a liaison between Robert, the sixth Duke of Normandy, and Herleve, a girl of Falaise who probably was the daughter of a tanner. Both Robert and Herleve were most likely about 17 at the time. Apparently they parted on good terms because after the affair ended, Herleve was married to Herluin, Vicomte of Canterville, with whom she had two sons: Odo, the future Bishop of Bayeux and Earl of Kent, and Robert, the future Count of Mortain. Both were to play prominent roles in their half brother's invasion and conquest of England.

Little is known of William's early childhood. Most likely, he was left in his mother's household and little attention was paid to him by his father until 1034. In that year, Duke Robert made the fateful decision to go on pilgrimage to Jerusalem, a fairly common action for medieval men who wanted to atone for their sins. And Duke Robert, a brutal, violent man *(not that that was unusual for the time)*, had many sins for which to atone. For starters, he was accused of killing his brother Richard in order to inherit the dukedom of Normandy.

Regardless of his reasons for making the journey, Duke Robert's decision caused an uproar in the duchy. Normandy was an unstable land, torn by factions with numerous border threats and no single strong leader who could be left in charge during the duke's absence—not to mention the fact that Robert had no legitimate heir. But Robert was a stubborn man and he was determined to go, no matter what objections his magnates threw at him. To quell some of their concerns, Robert finally produced William. He forced the nobles and churchmen to swear allegiance to William and to promise to uphold his right to succeed to the dukedom. This was a risky maneuver. At a time when might definitely took precedence over right, and a strong leader who could impose his will through force was greatly desired and admired, there was no guarantee that the magnates would keep their word.

Off Robert went, leading a lavish entourage and building a legend of his journey that lives today. But the worst fears of the nobles left behind were soon realized. Robert died suddenly in July 1035 in Asia Minor on his return journey. Only eight-year-old William, dubbed "the Bastard" by his contemporaries, was left to rule Normandy.

William must have been born under a lucky star, because no other strong candidate emerged right away to challenge his inheritance. However, the duchy did descend into chaos with no strong force in charge, and the years of William's minority were some of the darkest and most brutal in Normandy's history. In this atmosphere, young William honed his military and political skills.

The situation continued to spiral out of control until it reached its apex in 1046 with a well-organized, full-scale revolt. William barely escaped Normandy alive and fled to King Henry I of France, pleading for support. Henry gave it and led an invasion force into Normandy in early 1047 to recapture the dukedom for William. From this point on, William, who was around 20 years old, began exerting power over his duchy.

From 1047 to 1060, William, who was descended from Viking kings, set about grinding down his enemies, solidifying his authority and expanding the borders of his duchy. After 14 years of continuous warfare, he emerged a strong and independent leader, in firm control of his duchy and with ambitions for loftier titles. The tantalizing prospect of the throne of England lay before him.

❖❖

THE NORMAN INVASION

Edward the Confessor, a saintly, if rather odd, king of England, left a mess behind him when he died on January 5, 1066. Because he had taken a vow of chastity and therefore had no heir of the body to succeed him, Edward had created a situation in which competing claims of the right to the throne were bound to erupt into war. It did not take long for that to happen.

The very same day that Edward died, his brother-in-law Harold Godwinson, the most powerful man in the kingdom, had himself crowned king in the newly built Westminster Abbey. He claimed that the Confessor, on his deathbed, had named Harold the successor. But Harold, who had not one drop of royal blood in his body, also had more than his fair share of enemies, including some in his own family and especially among those who held competing claims to the throne of England.

The strongest of these was William the Bastard, Duke of Normandy. William maintained that Edward had promised in 1051 to name him heir to the English crown. Further, William insisted that Harold had vowed to uphold William's claim when Harold came to Normandy on a diplomatic mission in 1064.

Needless to say, William was incensed when he learned that Harold had seized the crown after Edward died. William promptly set about preparing to invade England and wrest the crown from Harold by force. This was a logistical nightmare, but William was not daunted by the challenge. He knew he was going to need a large force, thousands of horses, specially built ships and enough supplies and equipment to support his army until his forces could gain a secure foothold in England. He set about recruiting troops, promising rich rewards in exchange for support. "Volunteers" (i.e., mercenaries) were drawn from Normandy, Maine, Brittany, Burgundy, Anjou and other parts of the Continent. William had a huge fleet of ships built, probably in the neighborhood of 600 vessels. He even managed to obtain the support of the pope, thereby turning the invasion into something of a holy war. All of William's preparations for invasion, and all of the events that led up to it, including Harold's supposed promise of support for William's claim, are documented in the Bayeux Tapestry, a contemporary history embroidered on a long strip of linen that tells the tale (at least from the Norman perspective) of the invasion and conquest of England.

Harold's army was ready and waiting. All through the summer of 1066, they kept watch on England's southeast coast. But William did not come. The sheer magnitude of the logistical task of preparing for such an invasion meant that William was not ready to leave Normandy until sometime in August. Then, unfavorable winds kept him trapped in the Somme estuary for about six weeks, until the end of September.

This delay gave Harold's unruly brother Tostig and another claimant to the English throne, King Harold Hardraada of Norway, the opportunity to beat William to the punch. They led an invasion force into the north of England early in September.

Harold, acting impulsively and forcefully as always, swiftly led an army north to confront this challenge, leaving the southeast coast of England unguarded. On September 25, 1066, the opposing forces met at Stamford Bridge in Yorkshire. Harold and his troops crushed the foreign army. Both Tostig and Harold Hardraada were killed in the fighting.

On October 1, King Harold, who was still in York at the time, learned that William had finally invaded the southeast coast, landing unchallenged at Pevensey on September 28. Harold quickly gathered his forces and led a fast-paced march back to London, covering nearly 200 miles in less than a week. He arrived there on October 6 and began immediately recruiting more troops. Without waiting to finish the job or properly train and equip the new recruits, Harold began marching his army again on October 11, this time south to confront William. Harold and his exhausted soldiers began gathering outside Hastings, near an open field known as Senlac (now the village of Battle), on October 13. Altogether, they had covered more than 250 miles in just 12 days — not the best condition in which to fight a pitched battle with the determined, well-trained and well-armed (not to mention well-rested) Norman forces.

Thus the stage was set for the battle that would set the course for the new millennium.

◇ ◇

✛ Hastings

LOCATED
Where the A21 meets the A259, about 58 miles from London

TRAVEL
Train service runs frequently from Charing Cross and Victoria
Stations. Travel time is around 90 minutes.
>>>

The town of Hastings is located on a peninsula with a small harbor, but its land is much drier than the marshes that once surrounded Pevensey. This is what made it so attractive to William as the site for his second defensive position in England. In the early Middle Ages, Hastings developed as one of the Cinque Ports, but it never became one of the more important ones.

A wall, remnants of which can be seen today, was built around the town in 1385 after the French sacked and burned it in 1377. All seven of Hastings's medieval churches also were sacked and burned in this invasion, but two of them were rebuilt. **Borough Church of St. Clement's**, located near the old Seagate of the wall, the site of which is marked with a plaque, was rebuilt in 1390. **All Saints Church**, located at the northern end of the narrow All Saints Street, was reconstructed in the early 1400s. A highlight of All Saints is a fragment of a medieval wall painting, found above the chancel arch, that depicts the Last Judgment.

We warn you, though: this is one for the hardy and intrepid traveler determined to do it all. First, the castle ruins are located high on a cliff above the city and are reachable only by climbing 100 stairs or riding a railway up a very steep cliff. The rest of the ancient sites are spread all over Old Town, the medieval and Tudor part of the city, and the walking distance between them is much farther than it looks on the map distributed by the information center. In addition, the medieval churches are rarely open to the public. Old Town retains the narrow streets and byways of an ancient village and is dotted with historic buildings, but few of them are marked with dates or any other historical information. They also are hard by clusters of tourist shops catering to seaside resort–goers. Clearly, the town of Hastings does not value its medieval and Tudor history as much as some of us do, despite the fact that there is a modern painting of scenes from the Bayeux Tapestry on the walls of a pedestrian walkway between Old Town and the newer part of Hastings. *(Actually, we're being polite. Imagine the world's most run-down, honky-tonk boardwalk, overawed by the much-tattered remains of a castle that threatens, at any moment, to shower your cotton candy with medieval rubble — which will be your **only** taste of medieval history in Hastings.)*

~

✝ Hastings Tourist Information Centre
Queens Square
Priory Meadow
Hastings

>>>

PHONE
   01424–781111

E-MAIL
   hic_info@hastings.gov.uk

LOCATED
   In the back of a church located in the middle of a shopping area
   surrounded by pedestrian walkways

>>>

We found the staff at this information center to be pleasant and helpful, but not extensively knowledgeable about Hastings's medieval and Tudor history. The center was fairly well stocked with literature about sites in southeast England, but very thin on information about medieval and Tudor attractions in Hastings itself. A walking tour map of the city was available, but, as we said, we found it to be misleading in terms of distances between sites. All in all, we think there are information centers to be found in Kent, Surrey and Sussex that better meet the needs and interests of medieval and Tudor enthusiasts.

∿

 ## Hastings Castle
West Hill
Hastings

>>

PHONE
01424-781111 (Hastings Information Centre)

LOCATED
On a ridge overlooking the town of Hastings, near the top station of a cliff railway

OPEN
10:00 a.m.–5:00 p.m. daily, April–September
11:00 a.m.–3:30 p.m. daily, October–March

ADMISSION
£3.20 Adults
£2.10 Children
£2.60 Seniors
Family ticket available

CONVENIENCES
An audio/visual presentation entitled "The 1066 Story"

TIP!
This is not the easiest site we've ever tried to visit. The only way up is by climbing 100 stairs or riding a railway up a steep cliff. You have a choice of two: the East Hill Cliff Railway bills itself as "the steepest funicular railway in the UK"; the West Hill Cliff Railway offers the less vertical ascent. The East Hill Cliff Railway is located in Rock-a-Nore Road and is open 10:00 a.m.–5:00 p.m. in the summer and 11:00 a.m.–4:00 p.m. in the winter. The West Hill Cliff Railway is in George Street and is open 10:00 a.m.–5:30 p.m., April–October and 11:00 a.m.–4:00 p.m., November–March. Look for signs advertising "The 1066 Story"; you won't find any mention of Hastings Castle. Both railways charge 80p for adults and 40p for children and seniors.

>>

After William the Conqueror secured a base at Pevensey when he invaded England in September 1066, he began ranging farther up the coast, searching for a better logistical site from which to manage his campaign. He found it at Hastings, which had a good harbor and was situated at the end of a small peninsula, making it easily defendable. William moved cautiously, but quickly, occupying Hastings on September 29 and securing his line of retreat by building a castle in the town. Construction of this castle is depicted in the Bayeux Tapestry, the documentary report of William's conquest that is preserved at the Centre Guillaume de Conquerant in Bayeux, France. Basically, the castle was a simple motte-and-bailey type with a "prefab" timber tower brought over from Normandy.

✦✦✦✦✦✦✦✦✦✦✦✦✦✦✦✦✦✦✦✦✦✦

☞ Did you know?

Underneath the old moat of Hastings Castle is a network of caves with highly unusual acoustics. The slightest whisper carries eerily for long distances. Legend has it that prisoners in medieval times would be put in the caves and left alone while guards positioned themselves around a corner and listened to every word spoken.

✦✦✦✦✦✦✦✦✦✦✦✦✦✦✦✦✦✦✦✦✦✦

From this stronghold, William and his troops began rampaging all over southeast England, burning, looting, raping and killing as they went. They concentrated their efforts, whenever they could, on lands held by the Crown. Recognizing that his position was very precarious, William knew that his best chance for success in this audacious venture was to draw Harold south and to do it quickly before supplies ran short and men's enthusiasm for an invasion launched against incredible odds ran thin. William and his troops began a deliberate campaign of massive destruction to fire up Harold's temper.

There is little left of Hastings Castle to see, just a few broken walls and crumbling stone structures. And what does remain is not on the original site. The castle was moved to its current location in 1070, an action that turned out to be not such a wise decision. In the early 14th century, the part of the cliff on which the castle was located and some of the castle itself were swept away by the sea.

While you're in Hastings ...

✝ Old Town Hall Museum
High Street
Hastings

>>

PHONE
01424-781166

OPEN
10:00 a.m.–5:00 p.m. daily, April–September
11:00 a.m.–4:00 p.m. daily, October–March

ADMISSION
Free of charge

CONVENIENCES
Brass rubbings and creation of faux Saxon coins

>>

Hastings also boasts a museum in the Old Town Hall that focuses on the town's medieval history with displays, models and dioramas from the Middle and Tudor Ages.

∾

✝ Battle

>>

LOCATED
About 57 miles from London, 4 miles northwest of Hastings; turn off the A21 onto the A2100.

TRAVEL
Frequent trains run from London Charing Cross; the trip takes about 75 minutes. There is daily National Express Bus service from Victoria Coach Station in London.

>>

When the Norman invaders following William the Conqueror clashed with the Saxon forces of King Harold, it was in an open field then known as Senlac. The closest town was Hastings; hence, the name "The Battle of Hastings." It was only after William ordered the construction of a church to commemorate the battle and founded an abbey on the site that the town of Battle, taking its name from the abbey, sprang up. That is how the site of the Battle of Hastings and Battle Abbey came to be located in the town of Battle.

✝ Battle Information Centre
88 High Street
Battle

>>>

PHONE
01424-773721

E-MAIL
battletic@rother.gov.uk

>>>

If you haven't already collected enough brochures and other free information about the medieval and Tudor sites and history of southeast England, this little center is a good place to pick up more. Battle does a particularly good job at promoting its ancient attractions.

✝ Hastings Battlefield
Battle

>>>

OPEN
10:00 a.m.–6:00 p.m. daily, April–September
10:00 a.m.–5:00 p.m. daily, October
10:00 a.m.–4:00 p.m. daily, November–March

ADMISSION
£4.30 Adults
£2.20 Children
£3.20 Concessions
Family ticket available

CONVENIENCES

An introductory video and an interactive audio tour that walks you through the battlefield and abbey ruins are available for free. The full tour takes 45 minutes, although a shorter route can be done in about half an hour. Table models depicting the battle are located at various sites along the battlefield. There is also a children's activity and picnic area.

TIP!

Every October, on the weekend falling closest to October 14, a re-creation of this famous battle that changed the course of history is staged at Battle Abbey. The event is made even more festive with hundreds of re-enactors participating in demonstrations of the arts and crafts of the time.

»»

By all accounts, the last Saxon king of England, Harold Godwinson, was hotheaded, impulsive and overconfident. He had always achieved success through quick action and thought this strategy would work for him again after William, Duke of Normandy, invaded England to contest Harold's assumption of the crown. Harold responded to William's invasion by saying, "Show me the enemy!" Thus he threw away his greatest advantage — time — and took the fight to William instead of waiting for William to come to him.

William, in contrast, played it cool. He took his sweet time moving about southeast England, raiding and pillaging the land, particularly any that belonged to Harold personally or to the Crown.

Harold responded to the lure and quickly assembled a force of raw recruits. Without taking time to adequately equip and train his new "army," Harold led a forced march out of London on October 11. He and his troops covered more than 55 miles in just two days to wind up 9 miles from Hastings late in the day on October 13. The only "seasoned" troops he had with him had just fought — and won — a brutal battle at Stamford Bridge in Yorkshire against invading Viking forces led by Harold's brother Tostig and Norway's King Harold Hardraada. The Saxon king and his forces had then marched quickly back to London, only to regroup and promptly march again, this time south to combat William the Bastard's invasion. Needless to say, Harold would be fighting at less than full strength.

Learning of Harold's movements, William roused his better-armed and -trained forces and led them out of the hastily built fortifications of Hastings at dawn on October 14, 1066. The quick reaction caught Harold by surprise and he was forced to take the defensive position. Still, Harold was a great soldier (if not a brilliant strategist) and the position he chose was very strong. He massed his forces along the top of a ridge in a field called Senlac, thus forcing William's troops to fight uphill.

☞ **Did you know?**

So hastily did Harold assemble his troops and march them south that exhausted stragglers of the forced march from London were still wandering into the camp after the battle started and continued to do so throughout the day.

But William still held the advantage in this fight; his troops included a strong force of mounted knights and squires. In contrast, all of Harold's men fought on foot—the ancient, and by then outmoded, way of battle.

The battle probably began somewhere around 9:00 or 9:30 a.m. It looked at first as if Harold's "shield wall" along the ridge was going to hold and carry the day for the Saxons. One wing of William's troops broke against the relentless and bloody pressure of fighting uphill and turned to flee the field. The English line then broke—this time in jubilation—and, despite Harold's strict injunctures not to break the "shield wall," began running down the hill, chasing and killing their Norman quarry.

William stopped the rout by riding into the midst of his fleeing men, removing his battle helm so he could be seen and heard and rallying the troops to turn and fight again. The technique was so successful that the Normans repeated it a couple of more times during the day-long battle, pretending to break and run, only to turn and decimate their pursuers each time.

One would have thought that the Saxons would have caught

on after at least the second time the Normans played this trick, but apparently they did not. Eventually, the Saxon line was so weakened that a group of Normans was able to fight its way through to a wounded King Harold. He had been shot in the eye by an arrow and although he stayed to fight after pulling out the arrow, he was greatly weakened by the shock and pain. Despite a ferocious defense by Harold's personal guard, the Norman soldiers were able to break through the circle to reach the king and proceeded to hack him to death. That was the end of the battle. There was no one left to take command. Most of the Saxon leaders had been killed—a fortuitous development for William that greatly eased his task of bringing all of England to heel.

All was not sweetness and light after the Battle of Hastings for William, though. A significant number of English nobles and church officials, as well as the citizens of London, threw their support to Harold's surviving heir, Edgar the Ætheling, a great-nephew of Edward the Confessor. William didn't try to woo them with diplomacy or bribes; he simply employed the technique he had used so successfully before in subduing recalcitrant lands—he launched a ruthless campaign of suppression, burning, looting and pillaging his way through southeast England en route to London. Needless to say, this violent march made a great impression upon the Londoners.

◆ ◆

☞ Did you know?

Estimations of the numbers of men involved in the Battle of Hastings range from 3,000 to 10,000 on each side *(historians have a slight disagreement on this issue!)*. Most sources seem to think there were around 7,000 men on each side.

◆ ◆

They wisely agreed to accede to William's claim to the throne—on their own terms, of course. City leaders met with William at Berkhamstead in mid-December and swore their allegiance to him. A few days later, on Christmas Day 1066, William the Conqueror was crowned King of England in a coronation ceremony at Edward the Confessor's recently completed Westminster Abbey.

The Battle of Hastings not only marked the beginning of

Norman rule in England—an event that changed the course of history—but it also is notable as the last battle in which England was conquered by an invading foreign force.

Ghost Alert!

Not surprisingly, this battlefield supposedly is haunted by monks and knights. One in particular is routinely seen riding across the battlefield on October 14. In addition, the field is supposed to run red with blood when it rains. (*It was raining the last time we were there and we didn't notice anything unusual, but then we're not big on hanging around battlefields under the best of circumstances and certainly not in the rain.*)

❖❖❖

BAYEUX TAPESTRY

"A very long and very narrow strip of linen embroidered with figures and inscriptions representing the Conquest of England . . ."
—from a 1476 inventory of Bayeux Cathedral

The Bayeux Tapestry is arguably one of the most famous pieces of political propaganda ever created. Dating from the 11th century, it actually is not a tapestry at all but an extremely long strip of linen, 230 feet long by 20 inches wide. Embroidered with eight different colors of woolen thread, it depicts, through more than 70 individual scenes, the events leading up to William the Conqueror's invasion of England and subsequent victory at the Battle of Hastings.

Because embroidery was a distinctly Anglo-Saxon art at the time and because the tapestry bears a strong resemblance to some illuminated manuscripts at Canterbury Cathedral, many historians have concluded that the tapestry was made by English needlewomen from Canterbury. Most agree that it was done at the order of Odo, Bishop of Bayeux and half brother of William the Conqueror. Some of the facts that have led historians to conclude that Odo commissioned the tapestry are the decidedly "Norman" bent to the scenes depicted, the bishop's prominent role in several of them, the intimate knowledge displayed of the events depicted and, of course, the tapestry's winding up at the cathedral at Bayeux.

Clearly, the tapestry was meant as justification for William's actions. A prime focus is the alleged duplicity of Harold Godwinson. A key panel shows

Harold, while he was supposedly on a diplomatic mission to Normandy in 1064, swearing on relics at Bayeux that he would support William's claim to the crown of England. After detailing Edward the Confessor's death and Harold's immediate usurpation of the throne, the tapestry then outlines in great detail William's preparations for invasion, the sea crossing and the Battle of Hastings. It ends with Harold's death on the battlefield and the flight of the English. Because the tapestry contains such tremendous detail, it yields multitudinous clues about daily life in the 11th century, illustrating styles of dress, forms of entertainment, castle building, weaponry, battle tactics, religious beliefs and so on.

The tapestry has not always been treated with the respect it is due. First mention of it is found in a 1476 inventory of Bayeux Cathedral. The monks conducting the inventory certainly had no concept of the valuable piece of history they were recording. All they wrote, in addition to their description of its physical properties, was that the tapestry was used to decorate the cathedral's nave on sacred feast days.

Nor did Republican troops in the French Revolution have much regard for this fragile documentary. They tried to use it as a cover for an ammunition wagon. Fortunately for us, a Bayeux lawyer named Lambert Leonard Le Forestier intervened, found another piece of cloth for the soldiers and thus preserved the Bayeux Tapestry *(evidence that lawyers do occasionally perform valuable public services)*.

On the flip side of that coin, others have tried to use the tapestry for lessons about successfully invading England. Both Napoleon and Hitler had the tapestry brought to them so they could study it for inspiration when planning their own invasions of England. Fortunately, neither was able to match the Conqueror's feat.

◇ ◇

✝ Battle Abbey
Battle

>>

PHONE

01424-773792

LOCATED

South end of Battle High Street in the village of Battle

OPEN

10:00 a.m.–6:00 p.m. daily, April–October

10:00 a.m.–4:00 p.m. daily, March–November

Note: The medieval Abbot's Hall is part of a boarding school located

on the grounds of Battle Abbey. It is open to the public 10:00 a.m.–
6:00 p.m. in August only. Inquire at the abbey gift shop or call ahead
for touring permission.

ADMISSION
Included as part of the admission to the battlefield

CONVENIENCES
Museum about monastic life in the medieval gatehouse; bookstore
and gift shop

>>

After William had subdued most of England, his conscience
began to smite him for all the blood he had shed in his conquest
of the island nation, starting with King Harold. In 1070, he ordered an abbey built on the field where the Battle of Hastings
was fought. Specifically, he directed that the altar of the abbey
be placed on the spot where Harold died. Construction of William's church, probably the first Norman church built in England, was not completed until 1094. It was consecrated by the
Archbishop of Canterbury. William Rufus, the Conqueror's
son who inherited the throne of England, attended the ceremony.

The original church was rebuilt in the 13th century to accommodate the growing abbey's needs. At the same time, the
great gatehouse, the most prominent surviving feature today,
was built as a defense against French raids. It was constructed
alongside the earlier, 11th-century Norman gatehouse and some
features of the older gatehouse were incorporated into the
new one. Considered one of the finest medieval monastic gatehouses in England, it also is a very formidable one. It is a huge,
rectangular building with octagonal corner turrets, fortified
with battlements along all four sides and dotted with arrow slits
all over. The vaulted gate passages feature excellent decorated
arch bosses, including two heads facing northward that are said
to represent Harold and William. The sad-looking character
is, of course, supposed to be Harold while the beaming head is,
needless to say, William.

When William ordered the construction of this church, he also invited a group of monks to come over from the Benedictine abbey of Marmoutier on the Loire in France to found a new abbey. He ensured the prosperity of the abbey by endowing it with rich manors and granting the abbot supreme jurisdiction over all the land and people within a mile and a half radius. This meant that the abbey was exempt from the chain of command of the Church, a rare and wonderful privilege.

Unfortunately, this royal privilege was to be a source of conflict between the abbey and the Bishop of Chichester (under whose authority the abbey normally would fall) for several centuries. The trouble began in 1147 when Bishop Hilary of Chichester demanded that the abbey submit to his authority. Abbot Walter de Luci refused and appealed to King Stephen; Bishop Hilary appealed to the pope. Thus the battle began and continued through the reigns of Henry II and his son John. It

• •
☞ Did you know?

Edward II was the last medieval monarch to visit Battle. None of the Tudors ever came.
• •

ended in 1235 when a compromise *(naturally)* was reached and everybody managed to get along, to the abbey's great profit, until Henry VIII dissolved the monasteries in the 16th century. Henry gave the abbey to Sir Anthony Browne, who tore down many of the medieval structures, including the church, in order to make way for a grandiose Tudor mansion.

The most complete buildings left that were constructed from the 11th through the 16th century are occupied now by a boarding school that generally is not open to the public. The most impressive feature, accessible to the public only in August when the school is closed, is the Abbot's Hall, constructed in the 13th century. A 20th-century fire burned off the modifications that had been made to the hall over the centuries, leaving it near its original state. It is well worth seeing if you have the opportunity.

Otherwise, many of the medieval buildings that comprised

the abbey are in ruins and the church founded by William is gone. Remnants of it, part of a wall and what was once part of a great door to the nave, run alongside the ancient buildings that the school now occupies. You walk beside them as you exit the abbey grounds. The most prominent surviving feature, as we noted earlier, is the gatehouse that dominates the triangular marketplace of the town that grew up around the abbey. This is where the museum and gift shop are located. The most extensive ruins are the 12th-century dormitory, rebuilt in the mid-13th century. This dorter range housed the novices' rooms and the monks' common room, which have been impressively restored to close to their original state. There is also a marker indicating the spot where the high altar of the church founded by William once stood.

Ghost Alert!

Be alert as you wander among the abbey ruins, especially around the site that marks the spot where King Harold died. He is said to haunt the place.

~

While you're in Battle . . .

✝ St. Mary the Virgin Church
High Street
Battle

>>

PHONE

01424-773649

OPEN

10:00 a.m.–noon daily, April–September
10:00 a.m.–noon Wednesday–Friday, October–March

>>

This church was founded in 1070 by Robert, Count of Eu, whose descendants held Hastings Castle. Among its historic features today are its Romanesque nave, a Norman font with a medieval cover, wall paintings that date from the 14th century and crusaders' crosses carved by swords. There is also the gilded alabaster tomb of Sir Anthony Browne, to whom Henry VIII granted Battle Abbey after the Dissolution. The church's other claim to fame is that Thomas à Becket was dean of the college here before becoming Archbishop of Canterbury.

Battle Museum of Local History

Memorial Hall
High Street
Battle

>>

PHONE
01424-775955

OPEN
10:30 a.m.–4:30 p.m. Monday–Saturday, April–October
2:00–5:00 p.m. Sunday, April–October

ADMISSION
£1.00 Adults
Children free of charge if accompanied by an adult

>>

This small museum has a few displays that will appeal to the medieval enthusiast: a model of the Battle of Hastings, a print of the Bayeux Tapestry and a facsimile of the *Domesday Book*. It's worth a peek if you are not pressed for time. Ask to see the city guide that identifies all the medieval and Tudor buildings in town. Unfortunately, it's not available for sale.

☩ The Almonry
High Street
Battle

>>

PHONE
01424-772210

OPEN
10:00 a.m.–4:30 p.m. Monday–Saturday, year-round

ADMISSION
Free of charge

CONVENIENCES
Coffee and gift shop

>>>

This 15th-century building also serves as the town hall. It contains a model of Battle and its historic buildings.

While you're in the area . . .

If you are someone who enjoys the rugged outdoors and is longing for a chance to hike through the English countryside, you can combine interests by following the path of the 1066 Country Walk between Battle, Pevensey and Rye. Guided walks can be booked by contacting Walk Walk at 01424-754140 or by e-mail: info@walkwalk.com. The book *The 1066 Country Walk*, by Brian Smailes, can also help you plan your trip.

∿

☩ Bodiam Castle
Near Robertsbridge

>>

PHONE
01580-830436

LOCATED
2 miles east of A21 at Hurst Green, 3 miles south of Hawkhurst

OPEN
 10:00 a.m.–6:00 p.m. daily, March–October
 10:00 a.m.–6:00 p.m. Saturday and Sunday, November–February
ADMISSION
 £3.60 Adults
 £1.80 Children
>>>

Aside from Leeds Castle, Bodiam is probably England's most romantic castle. The sight of the peculiarly graceful fortress, reflected in the clear waters of its lake-like moat, fills fairy-tale expectations to the hilt. One of the last medieval castles in Britain, Bodiam was built in 1385 by Sir Edward Dalyngrigge, Keeper of the Tower of London, under license by Richard II.

Like so many of the castles in the area, it was intended as a defense against rumored French invasion. The invasion never materialized, but Bodiam continued to be a valuable deterrent to pirates who sought to penetrate the mainland from the once-navigable River Rother.

Typical of castles of this period, Bodiam combined plenty of domestic comforts with its imposing facade. There were an incredible 33 fireplaces in the castle, no fewer than 24 toilets and the medieval equivalent of a central heating system. Unusual for a defensive structure, Bodiam was designed to create a de facto caste system . . . the mercenary garrison was physically segregated from the luxury apartments of Sir Edward and his household. Clearly, this arrangement would have hampered communication in a crisis—luckily, the point was never tested. Bodiam was also designed so that no servant could venture from the kitchen or retainers' hall without passing through a courtyard under the watch of the castle owner. *(You would think that castellans would have more to do than keep an eye on the whereabouts of each and every servant!)* Conceived as a "courtyard castle," Bodiam had unusually open middle grounds that provided ample space for bakeries, brew-houses and the storage of goods that could be marketed for income during times of peace, or used to sustain the castle's defenders, should an anticipated attack ever come to pass.

Whether Bodiam ever contributed in a major way to national defense is not clear. Since the castle was built at the very advent of the cannon, Bodiam's builder did not anticipate the power of such mighty weapons, and the castle's walls were far too thin to resist serious cannon attack. Luckily, such a siege never came to pass. The only recorded conflict took place during the Wars of the Roses, and appears to have been easily settled. In 1483, a band of Lancastrians took refuge here under the protection of Sir Thomas Lewknor. Richard III's men, led by the Earl of Surrey, quickly ousted the rebels. The castle was abandoned in Tudor times, making it a cinch for parliamentary forces to seize Bodiam in 1643. Widespread robbing and vandalism destroyed the inside, but the exterior remained unscathed.

Today, Bodiam is technically a ruin—no furnishings or accouterments grace the interior. Although the castle is a shell, the grounds are fully accessible, allowing you to enjoy the architecture of one of the few completely preserved (and never architecturally altered) medieval castles in Britain. There are plenty of stone stairways to master and vistas to enjoy, and an on-site video gives the history of the castle.

While you're in the area . . .

The area around Bodiam Castle has two other medieval buildings. In the village of Bodiam stands the church of **St. Giles**, where the remains of a knight (1360) and a priest (1513) are buried. To the northwest of the castle, just outside the village of Sandhurst Cross, is historic **St. Nicholas Church**. Known for its amazing views of the Sussex valleys, this church provided a burial ground for 14th-century plague victims, which explains its location outside the town proper. The clerestory of the church dates from the 13th century, the west tower from the 14th. Look for the glorious 15th-century stained-glass window depicting St. Michael's struggle between the Cross and the Devil.

✝ Herstmonceux Castle
Hailsham

>>

PHONE

01323-833816

LOCATED

2 miles south of the village of Hertsmonceux off the A271; 10 miles west of Bexhill

TRAVEL

Go by car or train to Polegate Station.

OPEN

This privately owned castle generally is open to the public once a week; call ahead for details.

ADMISSION

£2.50 Adults

£1.00 Children

>>

Like Bodiam, Herstmonceux Castle (c. 1441) was built as a defense against feared French invasion. More manor house than castle, Herstmonceux does boast a moat, battlements, arrow loops, gun ports and lovely gardens. While the interior has been greatly altered from the original construction, the exterior brick walls are the real thing.

Tip!

If you are lucky enough to land in England during the August Bank Holiday, you may be able to catch the annual three-day medieval festival staged at the castle. Complete with twice-daily battle reenactments, archery contests and a medieval tournament, this festival is the largest of its kind in England. For more information about the festival, call 01891–172902 or visit the website at www.mgel.com.

❖❖

ENGLAND'S SOUTHEAST COASTLINE
AND THE FRENCH INVASION OF 1377

King Edward III was the eldest son of Isabella, the "She- Wolf of France," and the ill-fated Edward II. Although he was crowned at the age of 14 in 1327, while his father was still a prisoner in Berkeley Castle, it was mama Isabella and her paramour, Roger Mortimer, Earl of March, who wielded the power in England. Edward III wasted little time in securing his position, however. By 1330, he had arrested Mortimer for treason and had him hanged, drawn and quartered at London's Tyburn killing fields. His mother he sent to live out her days in genteel exile at Castle Rising.

That was not the end of the role Isabella would play in her son's life. The dowager queen was the sister of King Charles IV of France, who had died in 1328 with no male issue. The crown passed to Charles's cousin, Philip VI, but Edward firmly believed he had, through his mother, a more legitimate right to the throne of France. In 1337, Edward decided to press his claim, quartered the arms of France with his own, and raised an army to invade the Continent, launching what would come to be known as the "Hundred Years' War." In 1338, he ravaged the French countryside, bringing the nation to its knees and proclaiming himself King of France in 1340.

Once recovered, the French had other ideas. Although it took a while for them to succeed in wresting back the bulk of their lost turf, by 1370 the tide had definitely turned in favor of the French. By then, the mighty Edward was failing in health, while his brilliant foe Commander Bertrand du Guesclin recaptured castle after castle in France. By 1375, all of the English-held territories in France, save Calais, had been lost. Edward's much-acclaimed heir-apparent, Edward the Black Prince, was dead, and as England was poised to lay its crown on the head of a mere child, France was poised on the opposite side of the Channel, waiting for the opportunity to invade England.

The chance came in 1377 when the 10-year-old Richard II was crowned at Westminster. The first English territory to fall was the Isle of Wight. From there the French proceeded to raze the ports of Rye and Hastings. The invading army was driven back in fairly short order, but the threat of a second invasion kept the entire southeast coastline of England on constant alert for years. All of the existing defenses were fortified, and a host of new defensive structures were built with impressive speed—not only along the coastline but inland as well, wherever navigable rivers might provide potential access to the mainland. Although these castles never saw protracted battle—at least not from foreign forces—they were built to withstand the most violent of ravages, which is why so many punctuate your tour of Kent and Sussex today.

❖❖

ANCIENT INNS AND EATERIES

~ Almonry Coffee Shop
High Street
Battle
01424-772727

This coffee shop is in the 15th-century building that also serves as the town hall for Battle.

~ Blacksmith's
High Street
Battle
01424-773200

A restaurant with a continental menu in a 16th-century building.

~ The Pilgrim's Rest
Battle
01424-772314

A coffee shop/tearoom serving lunches only. Located opposite the gatehouse of Battle Abbey in a charming, half-timbered 15th-century house. Garden seating available.

-· Tea-on-the-Green
4 High Street
Battle
01424-775258

This 14th-century tearoom features homemade cakes and pastries.

~ Ye Olde King's Head
Mount Street
Battle
01424-772317

A 15th-century pub serving light fare.

~ Clematis Cottage
The Green
3 High Street
Battle
01424-772416

A 15th-century cottage with two rooms.

~ The Gateway
78 High Street
Battle
01424-772856

A 16th-century restaurant and inn.

~ Old School Cottage
66A High Street
Battle
01424-773825

A 16th-century cottage with one Tudor room featuring a queen-size, four-poster oak bed, en suite bathroom, adjoining lounge and private entrance.

~ The Brickwall Hotel
Sedlescombe
Battle
01424-870253

A Tudor manor located 3 miles east of Battle; heated swimming pool.

~ Lionsdown House
116 High Street
Old Town
Hastings
01424-420802

B&B in a 15th-century house with exposed timbers.

~ Seagull House
 96 High Street
 Old Town
 Hastings
 01424-447789
A 16th-century guest house.

~ Bell Cottage
 Vinehall Road
 Robertsbridge
 Hastings
 01580-881164
B&B in a 16th-century converted inn; beamed throughout.

~ Stone House
 Heathfield
 01435-830553
Built in 1495; 1,000-acre estate with a five-acre garden, two lakes, seven rooms; Michelin "red" meals for hotel guests only.

~ Waldernheath Country House
 Amberstone Corner, near Herstmonceux
 01323-442259
The main building of this charming B&B dates from the 15th century.

CONTENTS

Lewes

The Path to Parliament

ou probably have an inkling already, so let us confirm your suspicions: we never met a medieval monarch we didn't like. While we might not actually *like* their personalities (some, we will admit, were rather dastardly), there isn't one—with the possible exception of William Rufus—that we don't find absolutely fascinating. However, our focus isn't completely narrow! There are some pivotal personalities of the Middle Ages who, even in our eyes, outshine the royalty. Close to the top of our list is Simon de Montfort, rebel baron and leader of the 13th-century revolt that paved the way for England's parliamentary representation.

Closely associated with that 1264 uprising, Lewes Castle and the nearby Lewes Priory are steeped in the lore of Simon de Montfort, Henry III and the young Edward I. As if that weren't enough, add the charming Anne of Cleves House (something for the Tudor contingent) and the unusual ruins of Michelham Priory—a fascinating tour of this little-known pocket of Sussex.

✝ Lewes Tourist Information Centre
187 High Street
Lewes

>>

PHONE
01273-483448

LOCATED
Center of the town of Lewes

TRAVEL
Trains depart Victoria Station for Lewes at regular intervals; travel time is just over 1 hour.

ADMISSION
Free of charge

TIP!
Whether you look upon this as a warning or an invitation is up to you: November 5 is Bonfire Night in England and nowhere are tourists given a "warmer" introduction to the traditional celebrations than in Lewes. No fewer than five major bonfires are staged in town, each depicting a specific period of English history. One of the effigies that locals parade through town is that of Pope Paul IV, head of the Catholic church during Mary Tudor's reign. The burning of this effigy is an apparent backhanded reminder of the role this pontiff played in the deaths of 17 Protestant martyrs from Lewes who were burned at the stake between 1555 and 1557. A plaque at the Lewes town hall marks the site of their fiery deaths.

>>>

✝ Lewes Castle
169 High Street
Lewes

>>>

PHONE
01273-486920

E-MAIL
castle@sussexpast.co.uk

LOCATED
Not far from the center of the town of Lewes

OPEN
>   10:00 a.m.–5:30 p.m. Monday–Saturday, year-round
>   11:00 a.m.–5:30 p.m. Sunday, year-round

ADMISSION
>   £4.00 Adults
>   £2.00 Children
>   Combination ticket is available to include the
>   Anne of Cleves House:
>   £5.50 Adults
>   £2.70 Children

CONVENIENCES
>   Museum included in the price of admission
>>

One of the most pivotal battles in the protracted rebellion of Simon de Montfort's baronial supporters against the forces of Henry III took place in the town of Lewes. Although there is not much in modern-day Lewes to remind visitors of that bloody 1264 clash (which de Montfort and his sons decisively won!), you can visit one of the key royalist outposts with a stop by Lewes Castle.

Although relatively small, and essentially in ruins, Lewes Castle is not without its charm, including a spectacular view of the surrounding countryside. Originally built in 1070 by William de Warenne, the Conqueror's Chief Justiciar and Earl of Surrey, the castle has one particularly unusual feature, its dual-motte design; there is one at each end of the bailey. By the 1100s, the second William de Warenne had topped both mottes with shell keeps, the larger of which you can still poke around today. At the top of the battlement, numerous brass plaques provide helpful information about the movement of the warring forces at the Battle of Lewes. The massive 14th-century barbican gate, attributed to John, the last de Warenne earl, is also open for your touring pleasure. It features a museum that highlights Sussex County's past, with a fine sampling of medieval artifacts.

Upon the death of John de Warenne in 1347, the earls of Arundel inherited the Honor of Lewes. This castle, so close to their own massive Sussex stronghold, was never given priority. It eventually fell into ruin, and the majority of its ancillary buildings were eventually torn down.

◇◇

WILLIAM DE WARENNE (D. 1088)

If ever a character typified conquered England's new breed of Norman-French nobility, it would have to be William de Warenne. De Warenne was already a soldier of considerable stature when he crossed the Channel with William of Normandy to help the duke claim England's crown. His powerful performance at the Battle of Hastings earned him extensive lands in his newfound country, properties that by 1086 traversed 13 counties, including strategically pivotal sites centered around Lewes. By the time of the Conqueror's death, William de Warenne was one of the largest private landowners in England and one of the most powerful forces with whom his fellow barons had to reckon. He was instrumental in crushing the 1075 revolt by the earls of Norfolk and Hertford, and lent decisive support to the Conqueror's heir, William Rufus, in his struggle against Robert Curthose, Duke of Normandy, and Odo of Bayeux—support that earned him the title Earl of Surrey.

William de Warenne was wounded in battle during the siege of Pevensey. He died at Lewes Priory in 1088. He left as his legacy several of England's most strategic defensive structures and a line of powerful, wealthy descendants who were honored as Surrey's earls until 1347.

◇◇

While you're in Lewes . . .

You may want to try your hand at tracing the last vestiges of the ancient city wall, built in 1266, two years after the massive Battle of Lewes. Although the village was a defensive outpost as early as the Saxon era, memories of that fierce 13th-century fight prompted city officials to try to protect the village by building the wall. This is not one of the best-preserved or most impressive city walls you'll ever see; indeed, only the western part of the wall can be walked, and major stretches are blocked by modern buildings. If you insist

• • • • • • • • • • • • • • • • • • • •

☞ Did you know?

During the height of the Middle Ages, Lewes boasted ten churches within its city walls and another four, just beyond. Vestiges of many of these houses of worship can still be seen as you work your way through the village.

• • • • • • • • • • • • • • • • • • • •

on this adventure, begin below the Lewes Castle keep and follow Pipe Passage to High Street. Keep your eye out for the West
Gate bastion—it can be barely glimpsed behind a residence.
Continue your brief wall walk along Keere Street to the southwest.

✶

✝ Lewes Priory (a.k.a. St. Pancras Priory) and Battlefield Memorial

≫≫

PHONE
01273-474610 (Anne of Cleves House)

OPEN
2:30 p.m.–dusk Tuesday–Thursday, summer only
Tours leave from the Anne of Cleves House by prior booking only.

ADMISSION
£3.00 Adults
Children admitted free of charge

≫≫

Like its contemporary, Lewes Castle, this Cluniac priory—the
first in England—was established by William de Warenne, in
1080. Dedicated to St. Pancras, the priory was active for 450
years, before being suppressed during the reign of Henry VIII.
In the meanwhile, it had grown to become one of the largest
and most influential Cluniac priories in the world, with an
enormous church and an internationally renowned artistic reputation. Access to the grounds is very restrictive; you must arrange your visit in advance by calling the Anne of Cleves House
information line, listed above.

To us, the priory is a *priority*, because it is here that you'll
find the one and only monument to de Montfort's stunning
1264 victory at the Battle of Lewes. Finding it, however, is not as
simple as it sounds. You must wend your way between the priory
and the adjacent playground, traversing some challenging ter-
rain in the process. This search was one of the truest tests of our

perseverance, and when we came upon the marker, there was a moment of rather stunned silence.

This is one of the oddest-looking memorials we have ever encountered. Our traveling companion likened it to a "litter bin on steroids" and although we don't feel that shows *quite* the proper degree of respect, we secretly agree. The massive cast-iron "helmet" is large enough for a slim adult to slip into—though, believe us, you probably won't want to. Scenes from the Battle of Lewes and an appropriately solemn inscription decorate the memorial's base. In short, a true oddity for your medieval and Tudor scrapbook!

❖❖❖

LEWES, 1264:
BARONS, BATTLES AND THE BIRTH OF PARLIAMENT

If anything positive can be said to have come from such a bloody confrontation as the Battle of Lewes, then certainly the birth of England's parliament would qualify as a worthy gain. This was not the final battle between Simon de Montfort's rebel barons and the royalist forces of Henry III, but it was a decisive one—the crucial turning point when the monarchy was forced to concede that, sooner or later, the demands of the malcontents would have to be satisfied.

Of all the Plantagenet rulers, Henry III was arguably the least effective. Many historians have deemed him downright divisive. At a time when military prowess was the hallmark of a successful king, Henry lacked even the most basic battlefield instincts. His passions, such as they were, centered around religion, art and architecture. Indeed, his most impressive legacy is Westminster Abbey, that glorious confluence of Henry's primary interests. Nor was Henry a savvy politician. Obtuse to the point of blindness when it came to his barons' deeply ingrained nationalism, Henry was cowed by Rome and surrounded himself with foreign-born courtiers, most of whom were relatives of his French-born wife, Eleanor of Provence, or his own half siblings from his mother's second marriage to Hugh de Lusignan. Tensions between the xenophobic English lords and Henry's French counselors reached a peak in 1234 when the barons ousted two of the king's top foreign-born advisors. Jealousies at court, deepening resentment over stiff taxation, the miserable failure of Henry's foreign policy and a general discontent with the king's administrative style kept the political waters stirred for the next 24 years.

By 1258, the barons had plied enough pressure; Henry, at last, began to cede to their demands. The Provisions of Oxford established a "Great Council" of 15 barons ("parliament"), of which the king was deemed "first among equals." The

Great Council of 15, in fact, governed England for the next seven years, but it was a humiliation no absolute monarch would endure for long. By 1263, Henry began to reassert his power and the barons, as one might suppose, were having none of it. Under the leadership of the most powerful noble in England, Simon de Montfort, Earl of Leicester, an army was raised and by 1264 the barons' revolt had become a full-scale civil war.

De Montfort was, in many ways, the antithesis of his brother-in-law Henry Plantagenet. An inspired military leader, he was incredibly effective at rallying support, not only among the barons but among the "common" people as well, most notably the merchants of London. More importantly, he was a keen general, with a devastating ability to lead his largely untrained troops to stunning victories. It was at the Battle of Lewes that de Montfort's military prowess (aided in no small part by several catastrophic misjudgments by the royalist faction) had the most profound results.

By the spring of 1264, King Henry had begun to close the power gap between himself and the barons. He had reeked havoc on the pivotal towns of Northampton, Leicester and Nottingham and had turned his attention to Rochester, where de Montfort was staging a protracted siege. Under the leadership of Prince Edward (later Edward I), Rochester was relieved, and the royalist armies proceeded southwest to capture the castle at Tonbridge. De Montfort had hurried to London to muster additional troops; the king and his infantry, meanwhile, continued their southern progress toward the village of Lewes. The baronial forces made great haste to meet up with the royalist army, pausing in Fletching long enough to engage in a diplomatic, if perfunctory, exchange of written communication, before actual battle was waged.

On the morning of May 14, 1264, de Montfort assembled his troops on a ridge overlooking Lewes. In a particularly rousing speech, fraught with religious zeal and national pride, he instilled a wild enthusiasm in his army, which served him well in the hours ahead. Two of Simon's sons, Guy and Henry de Montfort, commanded the right column. The Earl of Gloucester (the "Red Earl," Gilbert de Clare) controlled the center, and the left column was composed of enthusiastic Londoners. De Montfort held his own column in reserve, an unusual, but ultimately very wise, maneuver.

There was a strong opening move by the royalist faction; troops led by Prince Edward stormed the cavalry. Unfortunately for the royal cause, this cavalry was shielding the London brigade. Young Edward, still harboring resentment against the Londoners for past rude treatment of his mother, stampeded the London troops and impulsively pursued them for miles. This rash action effectively cut him off from his father's army at a time when his support was most vital. Henry's army was left unprotected from the mighty descent of de Montfort's troops from the ridge above Lewes. Henry, despite a rather cowardly reputation, fought impressively—two horses were killed from under him before he finally was forced to retreat to Lewes Priory. Edward returned from his temper tantrum to find his father's troops roundly defeated. Despite his efforts to turn the battle around, it wasn't long before the prince was compelled to take refuge with his father, along with a large number of royalist supporters, at the Cluniac priory in town.

De Montfort won the day, but the fact that the monarch and his heir were in sanctuary posed a delicate problem—no competent leader would make the mistake of storming a religious safe house, for fear of the moral, spiritual and political repercussions. Still, the negotiated terms, known as the Mise of Lewes, provided the barons with a great number of the concessions they had struggled to achieve. The king agreed to uphold the Provisions of Oxford, to remove all "traitors" (foreign and English) from his council, and to pardon the rebels and restore all their lands and goods. The king remained in de Montfort's custody. Prince Edward, his uncle Richard, Earl of Cornwall, and Cornwall's two sons, Henry and Edmund, were confined in de Montfort strongholds.

In effect, Simon de Montfort had done more than win a battle: he had paved the way for the lords of the realm to have a stronger voice in their government. In fact, so great were his gains that de Montfort found himself in the awkward position of being the de facto ruler of England . . . not a comfortable position for the anti-establishment leader of notoriously mistrustful nobles. He summoned the Great Council to London with an eye toward creating an enlightened oligarchy that would replace the monarchical government. In effect, this was the first "parliament," and deliberately included two knights from every county and two citizens from nearly every English borough, in addition to the lords.

Still, it did not take long for the tide to turn against de Montfort. A total break with the monarchy was simply too radical a concept for the mid-13th-century nobility. This, in addition to de Montfort's autocratic nature and the barons' ingrained jealousies of one another, led to an eroding of Simon's support. Nobles who had once fought mightily against the Crown now renewed their allegiance to King Henry. De Montfort's fate was sealed when the 26-year-old Prince Edward escaped confinement and promptly raised an army to restore his father's powers.

Edward's troops met de Montfort at the Battle of Evesham in 1265. De Montfort was killed in that battle, his body brutally mutilated and sent in pieces to towns throughout the country as an example of the harsh treatment rebels could expect under the future King Edward. De Montfort's cause was largely demolished as well. Although minor skirmishes would be led by his sons over the next two years, they were ineffectual. The monarchy, under the leadership of Prince Edward, was back in control, albeit with somewhat limited powers, now under the watchful eye of the Great Council—England's future parliament.

❖ ❖

Also while you're in Lewes ...

✝ Anne of Cleves House

52 Southover High Street

Lewes

>>

PHONE

01273-474610

E-MAIL

castle@sussexpast.co.uk

OPEN

10:00 a.m–5:00 p.m. Monday–Saturday, March–October
Noon–5:00 p.m. Sunday, March–October
10:00 a.m.–5:00 p.m. Tuesday–Saturday, November and December
Noon–5:00 p.m. Sunday, November and December
10:00 a.m.–5:00 p.m. Tuesday, Thursday and Saturday, January
and February

ADMISSION

£2.60 Adults
£1.30 Children
Combination ticket available to include Lewes Castle and Museum

>>

An easy side trip during your Lewes visit is to the charming
Anne of Cleves House. Actually, the name is somewhat mis
leading. While it is true that the home was deeded to Henry
VIII's fourth wife in 1541 as part of her divorce settlement, the
German-born Anne never actually lived here. Still, the home
is particularly picturesque, with its timber-framed Wealden design. You may tour the furnished rooms, although the interiors
have been modeled after 18th and 19th century residences and
do not reflect the period when Anne "did not" live here. (*We
find it ironic that so many modern couples find this the ideal wedding venue—personally, we'd never hinge our love lives on anything linked to Henry VIII, but maybe we're just overly superstitious.*)

✝ Michelham Priory
Upper Dicker
Halisham

>>>

PHONE
01323-844224

LOCATED
2 miles west of Halisham, 8 miles northwest of Eastbourne

TRAVEL
Trains depart Victoria Station for Polegate; taxi service to the priory is available.

OPEN
10:30 a.m.–5:00 p.m. Wednesday–Sunday, April–July and September
10:30 a.m.–5:30 p.m. Wednesday–Sunday, August
11:00 a.m.–4:00 p.m. Wednesday–Sunday, March and October
Closed November–February

ADMISSION
£4.70 Adults
£2.30 Children

>>>

Michelham Priory is an amalgam of unusual features: an 800-year-old ruin, incorporated into a Tudor manor home, surrounded by England's longest water-filled moat. The gatehouse dates from the 14th century; the barn is from the reign of Elizabeth. The museum houses a wide array of artifacts, from ancient Augustinian religious treasures to 18th-century farming equipment. There is a watermill, a re-created medieval herb garden *(for all of us Cadfael groupies!)* and a fully realized Georgian child's bedroom. In short, a one-stop "something for everyone."

ANCIENT INNS AND EATERIES

~ The Old Parsonage
Westdean, near Seaford
01323-870432

Although not in the immediate vicinity of Lewes, this striking medieval home (with a relatively unobtrusive Victorian wing) is close enough for a convenient overnight rest. Three handsomely appointed bedrooms.

CONTENTS

Arundel

A Cache of Castles

ere's one for those of you who crave castles above all else—a trip devoted entirely to medieval castles. The three that you will visit on this tour span the spectrum of roles played by castles in ancient times. Bramber Castle was built entirely for defensive purposes with little to offer in the way of creature comforts. Arundel Castle, although essentially defensive, was also the primary residence of many a noble family; impressive accommodations were as important as oppressive intimidation in the development of Arundel. Defense played a very minor role in the design of the 14th-century Amberley Castle—it was built as a retreat for the archbishops of Chichester, presumably with the goal of shoring up spiritual rather than military strength.

Although Amberley Castle can be seen from the road, you can tour the property only as an overnight guest. If your budget and your schedule allow, we suggest you consider spending the night out of London, visiting the Arundel area one day and Chichester the next. Either way, you'll find much to enjoy as you venture out into the beautiful countryside of West Sussex.

✝ Arundel Castle
Arundel

>>>

PHONE
01903-883136

LOCATED
56 miles south of London, 4 miles north of Littlehampton on the A27

TRAVEL
Trains depart Victoria Station for Arun Station; travel time is approximately 1½ hours. The castle is a 10-minute walk from Arun Station.

OPEN
Noon–5:00 p.m. Sunday–Friday, April–October

Note: Arundel Castle is closed on Saturday. Also, it is open by pre-arrangement from November through March.

ADMISSION
£7.00 Adults
£4.50 Children
£6.00 Seniors
Family ticket available

>>>

Although Arundel Castle *looks* medieval, and is marketed by the trustees as such, the major portions of the castle are, in fact, the result of a "re-Normanization" dating from the Victorian period. It may be ersatz, but the architecture remains true, by and large, to the *spirit* of the Norman era. The restoration was modeled heavily after Windsor, and in fact is so convincing that *The Madness of King George III* used Arundel as the cinema substitute for the royal palace.

Architecture and movies aside, the history of Arundel Castle is ancient, indeed. This has been the seat of the earls of Arundel since 1067, when William the Conqueror gave Roger de Montgomery, Earl of Essex and Shrewsbury, one third of the county of Sussex, along with the earldom of Arundel. Although there was once a Saxon fortress on the site, the basic layout of de Montgomery's castle formed the boundaries of all future castles on the property.

Originally a strategic site for the defense of the Arun Valley, the castle soon became a pawn in early medieval politics, withstanding periods of violent civil discord. The castle was captured by Henry I in 1102, when the fair-weather Robert de Belleme, Earl of Shrewsbury, staged a rebellion, holding up in Arundel for three months. The castle was attacked by King Stephen's forces in 1139, after Empress Matilda and her Angevin retinue—intent on challenging Stephen's claim to the throne—were hosted at Arundel by Matilda's stepmother, Adeliza, and her new husband, Sir William d'Albini (a.k.a. Aubigny). The property passed down through the d'Albini and Fitz Alan families until 1556, when Mary Fitz Alan, last of the clan, married Thomas Howard, fourth Duke of Norfolk. Arundel Castel has been held by the dukes of Norfolk ever since.

Its owners may have lived turbulent lives, but the castle itself remained virtually unscathed for nearly 600 years. Henry I and Henry II both added considerably to Arundel's defensive stature; it was Henry II who added royal apartments as part of his building plan. It wasn't until the civil war of the 17th century that Arundel finally surrendered to a brutal 30-day onslaught by the Cromwellian forces. By the time the siege was over, Arundel Castle was a ruin, and so it would remain until Victorian renovators began restoration in the 1800s.

There are very few medieval remnants at Arundel, although that handful are worth the visit. A modern drawbridge crosses into the 1295 barbican, a long passage flanked by "new" towers. The gate tower beyond is from the early Norman period, predating Henry I's 1102 attack. The shell keep is entered through the ancient gatehouse, above which is "Queen Matilda's Room," presumed to have been built by Em-

• •

Did you know?

Mary Queen of Scots had more than a tangential association with the house of Norfolk. The fourth Duke of Norfolk was among the Catholic queen's staunchest supporters, and he made many brave, if foolhardy, attempts to come to her aid while she was held prisoner in England. His proposed betrothal to the Scottish queen proved to be the misstep that cost him his life. Elizabeth was so alarmed by the potential power of a Norfolk-Stuart alliance that she arrested the duke and had him beheaded in 1572.

• •

press Matilda's d'Albini stepfather. (Matilda, by the way, was never crowned Queen of England, so the garret's name is a misnomer!) At the foot of the post-Conquest motte, in the outer bailey, sits the late Norman—though heavily restored—Bevis Tower.

The artifacts inside the castle, by and large, date from later eras. The Baron's Hall was built in commemoration of Magna Carta, and in it you'll find a 1797 painting of Richard III's struggle at the Battle of Bosworth. Personal possessions of Mary Queen of Scots, including the enameled rosary beads she carried to her execution, and a selection of historical, heraldic and religious items connected with the Norfolk clan are on display in the Fitz Alan Chapel, where many of the early Fitz Alan clan are buried. The chapel was founded as the Collegiate Church of St. Nicholas in 1380 by Richard, fourth Earl of Arundel. It was served by secular canons until the college was dissolved by Henry VIII. From that point on, the Fitz Alan Chapel has been the private chapel of the earls of Arundel and dukes of Norfolk—one of the few English chapels to remain staunchly Catholic throughout its history. The handsome timber roof of the Fitz Alan chapel was constructed by Hugh Herland, whose most famous work is the stunning hammerbeam ceiling in Westminster Hall, London.

❖❖

THE HOWARD CLAN

The Howards had a long political career throughout medieval and Tudor history, and honors granted to the Howards for their service continued to add prestige to the titles of their descendants. Richard III conferred upon Sir John Howard the title "Premier Duke," which continues to distinguish the house of Norfolk. The dukedom also carries with it the hereditary offices of Earl Marshal of England and Chief Butler of England.

One of the most notorious of the Howard clan was Thomas, third Duke of Norfolk, uncle to two Tudor queens: Anne Boleyn (her mother was Lady Elizabeth Howard, Thomas's sister) and Catherine Howard. After both nieces lost their lives to Henry's axe, Thomas apparently abandoned his career as a misguided matchmaker. He barely escaped with his own life, saved only by the fact that Henry VIII died the day before Howard's scheduled execution. Thomas's son Henry was less fortunate. He was beheaded by Edward VI shortly before the young king's death.

Ever faithful to the Catholic creed, the Howards enjoyed a brief respite during Mary Tudor's reign, but suffered mightily (albeit largely due to their own indiscretion) during Elizabeth's tenure. Henry's son Philip perished in the Tower of London, where he was imprisoned for celebrating Mass in honor of the success of the Armada. Ironically, it was another Howard — Lord Howard of Effingham — who assisted Drake in repelling the Spanish fleet.

The romantic Earl of Surrey, Tudor poet and courtier (executed by Henry VIII on trumped-up charges; allegedly he had quartered the arms of Edward the Confessor, an aggressive heraldic assertion tantamount to treason), rounds out the roster of noteworthy Howards from this era.

◇◇

✝ Amberley Castle
North of Arundel

≫≫≫

PHONE
01798-831992

WEBSITE
there.is/amberley*castle

LOCATED
4 miles north of Arundel, off the B2139

OPEN
Amberley Castle is a privately owned, exclusive hotel; the grounds are open only to hotel guests.

≫≫≫

If you're looking for a true medieval immersion experience, consider stretching your budget to include a night of unabashed luxury at Amberley Castle. The fact is, this is the *only* way you'll have the chance to explore the stunning 14th-century castle . . . an extravagance we found to be worth every penny!

There is an eerie tension between the serene landscape of picturesque Amberley village and the foreboding castle that looms on its outskirts. Built in 1377 by the Bishop of Chichester, one William Rede, Amberley is yet another example of England's appropriately alarmed response to the French invasions of that year. The castle was sited at the farthest navigable point on the River Arun, making it a deterrent to pirates as well as to enemy forces. But defense wasn't the only role Bishop Rede had in mind for Amberley. The castle was designed to also serve as a luxury retreat for weary bishops, and it is this role that comes to mind when you visit Amberley today.

If it were not for its expansive green pastures, punctuated by ponds, waterfowl and grazing cattle, the exterior of Amberley would present a rather austere demeanor. Its imposing curtain wall is punctuated with narrow window openings and its gatehouse and flanking turrets are severe to the point of being forbidding. One wonders what welcome relief the good bishops felt upon approaching such a stern sanctuary. To this day, the 14th-century portcullis is lowered at bedtime. Ah, but once you are "locked" inside, any misgivings immediately give way to the castle's romantic lure. A sizeable portion of the original Great Hall and solar comprise the bulk of "modern-day" Amberley; an "L"-shaped wing, adjacent to the main building, embodies the 13th-century Bishop's Hall. Fifteen exquisitely detailed rooms provide accommodations in the manor house, tower, castle wall and Bishop's Hall. Most rooms are named after Sussex castles and each is furnished with contemporary luxuries that evoke the ambience one might imagine was enjoyed by a favored medieval courtier. We indulged in the quiet splendor of the two-story Bishop's Quarters, with exposed wood beams, opulent velvet draperies, a hand-carved bar fully stocked with libations and treats, an oversized Jacuzzi and bed linens adorned with images from illuminated manuscripts.

As you stroll to dinner, enjoy the castle's spectacular gardens — white peacocks wander under the flowering arbors and the numerous ornamental pools are stocked with rare koi and flowering water lilies. The Queen's Room Restaurant claims the oldest part of the castle. Its barrel-vaulted ceiling and lancet windows have witnessed glorious feasts for over 700 years. You'll dine like a monarch on imaginatively rendered British cuisine, accompanied by live light jazz. Not an experience you're likely to forget!

✝ Bramber Castle
Bramber

>>>

PHONE
  01732-778000

LOCATED
  Just north of the A283 in the village of Bramber

OPEN
  Daylight hours daily, year-round

ADMISSION
  Free of charge

>>>

The setting is what makes Bramber worth your while: the views of the Adur Valley are quite moving. The property itself is also visually striking, dominated as it is by the looming medieval monolith—all that remains of the castle's gatehouse. Bramber was awarded to William de Braose by William the Conqueror in appreciation of "services rendered" at the Battle of Hastings. De Braose built his motte and bailey castle in 1070; the size of the structure is alluded to by the scattered remains of the castle walls. Except for a brief period of confiscation by King John, Bramber remained a de Braose holding until 1324. It seems to have played no significant role in medieval and Tudor times, and suffered irreparable damage during the Cromwellian Civil War.

Ghost Alert!

"King John was not a good man, he had his little ways . . ." Well, one of John's ways was to be particularly cruel to those against whom he bore a grudge. One such unfortunate creature was William de Braose, a powerful baron of the Welsh marches whose falling-out with the king had horrific consequences for the rest of the de Braose household. In 1210, John confined William's wife, Matilda, and his son Will at Windsor Castle and left them to starve to death. Their ghosts are said to return to the family home at Bramber each December, skeletally thin, hands outstretched for food.

CONTENTS

TRIP 5

Chichester

Culture Clashes

 hichester traces its lineage to the Roman city of *Noviomagnus*. It continued to thrive, even after the Roman withdrawal in 420 CE, surviving a later Saxon onslaught and a series of routing attacks by the Danes.

After the Norman Conquest, Robert de Montgomery built a castle at the northeast edge of the ancient Roman wall in order to defend the town against further violence—civil or foreign-inspired. The castle was destroyed during the reign of Henry III and its site deeded to the Greyfriar (Augustinian) monks, whose church still dominates the property. Of de Montgomery's castle, only a ruined motte can be seen today; you'll find it in the priory park.

Although there are several attractions to enjoy in and around Chichester, the "main event" is clearly Chichester Cathedral. We have visited a wealth of medieval churches and cathedrals over the years—we'd rate Chichester right at the top, along with St. Bartholomew's and Southwark Cathedral, both in London. Should you be in the mood to break out of the medieval and Tudor mode for a moment, this trip also offers a very exciting Roman attraction: Fishbourne Roman Palace. We enjoyed the juxtaposition of the pagan and Christian sites . . . we're certain you will find it intriguing, too.

✝ ## Chichester Tourist Information Centre

29a South Street
Chichester

>>>

PHONE
01243-539449

LOCATED
A3 out of London to A27

TRAVEL
There is regular train service from London's Waterloo and Victoria Stations. Travel time is approximately 2 hours from London.

>>>

✝ ## Chichester City Wall

>>>

Like most Roman-era British towns, Chichester was enclosed by a defensive wall during the 3rd century. The existing city wall follows the original Roman alignment. The core of the wall is primarily authentic, but the masonry you see today is not Roman. Reconstructed in 1261, it was badly damaged and subsequently repaired after the French raids of the 1370s. The wall remained in commission until after the English Civil War of the 17th century. Rather than allow the wall to fall into decay, wealthy Chichester citizens repaired the wall at their own expense and as a result, Chichester has one of the best-preserved (if heavily restored) city walls in England. Unfortunately, not all of the restoration was done in the antiquarian spirit. Substantial alterations were done at the sites of the four original gatehouses in order to accommodate modern vehicles, and most of the semicircular bastions have been lost. The southwest stretch is, by far, the portion of greatest interest; here you'll see a number of the original bastions while enjoying a spectacular view of Chichester's famous Norman cathedral.

✠ Chichester Cathedral
West Street
Chichester

>>

PHONE

01243-782595

OPEN

7:30 a.m.–7:00 p.m. daily, April–October
7:30 a.m.–5:00 p.m. daily, November–March
Guided Tours: 11:00 a.m. and 2:15 p.m. Monday–Saturday,
year-round
Limited touring during church services

WORSHIP

Matins: 7:30 a.m. Monday–Saturday
   10:00 a.m. Sunday
Holy Communion: 8:00 a.m. daily
   1:10 p.m. Wednesday
   10:30 a.m. Thursday
   7:15 p.m. Friday
Sung Eucharist: 11:00 a.m. Sunday
Evensong: 5:30 p.m. Monday–Saturday
   3:30 p.m. Sunday

ADMISSION

Donation suggested

CONVENIENCES

Gift shop and tearoom; brass rubbing by appointment

>>

For over 900 years, Chichester Cathedral has been the hub around which the city's community life and Christian worship have centered. Founded by Bishop Luffa in 1091, the ancient cathedral was largely destroyed in 1114, but it was rapidly rebuilt and completed by 1123. As you tour the cathedral, you will find that much of the architecture dates from this Norman period: the nave, the transepts, the quire and three eastern chapels. The roof and clerestory are of a slightly later—but still Norman—vintage. Other portions of the cathedral date from the 13th century and exhibit that era's preference for the Early English style of design. On-site guides clearly delineate the specific age of each of the cathedral's main sections.

Amateur historians—especially those en route to or from Arundel Castle—will want to look for the cathedral's famous Arundel tomb. This is the sarcophagus of Richard Fitz Alan (d. 1375) and his countess. The tomb depicts the couple in the unusual posture of holding hands (*unusual for medieval effigies, that is!*). However, there is some conjecture that this sentimental touch was added during a 19th-century restoration. Look, as well, for the handsome vaulted Arundel screen, built in 1475 under the direction of John Arundel, Bishop of Chichester. Also of particular note is the recently restored effigy of the politically savvy Bishop Robert Sherbourne (d. 1536). Sherbourne had a distinguished career as counselor to Henry VII, ambassador and Dean of St. Paul's, London. He managed to navigate the troubled religious waters of Henry VIII's reign and lived to help Chichester adjust to the changes brought by the monarch's break from Rome. It is to Sherbourne that the cathedral owes some of its most beautiful panels—the north transept panels depict the bishops of Chichester; the south transept panels depict the kings of England from William of Normandy to Henry VIII.

Elsewhere in the cathedral are two outstanding 12th-century Romanesque carved panels depicting the Miracle at Bethany and the Raising of Lazarus. The cathedral also has an internationally renowned art collection, although there is little on display from the medieval and Tudor periods.

While you're in Chichester . . .

You may want to visit **St. Mary's Hospital**, a 13th-century almshouse, located in St. Martin's Square. Unfortunately, St. Mary's is closed on Sundays. If you're looking for an interesting, interactive experience that provides a broad look at British history, consider the **Weald and Downland Open Air Museum**. Located outside of Chichester in the village of Singleton, the museum features more than 40 historic residences and workplaces from medieval through Victorian times. With its working 17th-century watermill, live demonstrations, assorted farm animals and spacious picnic area, the museum is a welcome stop for families looking to expend some pent-up energy. Phone 01243-881348 for details.

❖❖

ST. RICHARD OF CHICHESTER (D. 1253)

> *Day by day*
> *Dear Lord, three things I pray:*
> *To see Thee more clearly,*
> *Love Thee more dearly,*
> *And follow Thee more nearly.*
> —Prayer of St. Richard of Chichester

Chichester Cathedral is revered throughout the world for its shrine to the venerable St. Richard of Chichester. Known to his contemporaries as Richard of Wych, he gained renown in his own age for successfully defeating Henry III's attempts to block his election as Bishop of Chichester. His stalwart attitude, coupled with his piety and extraordinary pastoral skills, led to his canonization in 1262; Chichester immediately became a popular destination for pilgrims seeking St. Richard's intercession. In 1276, his body was translated from the Chapel of St. Thomas and St. Edmund to a platform in the retro-quire; King Edward I presided over the solemn event (*perhaps hoping to quell any remaining doubt that his father and the saint parted as anything less than the closest of friends!*). It is appalling to think that such an important shrine would be desecrated during the reign of Henry VIII—despite Bishop Robert Sherbourne's decidedly "Henrican" posture. Today, the site of the original shrine has been endowed with a lovely altar and an Anglo-German devotional tapestry, fitting accouterments for what is, again, a much-loved destination for pilgrims from all over the world.

❖❖

While you're in the area . . .

✝ Fishbourne Roman Palace
Salthill Road
Chichester

>>

PHONE
01243-785859

E-MAIL
adminfish@sussexpast.co.uk

LOCATED
1½ miles west of Chichester in the village of Fishbourne, off
A27/A259

TRAVEL
Bus service is available from the city of Chichester.

OPEN
10:00 a.m.–5:00 p.m. daily, year-round

ADMISSION
£4.50 Adults
£2.40 Children

CONVENIENCES
Mosaic-making for children
>>

Wondering what life was like in Roman Chichester? Nearby
Fishbourne Roman Palace will answer many of your questions.
This is the largest known Roman residence in Britain, occupied
in 43 CE as a military base and rebuilt as a palace in 75 CE. The
carefully unearthed and painstakingly restored floor mosaics
are sensitively displayed in a brightly lit modern building; look
for the glorious "Cupid on a Dolphin." Numerous Roman artifacts are housed in the museum; outside you can stroll through
a reconstructed Roman garden. We *know* that Fishbourne well
predates our special era, but this is one exception to medieval
history you will not want to miss!

Want more?

We hope we haven't totally changed your alliance from the Middle Ages to the Roman era, but if Fishbourne has left you wanting more, then a side trip to **Bignor Roman Villa** may be worth your time. The star attraction is the spectacular 80-foot-long mosaic corridor, but the smaller mosaics depicting "Venus and the Gladiators," Medusa and Ganymede are also very special. The museum is located in Pulborough, West Sussex. Phone: 01798-869259. Call ahead for details.

ANCIENT INNS AND EATERIES

~ Spread Eagle
South Street
Midhurst
01730-816911

Not too far from the town of Chichester, you'll find this renowned 15th-century coaching inn that resonates with the atmosphere of our period. Thirty-six rooms, a serious health spa with swimming pool, hearthside restaurant and lovely rose gardens.

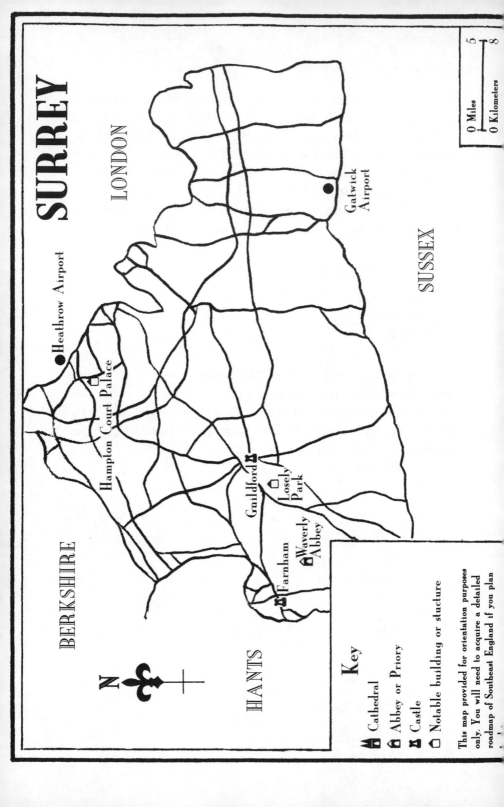

Surrey

◈   ◈   ◈

CONTENTS

TRIP 1

Guildford

Gilded History

f your idea of the ideal day trip combines castles, abbeys and stately homes, you'll want to be certain to include the town of Guildford on your itinerary. The county seat of Surrey, Guildford was established by the Saxons on the banks of the River Wey. By the time of the Norman Conquest, it was the principal town in west Surrey, with a population of between 300 and 400 persons inhabiting 75 houses. Throughout the Middle Ages, this was one of England's more prosperous cities, with a thriving wool business and a lucrative shipping industry.

What it lacks in historical "events," Guildford makes up for with historical "character." You can mosey along High Street, with its 500-year-old guildhall (open to the public on Tuesday and Thursday afternoons) and clusters of Tudor buildings. If you're looking for some ancient atmosphere in which to enjoy your lunch, try the Angel Inn or the Star. Be sure to scout down St. Mary's Church on Mill Lane — it is Guildford's oldest building, parts of which date from 1050. Then venture off to explore the ruins of Guildford Castle Keep, keeping your eye out along the way for an interesting medieval gate. Just outside of town is the handsome Elizabethan manor home Loseley Park, the evocative Waverly Abbey Ruins and the Bishop of Winchester's Farnham Castle and Keep. Enjoy!

Tip!

Because of the opening hours of several Guildford buildings, we recommend you plan your visit to Guildford for Tuesday through Saturday, preferably in the spring or summer, when the castle gardens offer a profusion of glorious color. Also (lest you think we are way, way, way too narrow in our focus), let us state for the record that Guildford has the best shopping we have found outside of London . . . so far!

✳

✝ Guildford Information Centre
14 *Tunsgate*
Guildford

>>

PHONE
01483-444333

LOCATED
33 miles southwest of London via A3

TRAVEL
Trains depart Waterloo Station for Guildford every half hour; travel time is under an hour.

ADMISSION
Free of charge

>>

In addition to providing a wealth of information, maps, brochures and the like, the Guildford Information Centre also conducts guided walking tours of the town from May through September. The tours meet at the Tunsgate Arch in High Street, opposite the **Guildhall** clock on Sunday, Monday and Wednesday at 2:00 p.m. There is also a Thursday evening tour,

• •
☞ Did you know?
The name "Guildford" derives from the Saxon name *Gyldford*, meaning "ford of the golden flowers."
• •

which meets at 7:30 p.m. We encourage you to consider one of these tours, since it may well provide you with your only chance to see the **Medieval Undercroft** in High Street. You must phone ahead for further information, as itineraries and schedules do tend to vary.

〰

✝ A lost treasure ...
The Dominican Friary

〉〉〉

As you meander the streets of Guildford, chances are you'll happen upon an enclosed shopping arcade sporting the incongruous logo of a medieval monk. This is the Friaries, named for the Dominican friary that for 250 years sat just north of the town center. It is believed that the friary was endowed in 1275 by the grandmother of young Prince Henry, son of Edward I, who died at the age of six while in residence at Guildford Castle. In the 1530s, the friary fell to the Crown, victim of the Dissolution of the Monasteries. (*We find it ironic that a site once condemned for its wealth and avarice would eventually become a mini-mall. That's progress for you!*)

〰

✝ Guildford Castle
Castle Street
Guildford

〉〉〉
PHONE
   01483-444718
LOCATED
   On Castle Hill
OPEN
   10:00 a.m–6:00 p.m. daily, April–September
ADMISSION
   90p Adults
   45p Children

TIP!

> As we've mentioned before, we are not "outdoors" kind of gals. However, even we were bowled over by the beauty of the Guildford Castle gardens. Eleanor of Provence, wife of Henry III, introduced colonnaded gardens to England, and although the current gardens were not planted by the queen, we are certain she would be well pleased with the castle's modern interpretation. We strongly suggest you plan your visit for spring or summer; you won't be sorry!

Although comparatively small for a Norman keep, Guildford Castle is believed to be one of the first Conquest-era castles in England. There is speculation that the original portion of the castle may have been built by William of Normandy as one of his "circle of nine," intended to embrace the City of London and overawe the newly conquered populace. Its recorded history begins in 1173 when the castle stood fast against the supporters of Prince Henry (a.k.a. "The Young King") in his dynastic struggle against his father, Henry II.

During the reigns of Kings John and Henry III, Guildford was a favorite royal retreat for hunting and fishing junkets; in its prime, it was considered to be the most luxurious of all royal residences in England (*so much for roughing it on those sporting weekends*). Like Farnham, Winchester and Reigate, Guildford Castle was one of four English defensive structures that fell into the hands of Louis, Dauphin of France, during the barons' revolt in 1216. However, by the 1360s the castle was largely abandoned and a mere decade later, it was essentially

☞ Did you know?

As you enter the main gate of Guildford Castle, take a second to look at the clock across the street behind you. This 20th-century representation is a tribute to Edward I and Eleanor of Castile. Their connection with the castle is particularly poignant. In 1274, their six-year-old son, Henry, heir to the throne, died at Guildford. (*We find it chilling that neither parent bothered to visit their dying child even though they were in nearby London.*) The town's Dominican friary was established in his memory, and his heart was buried at the friary church; young Henry was buried at Westminster Abbey. This sorrowful occasion may explain why Guildford Castle fell out of favor during Edward's reign.

a ruin. Eventually, the castle was appropriated by the town of Guildford to serve as a courthouse and local jail.

The only substantial part of the castle that remains is the Norman keep; the rest of the structure is all but destroyed. The imposing facade is tempered somewhat by large Tudor-era windows. We found the first floor mural chapel, with its evocative prisoners' graffiti, the most interesting feature of the

> ◆
>
> 🏴 Did you know?
>
> King John and his wife Isabella of Angoulême held their first Christmas court at Guildford.
>
> ◆

building. Beyond the keep, you will find random portions of a later-era shell keep and portions of the residential buildings built under the direction of Henry III.

Just downhill from the keep, at the corner of Castle Hill and Quarry Street, is the arch of the medieval gatehouse; it was built in 1256 by Henry III's master mason, John of Gloucester.

∿

✝ Guildford Museum
Castle Arch
Guildford

>>

PHONE
01483-444750

OPEN
11:00 a.m.–5:00 p.m. Monday–Saturday, year-round
Closed Sunday

ADMISSION
Free of charge

CONVENIENCES
Bookstore

>>

Guildford is a village that takes its history to heart, a fact that we greatly appreciate equally as history buffs, travelers and authors. Although the Guildford Museum does not display a tremendous amount from our era per se, the museum staff were a wealth of information about Guildford, its ancient past, and other sites of interest throughout the town. Come with any questions you might have, as well as to enjoy displays on subjects as diverse as Saxon burial rites and Lewis Carroll.

~~

Guildford Guildhall
High Street
Guildford

>>>

PHONE

01483-444035

OPEN

Tours at 2:00 p.m. and 3:00 p.m. Tuesday and Thursday, May–September
Pre-booked tours are available year-round.

>>>

Unfortunately, our schedule did not allow for us to take a peek inside Guildford's handsome guildhall. The distinctive building with its signature gilded clock (c. 1683) dominates the city's commercial corridor. The ground floor of the building dates from the Tudor times, and there are civic records, plate and memorabilia on display.

~~

St. Mary's Church
Quarry Street at Millbrook
Guildford

>>>

PHONE

01483-444751

OPEN

11:00 a.m.–5:00 p.m. Tuesday–Saturday, year-round
Limited touring during worship

ADMISSION
Donation suggested

CONVENIENCES
Well-stocked bookshop focusing on spiritual topics

>>

With its sturdy, square Saxon tower, St. Mary's Church is Guildford's oldest building. Most of the church dates from the Norman era.

~~

The Medieval Undercroft
72 High Street
Guildford

>>

PHONE
Contact the Guildford Museum for details: 01483-444751.

OPEN
Limited access during summer afternoons; the undercroft is also sometimes included on the Guildford guided walking tours. Contact the Guildford Information Centre for schedule.

>>

Built in the 1300s, this exceptionally well preserved undercroft was once the shop of an affluent Guildford merchant, perhaps in the wool or wine trade. Evidence of the owner's wealth can be found in the numerous carved corbels that bracket the vaulted ceiling—only the most well-to-do could invest in so many carefully detailed carvings. Although this is not the only undercroft in Guildford, it is one of the two that remain open for public view—the other is the subterranean Crypt Restaurant at the Angel Posting House Hotel. By the way, "crypt"

☞ **Did you know?**

One of the most unusual crypts to be discovered in Guildford is that of an ancient synagogue. For safety reasons, the space is not open to the public, but the museum features a very interesting display on the vestiges of Jewish culture in Surrey excavated from the site.

in this instance is a misnomer: crypts are unique to churches, while undercrofts are specific to homes and commercial space. *(Carole wants to be certain you properly differentiate her favorite medieval spaces!)*

~~

✝ Loseley Park
Guildford

>>>

PHONE
   01483-304440

WEBSITE
   www.loseley.park.com

LOCATED
   Off A3, south of the village of Guildford, on B3000

OPEN
   2:00–5:00 p.m. Wednesday–Sunday, June–August

ADMISSION
   £5.00 Adults
   £3.00 Children
   £4.00 Seniors

CONVENIENCES
   Tearoom and gift shop

>>>

Whether you choose to take the guided house tour, or simply to relax over tea and cakes, a visit to Loseley Park offers a charming afternoon out of London. This handsome Elizabethan manor home was built in 1562 by Sir William More. His descendants are still in residence. One of the remarkable features of the estate is its unusual stone, salvaged from the ruins of nearby **Waverly Abbey**. The stone itself is nearly 900 years old. The interior furnishings, by and large, postdate our particular period of interest, although there is some fine paneling from Henry VIII's Nonsuch Palace. Even so, you may prefer to spend your time strolling through the myriad of lovingly tended gardens and enjoying the charming Loseley Park lake. A particularly pleasant culmination of your visit to Guildford!

∿

✠ Farnham Castle and Keep
Castle Hill

Farnham

>>>

PHONE

01252-713393

E-MAIL

info@cibfarnham.com

LOCATED

On A287, ½ mile north of Farnham town center

OPEN

Keep:

10:00 a.m.–6:00 p.m. daily, April–September

10:00 a.m.–5:00 p.m. daily, October

Closed November through March

The castle generally is not open to the public; call for details

ADMISSION

£2.10 Adults

£1.10 Children

£1.50 Seniors

>>>

Being the brother of the king in the middle of a bloody civil war cannot be the most secure of positions. Clearly, Henry of Blois, Bishop of Winchester and brother of King Stephen, felt the heat. By 1138, Henry had done some serious renovation on all of his castle-palaces, with an eye toward fortification against Empress Matilda's rebel forces, and it was about this time that he began construction of Farnham Castle. Strategically located between Winchester and London, Farnham Castle remained a primary seat of the bishops of Winchester from the 12th century until 1927. Today, the keep is owned by English Heritage and the castle is privately maintained by the Church of England. Farnham Castle is a foreboding presence. It looms over the lovely village of Farnham, a rather incongruous feature of an otherwise congenial landscape. Even at a distance you will note that the main castle has suffered the vestiges of several misguided attempts at "modernization." This is due, in part, to the fact that the original castle buildings were made of an inferior-quality chalk, which has weathered badly over time. During the Middle Ages, some attempt was made to seal the surface, but erosion has prompted subsequent generations to replace the chalk with hard stone or brick. The result is a peculiar sort of mosaic effect, which makes it difficult to determine, without a guidebook, the ages of the various structures on the property. As a visitor, your tour will center on the castle keep, with the foundation of Henry's no-nonsense Norman tower and the massive 13th-century shell and gatehouse. The buildings of the actual castle-cum-palace are well removed from the keep, and are not open to the public on a regular basis.

◆ ◆

☞ Did you know?

Farnham Castle was one of four English strongholds surrendered to the Dauphin of France in May 1216. Louis and his French forces landed on English soil at the invitation of the rebel barons who were so disgruntled by John's sinister rule that even the prospect of a French monarch seemed preferable . . . although John's sudden death, close on the heels of the French "invasion," rendered the issue moot. The castle remained under French occupation for 10 months; in March 1217, it was reclaimed by William Marshall, Earl of Pembroke and Protector of the young King Henry III. In a very short period of time, Pembroke had been able to marshal hearty support among the barons for the new monarch, and Louis's aspirations of ruling England were ultimately dashed.

◆ ◆

Ghost Alert!

We're not convinced that this is the best marketing gimmick we've come across, but the village of Farnham claims to have more ghosts than any other town in England. Farnham Castle itself is notorious for the bleak form of a misery-wracked woman who wanders the ruined keep, while Waverly Abbey is rumored to be haunted by a spectral monk. This unfortunate soul was apparently hanged, drawn and quartered and is perusing the grounds in search of his, er, "inner self." Yetch!

✤

✝ Also in the area . . .
Waverly Abbey Ruins

>>

LOCATED
Approximately 2½ miles south of Farnham, off B3001; follow signs to "Waverly House."

OPEN
Daylight hours daily, year-round

ADMISSION
Free of charge

>>

Located on the grounds of the stately Waverly House, alongside the peaceful River Wey, the remains of Waverly Abbey make a lovely side trip to your visit to Farnham. This is the site of the first Cistercian abbey in Britain, erected in 1128, although the ruins you'll see are of 13th-century origin.

> **☞ Did you know?**
> Waverly Abbey's idyllic setting served as the inspiration for Sir Walter Scott's novel of the same name.

❖❖❖

HENRY OF BLOIS
(a.k.a. HENRY OF WINCHESTER; 1100–1171)

One of the more ironic twists of fate in English history is the birth order of the brothers Blois. These grandsons of William the Conqueror were simply born with the wrong set of talents for the roles they ultimately assumed. Affable, eager-to-please Stephen lacked the decisive leadership skills so critical in a monarch; one can imagine him, however, as an effective diplomat. Henry of Blois, on the other hand, seems far too ambitious, urbane and political to be a "man of the cloth" . . . not that he didn't share those traits with a host of other medieval churchmen, but *still!*

Well, regardless of *our* opinion, Henry was, indeed, a fourth son, and as such was destined for life in the church. True to his nature, he determined from the start to make the very best of the situation. By virtue of his noble lineage, Henry was both "prince" and bishop, and throughout his career he never lost sight of that first, important honor. He entered monastic life at Cluny, arguably the world's most influential monastery. In 1126, with the aid of his uncle King Henry I, young Blois became abbot of Glastonbury; by 1129, he had added the affluent See of Winchester to his honor. He held both bishoprics for the rest of his life, a fact that put many an ecclesiastical nose out of joint.

Henry may have fostered a taste for the finer things in life — fine art and expensive jewelry being particular fancies of his — but he did not bleed his bishoprics dry. On the contrary, his keen administrative skills ensured that the abbeys and sees under his jurisdiction continued to flourish. Nor was Henry without some modicum of a true religious vocation. Indeed, he was the archetypical medieval multi-tasker, balancing an active — and impressive — involvement in English politics, foreign affairs, culture and, yes, religion. If he could not wield power with a scepter, he would do so with a bishop's mitre. In exchange for helping his brother Stephen secure the throne of England, Henry negotiated formal freedoms for the Church. He maintained close ties with the Vatican and in 1139 was appointed papal legate to England, a role he used continually to remind his fellow bishops, as well as his brother, of the scope of his authority. Henry did not hesitate to call the king before the legatine court to explain his arrest of the Bishop of Salisbury — that Stephen complied says as much about Stephen as it does about the power of the medieval Church.

During the war of succession between Stephen and their cousin Empress Matilda, Henry sought a policy of neutrality for the Church, although he personally found himself torn between pope, brother and cousin throughout the prolonged discord. Although he tried to mediate a treaty between Stephen and Matilda in 1140, he was not successful, and with Stephen's defeat at Lincoln, he sought temporary terms with the empress. It was a short-lived political honeymoon. Returning to Stephen's side, he was instrumental in the rousing royalist victory at Winchester, a decisive battle in the bloody civil war. In 1153, Henry was also a primary player in drafting the peace terms that eventually ended the conflict, assuring the Angevin succession of Matilda's son Henry Fitz Empress.

Henry of Blois may have been a churchman, but throughout Stephen's reign, he expanded the holdings of the Bishop of Winchester with a military commander's eye. He built strategic fortifications at Winchester, Taunton and Farnham. His palace in Southwark, just outside of London, while luxurious, was not without its defenses and its underground prison was infamous in its day — and for years to come! Understandably, the new king Henry II found the bishop's castles both tempting and a threat; he confiscated them in 1155, and Henry of Blois withdrew to Cluny in temporary retirement.

Politics was in Henry's blood, however. He did not stay away from court for long. By 1158, he was welcomed into King Henry II's inner circle, regarded as an elder statesman, but stripped of any significant political clout. However, he did preside over the election of Thomas à Becket as Archbishop of Canterbury. He was an outspoken advocate of Becket in the 1160s, believing strongly in the archbishop's controversial view of an independent Church, protected — but not interfered with — by the monarchy. Indeed, on his deathbed in 1171, he was still berating Henry II for his handling of the Becket affair: outspoken and independent to the very end.

❖❖❖

ANCIENT INNS AND EATERIES

~ Angel Posting House & Livery
91 High Street
Guildford
01483-564555

This handsome black-and-white coaching inn dates from the 1500s. Located on a cobbled street. Well-regarded restaurant in 13th-century crypt. Twenty-one rooms.

~ Star Inn
2 Quarry Street at High Street
Guildford
01483-532887

Share your sandwich with a ghost at this ancient pub.

~ Olivetto
124 High Street
Tunsgate
Guildford
01483-563277

Italian cuisine in a 16th-century environment.

CONTENTS

TRIP 2

Hampton Court Palace

✝ Hampton Court Palace

>>

PHONE
  020-8781-9500

LOCATED
  Off the M25, junction 15, then A312, A308 or A307

TRAVEL
  Trains travel from Waterloo Station to Hampton Court; travel time is
  approximately ½ hour.

  During the summer, Hampton Court is also approachable by
  river from London. The leisurely journey takes 3 hours each way,
  although you may arrive by boat and return by train if you so desire.
  For information on schedules and fares, call 020-7930-4721

OPEN
  9:30 a.m.–6:00 p.m. Tuesday–Sunday, April–October
  10:15 a.m.–6:00 p.m. Monday, April–October
  9:30 a.m.–4:30 p.m. Tuesday–Sunday, November–March
  10:15 a.m.–4:30 p.m. Monday, November–March

ADMISSION
  £10.00 Adults
  £6.60 Children
  £7.60 Seniors
  Family ticket available

>>

When King Henry VIII died in 1547, he left his heirs far more
than the crown of England. Traces of his fiery, erratic personality surfaced in his son Edward on more than one occasion, as

well as in his daughters, Mary and Elizabeth. His troubled marital history may well have set the stage for his children's conflicted intimacies, while years of Henry's conspicuous consumption left them with depleted royal coffers and staggering national debts.

However, one of the *pleasant* legacies Bluff Hal left his children was a vast portfolio of royal real estate. In addition to the numerous castles and defensive structures conferred with the title "monarch," Henry passed along more luxuriously appointed palaces and sumptuous manor homes than any ruler before him—66 in all! Unfortunately, many fell during the Cromwellian conflict and many more were vastly remodeled to reflect the radically different tastes of the Georgian era. Today, there is no finer example of Henry's overactive nesting instinct than the awe-inspiring palace of Hampton Court, portions of which provide an impressive glimpse at the grandeur of the Tudor court.

PRIDE: A "CARDINAL" SIN

Although Henry would eventually confer regal status on the palace, Hampton Court was truly "palatial" from the get-go. Work on the sumptuous estate was begun by Henry's chief minister, Cardinal Wolsey, in 1514. A prime example of status-symbol construction, Hampton Court was spared no opportunity to reflect Wolsey's inflated sense of importance. The site —originally home to a priory and estate offices of the Knights Hospitaliers—was ideal: equally accessible to London by carriage or barge, with a plentiful supply of sweet Coombe Hill water, which the cardinal funneled to the property by way of special lead pipes. (The cardinal's contemporaries found this a terribly affected gesture—if Thames's water was good enough for *them* to drink, by Jove, it was good enough for the Lord Chancellor of England!)

Six years later, Wolsey's grand home was complete. The exact outline of his splendid domicile has been consumed by many later additions, but by all accounts the cardinal's Hampton Court was truly vast: his base court included 44 separate lodgings and grand three-story apartments constructed for the sole purpose of entertaining the king. The incredible Hampton Court Great Hall and the south side Presence Chamber are also part of Wolsey's original scheme.

❖❖

CARDINAL THOMAS WOLSEY (1475–1530)

The son of an Ipswich butcher, Thomas Wolsey was educated at Oxford and ordained to the priesthood in 1498. No cooling his heels in some backwater parish for Tom—no sirree! Almost overnight he was appointed chaplain to the dour and devout Henry VII, a position that brought him into the confidence of the young Prince Harry. With the younger Henry's ascension to the throne in 1509, Wolsey's rising star began to shine very brightly, indeed. In very short order, he amassed an impressive résumé of powerful secular titles, starting with that of Privy Councilor in 1511.

Wolsey's rise to prominence was not unwarranted. A natural statesman with innate political savvy, Wolsey strategized and implemented England's successful 1513 invasion of France and negotiated a favorable peace treaty with the French the following year. So great were Wolsey's successes and so deep was Henry's admiration of his statecraft that by the sixth year of Henry's reign he had ceded the bulk of his affairs to Thomas, elevating him to Lord Chancellor in 1515.

Wolsey's ascension in the Church's hierarchy was equally rapid. By 1514, he was both Bishop of Lincoln and Archbishop of York The following year, he was made cardinal and by 1518 he had been named papal legate. For the ever-ambitious Wolsey, this was not quite good enough—all his life he harbored the hope that he would be elected pope, a wish that would never be fulfilled.

Despite—or perhaps because of—his meteoric ascent, Wolsey was not well liked. He was haughty, egotistical and perpetually self-serving. He could be extremely harsh, brutal even, as witnessed in the relish with which he executed his role as Henry's henchman during the suppression of the monasteries. These off-putting qualities, coupled with his great influence over the king, won him more than the usual share of enemies at court. Regardless of his elevating England to the forefront of foreign policy, and despite his numerous charitable gestures (including the founding of Christ College, Oxford), public opinion of Wolsey remained dim.

Spectacular rises often pave the way for spectacular falls; Wolsey's was no exception. His failure to secure Henry a speedy divorce from Katherine of Aragon spelled the beginning of the Lord Chancellor's end. In 1529, Pope Clement VII appointed two legates, Compeggio and Wolsey, to hear the king's case in England and advise the Vatican on its merits. When Compeggio was called back to Italy, Wolsey found himself in the uncomfortable position of arguing on behalf of the king before a pope who was, inconveniently, controlled by Katherine's nephew, the Holy Roman Emperor Charles V. Needless to say, the divorce was not granted, and Wolsey had to admit failure. A furious Henry, fueled by an embittered Anne Boleyn, sought revenge. Accused under an arcane law that forbade holding foreign court on English soil, Wolsey was found culpable of serious crimes against the state.

Stripped of all his honors and power (with the exception of the York bishopric), Wolsey retreated in shame to his headquarters at York. The worst was yet to come. He was subsequently called to London to answer charges of treason. Broken and beside himself with fear and grief, he fell ill and died en route to London on April 29, 1530. Wolsey was buried at Leicester Abbey, not far from the tomb of Richard III, a move that caused many to disdainfully refer to the church as the "sepulchre of tyrants." *(How rude! We have never regarded Richard as particularly tyrannical.)*

◇ ◇

Somewhat of an architectural trendsetter, Hampton Court has many distinctive features, including all-brick construction, high-pitched gables, expansive leaded-glass bays, and a bevy of graceful chimneys, which hinted at the numerous (24!) fireplaces within. There were 280 rooms (many have since been demolished), the most "public" of which were adorned with gilded ceilings, exquisite linenfold paneling, a rotating display of expensive tapestries, and paintings by Italian masters.

Many of the most renowned craftsmen of the time left their imprint on Hampton Court. Henry Redman—whose portfolio included portions of Westminster Abbey, St. Margaret's, Windsor Castle, Eton and Cardinal's College at Oxford— served as the "general contractor." The highly skilled master car-

☞ **Did you know?**

As one may suspect, Wolsey was hardly homeless after surrendering his showpiece to the king. Not only did Henry provide a suite of apartments at both Richmond Palace and Hampton Court for the cardinal's exclusive use, but Wolsey was practically finished with work on a second lavish estate, York Place, on the bank of the Thames. This sumptuous London home nearly outstripped Hampton Court in both size and opulence and it, too, would eventually fall into the hands of the king. York Place is better known to history as the royal palace of Whitehall.

penter Humphrey Coke crafted the rood and timber work, while another famous carpenter, James Needham, designed the spectacular Great Hall roof. Italy's pride, Giovanni di Majano, carved most of the bas relief ornaments: terra cotta busts of mighty emperors and numerous renderings of Wolsey's coat of arms.

Wolsey was clearly trying to call attention to himself and, unfortunately, he succeeded. Hampton Court far surpassed any of King Henry's royal palaces. Needless to say, this did not bode well for Wolsey's long-term occupancy. So disgruntled was the king over being outshone by one of his ministers that Wolsey was compelled to an act of uncommon generosity. In 1525, he graciously "gifted" Hampton Court to Henry.

HENRY, HONEYMOONS AND THE HEIR-APPARENT

Like so many new homeowners, Henry wasted no time remodeling his recent acquisition, the better to make it "his own." For starters, down came Wolsey's coat of arms and up went Henry's. He tore down sections of the cardinal's palace in order to reconfigure or enlarge the property to better suit the needs of his court. He commissioned his own lavish murals for the palace walls, although none as important as the Italian masterpieces Wolsey had commissioned. Two of Henry's propaganda-style paintings are still on display: *The Battle of the Spurs* and *The Field of the Cloth of Gold*; both show King Henry at his diplomatic "best." Countless extravagant tapestries were commissioned for the palace, several of which were embroidered by Anne Boleyn—apparently, Mistress Anne was quite accomplished with the needle. In his lifetime, Henry amassed more than 2,000 tapestries; 28 survive at Hampton Court.

One of the most interesting contributions Henry made to

> 🔖 Did you know?
> Hampton Court was one of the only Tudor palaces big enough to house Henry's entire court (over 1,000 people!).

Hampton Court can still be admired. The palace's inner court-yard is graced by a most unusual clock, crafted for Henry VIII by Nicholas Oursian in 1540. No ordinary timepiece this! The splendid machine functioned more like an almanac, displaying not only the time of day but also the days of the week, the month, the phases of the moon, the sign of the zodiac, and high tide at London Bridge.

An avid sportsman, Henry took an active interest in the grounds surrounding Hampton Court. There were extensive butts for the practice of archery and a most innovative tennis complex; Henry's enclosed hard courts can still be seen at the palace.

Because of its connection to Wolsey, many people tend to associate Hampton Court with Anne Boleyn. In fact, all six of Henry's wives spent *some* time at Hampton Court. Three of them spent their honeymoons

• •
☞ Did you know?

Security surrounding the monarch was as much an issue in Tudor times as it is today. In order to curtail violence at court, an Act of Parliament was passed dictating that anyone who shed blood within the vicinity of the king's presence would lose his (or her) hand. In 1541, during a hotly contested match at the Hampton Court tennis net, one of the king's "gentlemen" drew his sword and wounded his partner in anger. He was duly sentenced to have his hand lopped off in public. The king's Master Cook was on hand with the cleaver, the Sergeant of the Scullery was there with his mallet, and the royal Master Surgeon was standing by with searing iron and bandages, when lo! word came from King Henry pardoning the hot-tempered tennis player *(causing us to wonder how Good King Harry got such a nasty reputation).*
• •

at the palace, and one of them, sadly, lost her life here. Wolsey took great pride in the fact that the luxurious apartments he had built for Katherine of Aragon and Princess Mary met their favor; they were frequent visitors in the years prior to "The King's Great Matter." Anne Boleyn and Princess Elizabeth spent time here as well. On October 4, 1539, Thomas Cromwell witnessed the marriage treaty between Henry and Anne of Cleves—an ill-fated alliance, masterminded by Cromwell, which would become one of the contributing factors in his arrest and execution. In fact, on the very day of Cromwell's beheading—

June 28, 1540—Henry secretly married at Hampton Court the woman who had *really* caught his fancy, Catherine Howard, the flighty young niece of the Duke of Norfolk. Mistress Howard's romantic associations with the palace, unfortunately, were not limited to the king. She was accused of engaging in adulterous liaisons while at Hampton Court, and it was here that she was arrested and dragged away in tears, while her cuckold husband attended mass in the palace's Chapel Royal.

Ghost Alert!

For nearly 500 years, visitors to Hampton Court Palace have reported the hair-raising screams of a woman in anguish. It is believed to be the ghost of Catherine Howard, who was hauled off in a state of advanced hysteria, while desperately trying to gain access to King Henry in order to plead for mercy. At the time, her wails fell upon deaf ears. Five centuries of subsequent witnesses have not remained so unmoved. Recent scientific studies have attributed some of the spooky "cold spots" in the palace to concealed doorways and architectural nuances. Auditory and visual brushes with Queen Catherine, Edward IV's nursemaid and other visitors from beyond have yet to be scientifically explained away.

However, it is Henry's best-loved queen, Jane Seymour, who rightfully holds pride of place at Hampton Court. Following the execution of Anne Bolcyn, Henry made straightaway for Hampton Court and began to lay the groundwork for his pending marriage to Jane. At six o'clock in the morning on May 20, 1536, Jane arrived at the palace by barge. The couple was betrothed in a very brief ceremony just after breakfast. So hastily did workers move throughout the palace to replace Anne's carved initials with Jane's that "A"s are still visible beneath the "J"s on many of Hampton's Tudor motifs.

Hampton Court soon became Jane's favorite royal residence. So comfortable did she feel here that she chose the palace for her lying-in as she awaited the birth of the king's presumed heir. The entire court moved to the palace in early September 1537 for the anticipated arrival. Jane was ensconced in Anne Boleyn's former apartments—they were near the Silver Stick Gallery but have long since been demolished. On October 12, after an arduous three-day labor, Jane gave birth to the bonny, fair-haired son that King Henry—for over 27 years—had so longed for. Born on St. Edward's Day, the royal heir was named Edward, and was immediately honored as Duke of Cornwall. (Ironically, the long-awaited prince was never formally created Prince of Wales.)

• •

☞ Did you know?

Prince Edward was not the only baby, nor the only Seymour, nor the only *Edward* born at Hampton Court on October 12, 1537. The prince's aunt Lady Beauchamp provided him with a cousin and future playmate at virtually the same time, albeit in separate palace apartments.

• •

Prince Edward was immediately awarded his own suite of apartments at Hampton Court, as well as his own royal retinue. He was baptized in the palace's Chapel Royal on Monday, October 15. A mere 400 guests attended the midnight service—fear of the plague induced the king to keep the guest list to such a "modest" size. The Chapel Royal still bears the magnificent ceiling from this era. The prince was carried to the ceremony by Lady Exeter; Archbishop Cranmer, the prince's sister Mary Tudor, and the dukes of Norfolk and Suffolk stood as godparents. Edward's other sister, three-year-old Elizabeth, carried the chrisom; she, in turn, was carried by the prince's uncle Lord Beauchamp. All in all, a stellar retinue—as would befit a future king.

Tragically, what should have been a happily-ever-after story took a sudden turn for the worse. That all-too-common ancient malady, puerperal (or "childbed") fever, claimed the life of Queen Jane on October 24; her baby was only 12 days old. By all accounts, the funeral was appropriately magnificent. For seven days, Jane lay in state in the Hampton Court Presence Chamber. For a second week, she lay in state in the palace's Chapel Royal, where her entrails had been buried. Mary Tudor was her stepmother's principal mourner; the two had fostered a close, if brief, relationship and Mary was exceedingly appreciative of Jane's efforts to reconcile the disavowed princess with her father, King Henry. The funeral procession departed Hampton Court on November 8 for Windsor Castle. Both Jane and Henry VIII are buried in the St. George's Chapel at Windsor.

ELIZABETH'S ENTERPRISE

As much as her father may have loved Hampton Court, Queen Elizabeth had no particular fondness for the sumptuous palace. As a matter of fact, it wouldn't be much of an exaggeration to say that she loathed it. Who can blame her? Associations with her own mother aside, the palace was closely linked to the demise of two of her stepmothers. Any flicker of affection she might have harbored for the place was ultimately snuffed by her own near brush with death.

On October 10, 1562, while in residence at Hampton Court, Elizabeth began to feel out of sorts. Swayed by an old wives' tale, the queen steeped herself in a very hot bath, then went for a vigorous walk in the cool autumn air. Not surprisingly, this did little for her health; by the end of the day, she was bedridden with a high fever. Six days later, she was gravely ill, eventually losing consciousness for a full 24 hours. Those close at hand were convinced that death was inevitable, and the queen's closest councilor, William Cecil, was summoned to her bedside. Even Elizabeth, as she began to regain consciousness, was well aware of the gravity of her condition and the perilous position in which her death would place England. With no heir

> **Did you know?**
>
> The royal sensibilities are so easily offended! With her highly cultured sense of smell, Elizabeth was particularly offended by kitchen odors. This was a bit of a problem, since her accommodations at Hampton Court were perched directly above her father's enormous, malodorous sculleries. Attendants tried in vain to mask the aromas with Tudor aromatherapy: essence of rosewater. Needless to say, this didn't work, and the queen was quite displeased. In 1567, Elizabeth ordered that a new kitchen be built. You can visit it today: the divinely scented Hampton Court Tearoom.

to take her throne, the queen commanded that her council appoint her "good friend" Robert Dudley to serve as Lord Protector of England—conferring upon him a kingly salary of £20,000 per year for good measure. This overt favoritism shown to her Master of the Horse did little to quell the rumors that Dudley was, indeed, more than a "good friend" to the Virgin Queen. Once she regained her health, Elizabeth doggedly avoided Hampton Court for quite some time.

Despite her personal dislike for the palace, Elizabeth—ever the savvy businesswoman!—recognized the value of Hampton Court as a showpiece. She made a point of making certain that the palace was maintained to its maximum glory—and then charged the "well-dressed public" for the privilege of gawking at the trappings of royalty. Indeed, Hampton Court may well have been England's first "admission charged" tourist attraction. Visitors to the lavish Paradise Chambers were not disappointed. The walls were gilded in silver and gold, with brightly colored woodwork in hues of red, yellow, blue and green. The gilded ceiling fretwork glistened in the light of countless candelabra and there were numerous trompes l'oeil to delight the eye. The furnishings were equally impressive: tables inlaid with mother-of-pearl or edged in genuine pearl on which were displayed such queenly accessories as a gilt mirror, a backgammon set with dice of solid silver, an ebony draughts board, and chess boards of ivory. Elizabeth's love of music was clearly in evidence; there was a collection of ivory and gold whistles that produced a range of animal sounds and an assortment of unusual musical instruments. The queen's prowess as a huntswoman was underscored by a visit to the Horn Room, where the antlers of various game killed in royal hunts were hung with pride. (*We don't know about you, but we have seen this kind of display throughout our travels and it's never done much for us—in fact, we usually jump queue when we come to this part.*)

One of Elizabeth's most important contributions to Hampton Court was her cultivation of the palace gardens. Understandably proud of her role in New World exploration, the queen commanded that as many imports as possible be show-cased at Hampton Court. Tobacco and potatoes were just two of the "new" varieties of produce that were planted on the palace grounds.

YOUR VISIT TO HAMPTON COURT

True Anglophiles will find enough at Hampton Court to keep them happily engaged for a full day. The extensive gardens and beautiful parkland alone can easily consume several hours on a summer afternoon. Within its walls, Hampton Court provides a visual encyclopedia not only to the Tudor period but also to the subsequent reigns of the Stuarts, William and Mary and the Georgians. Even the Windsors are represented, with a glorious selection of paintings from the Royal Collection of Queen Elizabeth II.

Being somewhat myopic in our approach, we have focused each of our many visits to Hampton Court on the Tudor treasures alone *(surprised, huh?)* and have found that even such a limited sampling of the palace's pleasures can take a half day, depending on your propensity to linger. Here is an overview of what awaits you from the days of Henry VIII, his queens and Elizabeth.

Hampton Court has been divided into six separate tours, or "routes." Each tour meets at a specific gathering point on the palace grounds and focuses on a particular theme. You will be able to obtain the start times and meeting places for each tour from the **Hampton Court Visitor Centre**, which is on your left just after entering the main gates of the palace grounds. Some of the tours are self-guided; you can venture on your own, with the help of directional signs and/or audio cassettes. Others are docent-led. All are very well executed and there are a plethora of entertaining and knowledgeable guides throughout the palace to answer any questions. The tours that focus on the Tudor era are Tour One: **Henry VIII's State Apartments**, Tour Five: The **Wolsey Rooms and Renaissance Picture Gallery** and Tour Six: **The Tudor Kitchens**. *(Some of Henry's magnifi-*

cent tapestries are on display in the King's Apartments, Tour Four. The apartments, however, were built and furnished for William III, and we did not find the tapestries a strong enough temptation to endure so much Baroque decor!)

~ Henry VIII's State Apartments

On this tour you will visit the spectacular Hampton Court Great Hall, King Henry's Great Watching Chamber and the lovely Tudor Chapel Royal, as well as several smaller attractions. The Great Hall's carved hammerbeam roof is truly breathtaking—you'll think so, too, no matter how many *other* hammerbeam roofs you've seen in your day. Unfortunately, Henry's bright paint was stripped from the ceiling in the 1920s.

Next to the Great Hall is the Great Watching Chamber; although this was substantially altered by Christopher Wren in the late 1700s *(you can imagine what we think about **that**!)*, the handsome gilded ceiling sets the tone for the chamber's former glory. The hall is hung with several of Henry's illustrative Flemish tapestries, which, though somewhat faded, are still amazing works of art. The two smaller rooms of the Great Watching Chamber are the garderobe and the Page's Chamber, where servants waited to be dispatched to their duties.

While traversing the so-called Haunted Gallery (a.k.a. the Long Gallery), don't be surprised if you feel a sense of dis-ease; Catherine Howard is believed to wander this hallway, still desperate to gain access to her husband in the Chapel Royal. In this gallery, you will find the famous *The Family of Henry VIII* portrait, which sets the stage for the late Tudor dynasty.

The Chapel Royal was originally built by Cardinal Wolsey. The Royal Pew allowed the monarch and his family to attend Mass, separated from the rest of the congregation. Be sure to pay close attention to the glorious, richly painted vaulted ceiling—it is widely regarded as the most important Tudor ceiling in Britain. The lovely oak reredos, however, dates from the reign of Queen Anne. As you leave the chapel on your way to the North Cloister, look for Henry and Jane's coats of arms; they flank the chapel door.

~ The Wolsey Rooms and
  Renaissance Picture Gallery

This is the oldest portion of Hampton Court Palace, built by Cardinal Wolsey between 1515 and 1526. Appropriately, it displays a vast collection of important Renaissance paintings from the Royal Collection of Elizabeth II. Although most of the subjects of these masterpieces are people and places outside the realm of England, there are several portraits of Tudor monarchs and two early renderings of Hampton Court itself. Also on display is the only painting of Henry VIII's known to have hung in the palace during his reign: *The Four Evangelists Stoning the Pope*, which the king commissioned as a not-so-subliminal Reformation missive.

~ The Tudor Kitchens

We are typically not big fans of "slice-of-life" vignettes and reenactments, which—in our opinion—usually fall into the "McHistory" trap. The Tudor kitchens at Hampton Court are

* * * * * * * * * * * * * * * * * * * *
☞ Did you know?
One of the most famous portraits of the Tudor dynasty was painted by Hans Holbein during the winter of 1536–37 as a mural for the Presence Chamber of Whitehall. In the painting, Henry VIII is pictured with his current wife, Jane Seymour, his father, Henry VII, and his mother, Elizabeth of York. The painting was one of the first works of art to depict full-length likenesses of royal personages. During her reign, Elizabeth liked to receive visitors to Whitehall standing in front of the mural to emphasize her right to the throne as a direct descendant of Henrys VII and VIII. The mural was destroyed when the palace burned, but fortunately Charles II had the foresight to commission the Dutch artist Remigius van Leempert to make a copy of it. The copy now stands in the Renaissance Picture Gallery at Hampton Court. The left-hand section of Holbein's draft for the portrait, picturing the two Henrys, can be seen at the National Portrait Gallery in London.
* * * * * * * * * * * * * * * * * * * *

a rare exception: a re-created still life so real that you can actually lose yourself in the sights, sounds and *(sorry, Elizabeth!)* smells of Henry's massive scullery. Occupying over 50 (!) rooms and spanning 3,000 square feet, these kitchens once provided 1,600 meals a day whenever Henry's court was in residence. Although only a relatively small part of the kitchens is included on the tour, what you see is fascinatingly detailed, as if preparations are well under way for a feast of royal proportion. We don't want to spoil the surprise for you—all we can say is, allow enough time to stroll through the kitchens again and again on your visit . . . there is truly that much to take in!

~ The Palace Gardens

Spanning 60 acres, the Hampton Court gardens are a not-to-be-missed stop for any horticulturalist. The basic layout dates from the reign of Henry, although all the gardens—with the exception of the Pond Garden—have been radically altered over the years. The Pond Garden is somewhat removed from the hub-bub of the rest of the palace. The ornamental ponds were once stocked with freshwater fish to supply Henry's kitchens. There are numerous statues of cherubs and a striking figure of one of our heroines, the love goddess, Venus; in Henry's time, heraldic beasts were also part of the mise-en-scène.

ANCIENT INNS AND EATERIES

~ Hampton Court Lodging

Fancy yourself suited for the royal life? The lodgings at Hampton Court are your chance to find out! Available for self-catering vacations, the six-person apartment at the palace's Fish Court, or the separate (and "newer") 8-person "Georgian House," provides a unique opportunity to live within the confines of the spectacular palace.

CONCLUSION

One of the wonderfully rewarding things about being an amateur historian is wallowing in the domino effect—the tale of one queen or noble opens the page on a "new" personality, the investigation of one site leads you to explore its connection to another . . . where does it end? Hopefully, it doesn't! We feed on the perpetual excitement of discovery, linking the people and places and events of medieval and Tudor history, then following the traces throughout England. We are confident you feel the same way, too.

In the process of writing our first book on London, we were steered toward the wealth of castles, abbeys, cathedrals and homes that lay just beyond reach of the City. Some, to the southeast of London, you are now familiar with; we hope we have helped bring their history to life for you. Still others will be the topic of our next book, *Medieval and Tudor England: The Midlands*. We've already started our travels in that area and are thrilled by what we have to share! Once again, for most of the trips, you'll be able to head into the nearby countryside, poke into the fascinating vestiges of days gone by and *still* be back in the capital city with time for a night on the town.

You didn't *really* think we'd leave London for good, did you? Happy travels!

Carole and Sarah
The Amateur Historians
www.amateurhistorian.com

GLOSSARY

After years of lapping up medieval literature and lore, we find ourselves sprinkling our own writing with medieval and Tudor "lingo" as if they were household words. Here are some terms you might run across that could otherwise give you pause.

Abbey: A religious enclave headed by an abbot or abbess. Also known as a *monastery, cloister, priory* or — if housing female monastics — *convent, nunnery* or *convent monastery.*

Aumbury: A cupboard or recess in the wall for storing sacred vessels.

Bailey: The protected outer courtyard of a castle, also known as a *ward.*

Baron: A tenant-in-chief of the monarchy who held land and titles specifically granted by the king or queen.

Bosses: Carved ornaments, often gilded or painted, that disguise the joint between rib vaults.

Buttress: A vertical stone projection from a wall that supports (or resists) the lateral thrust of a roof.

Canon: An ordained, non-monastic priest living communally with others in observance of a Rule, typically that of St. Augustine of Hippo. A canon's main role was to officiate at religious services.

Cathedral: A Christian house of worship that contains a *cathedra* or bishop's chair/throne. The bishop (or archbishop) is the presiding religious authority at a cathedral.

Chancel: The east end of a church or cathedral closest to the high altar; reserved for clergy.

Chantry: A small chapel (in some cases simply an altar), endowed with funds to maintain a priest to pray for the repose of the founder's (or loved one's) soul.

Charter: The formal written record of the royal transfer of rights or property.

Clerestory: The part of a building that rises above standard roof level and contains a window that lights the core of the building. Also, the upper story of a church nave, providing light to the center of the church.

Corbel: A stone or timber wall projection that supports a beam or overhead platform.

Crenelation: Parapets of a castle that are divided into distinctive, solid chunks of wall (used as shields) interspersed with gaps ("crenels") used for aiming weapons at one's enemy. Also known as *battlements*.

Curtain Wall: A (typically) free-standing wall with interval towers that encloses the castle courtyard.

Donjon: The keep or great tower of a castle.

Friar: A member of one of the mendicant orders, who has taken a vow of material poverty.

Garderobe: Your basic medieval loo or latrine.

Grotesque: Used to describe a style of medieval woodcarving found particularly in church decor. Although some of the faces depicted are, indeed, "gross," the word really stems from the Latin word *grotto*—the Roman grottos being inspiration for this art form.

Hammerbeam: A horizontal beam that projects at a right angle from the top of a wall in order to support a wooden roof.

Lady Chapel: A chapel dedicated to the Blessed Mother, usually located in the east end of a major church or cathedral.

Misericord: A ledge located beneath the hinged seat in a choir stall, allowing the seat to be adjusted for the comfort of its occupant. These ledges and their brackets are often intricately engraved.

Monastery: A community of persons who have retired from the world under religious vows. When referring to collected monastic buildings, *monastery, abbey* and *priory* are frequently interchanged.

Motte: The rounded castle mound.

Nave: The west wing of a church or cathedral.

Piscina: A sink, set into the recesses of the altar area, used exclusively for the washing of sacred vessels.

Portcullis: A heavy grate, which slides vertically, designed to close off a passageway.

Presbytery: The east wing of the church where the high altar is located; also known as the *sanctuary*.

Priory: A religious house that is headed by a prior or prioress. Although a prior is technically one step below an abbot (making a priory subordinate to an abbey), the terms *priory, abbey* and *monastery* are commonly interchanged when referring to an enclave of monastic buildings.

Quire: The portion of the church between the presbytery and the pulpit. The quire was composed of stalls where monks sat to sing the Offices; modern use: *choir.*

Rape: A governing jurisdiction created after the Norman Conquest that empowered Norman nobles with military power and administrative control, centered in an English castle.

Relic: A part of a saint's body or personal belonging, believed to be a medium of intercession to God; relics of holy people were often preserved in ornamental caskets known as *reliquaries.*

Romanesque: An architectural style very similar to Norman; popular in the 11th and 12th centuries and characterized by rounded arches and groined or barrel vaults.

Rood Screen: The division between the nave and the quire of the church, adorned with a crucifix.

Sanctuary: 1. The area of a church or cathedral containing the high altar (see *presbytery*). 2. The medieval practice of granting refuge to fugitives who sought official shelter within the church walls.

Sarcophagus: A stone coffin, typically adorned with an effigy and inscription.

Sedilia: The trio of recessed wall seats made of stone for officiating clergy; located on the south side of the quire and usually topped with a decorative canopy.

Seneschal: The official deputy in a medieval great house.

Shield Wall: A virtually impregnable defensive stance formed by warriors standing shoulder to shoulder and shield to shield.

Transept: The transverse (north-south) part of a cruciform church or cathedral, set at a right angle to the main axis. The transept links the nave and the chancel.

Translation: A solemn ceremony in which the remains of a dead person are moved from one burial site to another.

Undercroft: A vaulted underground room or cellar that supports the principal chamber above; Carole's favorite part of any medieval building *(not!).*

Vault: An arched stone ceiling or roof, sometimes punctuated with ribs; a "barrel vault" is an arched, semi-cylindrical vault.

Wall Walk: The fighting platform directly behind the parapet of a curtain wall.

Ward: A castle's courtyard or bailey.

INDEX

Bold type indicates places or touring information. (It does *not* mean that a place still exists.) *Italics* indicates location information. Standard type indicates historical events or people.